I Give You
Authority

Some other books by Charles H. Kraft

Anthropology for Christian Witness
Behind Enemy Lines
Christianity in Culture
Christianity with Power
Communicating Jesus' Way (formerly *Communicating the Gospel God's Way*)
Communication Theory for Christian Witness
Deep Wounds, Deep Healing
Defeating Dark Angels

I Give You Authority

Charles H. Kraft

Chosen

a division of Baker Publishing Group
Grand Rapids, Michigan

© 1997 by Charles H. Kraft

Published by Chosen Books
A division of Baker Publishing Group
P.O. Box 6287, Grand Rapids, MI 49516-6287
www.chosenbooks.com

Printed in the United States of America

Library of Congress Cataloging-in-Publication Data
Kraft, Charles H.
    I give you authority / Charles H. Kraft.
        p.   cm.
    Includes bibliographical references and indexes.
    ISBN 10: 0-8007-9256-4 (pbk.)
    ISBN 978-0-8007-9256-5 (pbk.)
    1. Authority—Religious aspects—Christianity. I. Title.
BT88.K73   1997
262'.8—dc21   97-18563

10   11   12   13   14   15   16   18   17   16   15   14   13   12

Contents

to Human Authority • The Paradox of Submission • The Ten Commandments of Spiritual Authority

Introduction

Authority was an important issue in the New Testament. I believe it is an important issue for all Christians to this day. But before we tackle the substance of this issue, there are two important foundational areas I want to discuss: Scripture and experience.

The Bible, Our Tether

When my wife and I were missionaries in Nigeria, we frequently saw horses or smaller animals such as goats with one end of a rope tied around a back leg and the other end to a post that had been driven into the ground. If the horse or goat moved as far as possible from the post and began to walk, it would create a circle. Within that circle the horse or goat lived and grazed. But because of the rope tethered to the post, the animal could not venture beyond the circumference of that circle. The tether defined for the animal the range within which it could move.

Sometimes the rope was fairly long, giving the animal lots of room within which to graze. Sometimes, though, the rope was short and the area small within which the horse or goat could move. I often found myself feeling sorry for an animal tied with a short rope as it strained to reach grass at the outer periphery of its circle. We say of such an animal, "It was given a short tether."

Another use of the word *tether* is in the game called tetherball, in which a volleyball-sized ball dangles from the top of a post by a rope about five feet long. One person tries to hit the ball so that the rope wraps around the pole in a certain direction, while the opponent tries to stop the ball and wrap it around the pole in the opposite direction.

The length of the tether—whether the one tying the animal or the one used in the game—sets the limits within which the animal or those playing the game must function.

For us, the Bible is the tether that sets the limits. We seek to learn about Christian authority by looking within the Scriptures for examples and teaching that set the parameters within which we work in our daily lives. To learn about authority *in* Scripture, therefore, we submit ourselves to the authority *of* Scripture.

Since Scripture is our guide and tether, we must take seriously everything the Bible states regarding authority, and be guided by its general principles whenever it makes no specific statements. This is my aim throughout the following chapters, though you may question some of my interpretations. Since all interpretation is influenced thoroughly by experience, it is probably differences in experience that lead to differences in interpretation. More on that in a minute.

I believe the Bible, the 66 canonical books accepted by Protestants, to be inspired by God Himself (2 Timothy 3:16). Though the Bible nowhere defines what inspiration means, the fact that the Source of the inspiration is God, rather than the humans who did the writing, means it is trustworthy and authoritative as the conveyer of God's truth. This truth is conveyed in statement form (for example, the Ten Commandments or the Beatitudes) and through the examples of those whose stories are recorded there. We are told negatively that we are not to follow the examples of those who disobeyed God (1 Corinthians 10:11) and, positively, that we should imitate the faithful such as Jesus (John 13:15; 14:12), Paul (1 Corinthians 4:16; 11:1; Philippians 3:17) and the prophets (James 5:10).

Since it is the practice of some to pretty well ignore the Old Testament, I need to say explicitly that I consider the inspiration of the Old Testament equal to that of the New Testament. You will note, therefore, that in the chapters that follow, I take instruction and examples from the Old Testament just as seriously as from the New Testament (except when these have been specifically done away with by New Testament teaching—for example, animal sacrifices). There are those who deny that we are to derive doctrine from historical passages. I consider such a position misguided. Some of the most important teaching of Scripture lies in the ways in which God's servants demonstrate what life and ministry with Him are supposed to be.

So it is that I derive teaching ("doctrine") from the whole of Scripture, New Testament and Old, and from both direct statements and the descriptions recorded there of how God's people worked in the authority He granted them. All of Scripture is available for our instruction and guidance.

Personal Experience

Again, the way we interpret Scripture (and all else that goes on) is influenced pervasively by our experi-

11

ence. Jesus said that as we obey Him, we will *experience* (the Greek means "know through experience") the truth (John 8:31–32). The material in the following chapters comes out of the interaction between my commitment to Scripture (and, supremely, to the Lord of Scripture) and my experience working in the authority and power of Jesus in life.

I was raised in evangelical, noncharismatic churches, accepted Jesus as my personal Savior at age twelve and went to an evangelical college and seminary. To me, charismatic and Pentecostal expressions of Christianity were too far out to be taken seriously. I considered myself a strongly committed Christian and gave myself for missionary service in Africa. But I remember wondering if there might not be something more to Christianity than I was experiencing. I had no idea what the missing element might be.

My wife and I served as pioneer missionaries in northeastern Nigeria in the late 1950s. As I worked with the leaders there, I found there was an area of the Scriptures I could not handle.

I had been taught well in church, college and seminary in the areas in which evangelicals specialize: scriptural truth that can be understood rationally, and the need for commitment to Jesus Christ. Emphases considered charismatic were never dealt with, unless it was to make fun of a branch of Christianity we considered weird and off-balance. But now the Nigerian leaders wanted to learn how to handle evil spirits.

I could deal with just about everything else in Scripture, but this one was beyond me, except to teach that Jesus was able to cast evil spirits out. (I assumed He was able to handle them because He was God.) In my systematic theology class in seminary, our three-volume textbook had only a few references to Satan and demons, and the professor made no attempt to deal with that subject. I believed demons existed but considered myself fortunate never to have met one; and I certainly had no idea that I had any authority over them, though I had heard stories of other missionaries (none on our field) who had been successful in encounters with demons.

In any case, the Nigerians were gracious and did not press the issue. They knew I could not help them in this area.

With questions about demons deep in my subconscious, then, I found myself by the early 1980s firmly established on the faculty of the School of World Mission at Fuller Theological Seminary. Neither colleagues nor students at this prestigious missions institution expected me to radically change the solid, evangelical approach to Christianity and its relationship to culture that I had been teaching for more than a decade. But when it was suggested to our faculty that we invite John Wimber to teach a course entitled "Signs, Wonders and Church Growth," I remembered the embarrassment of the questions in Nigeria that I could not answer. I strongly supported the offering of the course and decided to attend.

A new phase of my life commenced with the start of that course in January 1982. I began to see what it is like to assume that Jesus *meant* it when He said, "Whoever believes in me will do what I do . . ." (John 14:12). We saw many people healed before our eyes because Wimber and his ministry team members asserted the authority of Jesus over whatever problems people came with. And in due time I began to claim the same authority, and to experience similar results. It became clear to me that for years I had been longing for the kind of authority and power we see in the pages of the New Testament.

Now, fifteen years later, I have found meaning, excitement and spiritual enrichment beyond measure as I work in Jesus' authority to bring freedom to those who are hurting. Although the class Wimber taught focused on physical healing, I soon discovered that God has gifted me in dealing with the deeper emotional and spiritual areas that often underlie physical problems. For twelve years I have been involved in what I call deep-level or inner healing. This ministry frequently brings me face to face with demons. Probably at least half of the thousand or more ministry sessions I have led have involved demons.

With demons, even more than with emotional or physical problems, it becomes obvious that we are working both under and with Jesus' authority. Often I will ask a demon if he recognizes that I come in the authority of Jesus. The answer is always yes; and he has to submit to that authority, since it is much greater than his.

But the authority of Jesus has many more dimensions than simply dealing with demons. It is about this authority, and these various dimensions, that I write—an authority in the spiritual realm that many Christians (including me, up to 1982) have known little about. It is as if God has deposited a million dollars in a bank for us and either we do not know it or we cannot find the checkbook. Meanwhile, the enemy—who has less authority than we have—goes about his business of disrupting God's plans and tormenting God's people, and we do not know what to do about it.

This book is dedicated to our being tools in God's hands to alert and instruct His people concerning the truths of this part of His Kingdom.

Bringing Tether and Experience Together

Both Scripture and Christian experience, it seems to me, can help us sharpen three primary focuses: allegiance, truth and power. (I will develop these in chapter 10.) For now, as I look back over my life, I can see that before 1982, I had gone a long way in experiencing the allegiance and truth dimensions of Scripture, but had almost no experience in the power dimension.

I had pledged allegiance to Jesus Christ and grown considerably in the depth and intensity of my relationship with and commitment to Him. In addition, I had learned enough scriptural truth to have a depth of understanding as to what the Christian life is all about. But I was almost totally ignorant of the power dimension of Christianity (apart from the power of love and faith) that Jesus and the apostles demonstrated in opposition to Satan—a power often spoken about and demonstrated in Scripture. I had two-thirds of Scripture fairly right. But that one dimension was foreign territory to me.

So as I have moved into the realm of spiritual authority and power, I feel I have become more biblical than I was before.

All of us have a major problem stemming from the fact that many situations we face in contemporary life are neither exemplified nor discussed in the Scriptures. We have gotten used to most of the techniques our churches have come up with to fill in the blanks in the allegiance and truth areas. We endorse evangelistic rallies in which appeals are made for commitment; we approve of educational techniques that train people in the truths of Scripture; and we are comfortable with a variety of other approaches not specifically endorsed by Scripture. These approaches, we feel, fall safely within the tether of Scripture.

But due to our unfamiliarity and discomfort with the power area, we often hear questions (or even raise them ourselves) concerning whether certain techniques are scriptural or not. Or else, as we ask God for guidance in situations involving spiritual authority and power, we

15

find ourselves doing things that cannot be supported by biblical chapter and verse.

In this book, as in my own ministry, I try to work within the limits imposed by Scripture, being careful not to claim as the voice of God any direction that ventures outside scriptural guidelines. As in the allegiance and truth areas, though, I find a lot of room within the tether for God to lead us creatively. The Scriptures themselves give us plenty of evidence that God can and will lead us both directly and creatively.

I would like to acknowledge the assistance of a number of people who have helped me in the writing of this volume. Most of them are also ministry associates, so my gratitude to them goes much deeper than for the help they have been to me in writing.

Special thanks to Sam Fraser, Ellyn Kearney, Jim Wilder, Bill Dancy, Mike Crow, Tom Harang, Gary and Betsy Runkle-Edens and Mark White. And extra-special thanks to Jane Campbell, faithful, conscientious and encouraging editor of Chosen Books.

Charles H. Kraft
South Pasadena, California

1

God's Authority Challenged

In the beginning, God. . . ." God was already there when history began—supreme in power, total in authority over all that existed. With Him were angels and perhaps other heavenly beings that He had created. These lived under His authority and did His bidding.

At least certain of these angels seem to have had authority delegated to them. The archangel Michael is said to have been assigned at a later date to protect Israel (Daniel 12:1). And Gabriel, who described himself as one who "stand[s] in the presence of God" (Luke 1:19), seems to have been given authority to interpret God's revelations to humans (see also Daniel 8:15–27; 9:20–27).

Then there was an angel named Lucifer. He was one of the archangels, perhaps the highest of them. We are not told what his assignment was, only that he rebelled. As Isaiah puts it,

> You were determined to climb up to heaven and to place your throne above the highest stars. You thought you would sit like a king. . . . You said you would climb to the tops of the clouds and be like the Almighty.
>
> Isaiah 14:13–14

We do not know why this being now known as Satan sacrificed his position as second in command to fight his Master. Perhaps what tipped him in that direction was the rumor that God planned to create a new being, a human, who would carry God's own image and displace Lucifer from second place in the universe. My theory is that this plan of God angered him beyond his willingness to remain obedient, so he rebelled and set up his own kingdom.

Whatever the reason, when Lucifer rebelled he became an enemy of God. But he left the presence of God with considerable authority and power. We do not know just how much of his authority and power as an archangel Lucifer was able to keep. Perhaps God allowed him to retain as much as he had had when he was serving Him. Whatever the amount, Lucifer seems to have a good bit of ability to disrupt the plans of God and His creatures. This situation has resulted in one of the great ironies of history: a being who uses the very power God allows him to oppose the God who gave it to him.

But this irony is paralleled by another: the fact that God has done the same thing with humans. God has set certain limitations on Himself by giving to humans (and apparently to angels) a certain amount of autonomy that we can use, if we choose, even to oppose the One who gives it to us.

At Creation

At the right time, God created the earth and all that He put in it, culminating His creation with His masterpiece, human beings. Having provided a lovely garden for them to live in, God made Adam and then Eve, placing them high above all other created beings. God made them in His image, like Him, resembling Him and having authority over all creation (Genesis 1:26). He then commanded them to "have many children" who will "bring [the earth] under their control" (Genesis 1:28). As the psalmist says,

> You made him inferior only to yourself; you crowned him with glory and honor. You appointed him ruler over everything you made; you placed him over all creation.
>
> Psalm 8:5–6

It is a shame that many translations, following the Greek Old Testament, misrepresent what I believe the psalmist is getting at here by translating the first part of this verse, "You have made him a little lower than *the angels*" (NKJV, italics added). The Hebrew word used here is *Elohim*, the word ordinarily translated "God." Perhaps they translated *Elohim* this way because they could not believe the position this verse and the creation account claim for us.

Since we are definitely *not* created lower than the angels, however, and since that Hebrew word is almost always translated "God," it seems strange that the English translators would perpetuate the mistake

19

made long ago by those who translated the Old Testament into Greek. See the next section for a discussion of Hebrews 2:7, in which the Greek version of the Old Testament of this verse is quoted with regard to Jesus living for a little while below the (satanic) angels.

At creation, therefore, authority of several kinds was given to Adam and Eve: authority to carry the image of God; authority to create children in God's image; authority over all creation. All would have gone well—with God over everything, humans under Him and angels serving them both—if God's enemy, Lucifer, had not succeeded in enticing Adam to misuse his authority by giving it all away.

But Adam, as we know all too well, fell for Satan's deceit. God's enemy led Eve to doubt the truth of what God had said by offering her the possibility of knowing as God knows (Genesis 3:4–5). Foolishly Eve, and then Adam, agreed to doubt, then disobey God, and in the process become obedient to Satan. In obeying Lucifer, Adam gave away the authority God had given him over the creation.

All that was under Adam's authority fell when he fell. His disobedience brought a curse on God's creation and gave Satan authority over all that God had given Adam and Eve. Satan had a right, therefore, in his discussion with Jesus, to claim that all the power and wealth of the world "has all been handed over to me, and I can give it to anyone I choose" (Luke 4:6).

The Fall did something to our status in the universe. Though we were created above the angels, including Satan, we now fell below him. This delighted Satan, of course, since it restored him to second place in the universe. We may picture the three situations as follows:

20

Before Creation (Genesis 1:1)	Just after Creation (Psalm 8:5)	After the Fall (Luke 4:6; Hebrews 2:7–9)
1. God	1. God	1. God
2. Archangels	2. Human beings	2. Satan (an archangel)
3. Angels	3. Archangels (including Satan)	3. Human beings
	4. Angels	4. Archangels
		5. Angels

From that day to this, there has been war between the two kingdoms, as Satan uses the authority given him by God to oppose God.

At Redemption

The news, however, is not all bad. God Himself worked out a plan to redeem us, and in so doing, to restore us to our rightful position in the universe. Into situation number three above, Jesus came as a human being, living in our post-Fall human context "for a little while lower than the angels" (Hebrews 2:7). As a man He retraced Adam's footsteps up to the point of temptation, facing temptation after temptation and succeeding in obedience where Adam had failed.

Jesus' life was a continual exhibition of the obedience in which humans were intended to live. We were made to function in dependence on and obedience to God, and things have not been right since our ancestor chose not to depend and obey. But Jesus came as Adam came, innocent of sin, and committed Himself to win the battle Adam lost and show us the way we were intended to live. Jesus came under an agreement with God the Father not to use His divine abilities while on earth. According to Philippians 2:6–8, Jesus, though fully God,

21

encapsulated that part of Himself and chose to function totally as a human, modeling what true humanity was intended to be. (See *How to Have a Healing Ministry* by C. Peter Wagner [Regal, 1988], pp. 113–132, for an excellent discussion of this point.)

Jesus did no mighty works before the Holy Spirit came on Him at His baptism. Indeed, He lived such an ordinary life before that time that the people of His hometown, Nazareth, were startled when He began asserting Holy Spirit authority in ministry (Matthew 13:54–57).

Jesus' obedience, then, took Him even to the cross, and through that to the empty tomb. Thus He won the battle over Satan from behind enemy lines—won it as a man for both humans and God. When the Father resurrected Jesus, a cosmic battle was won, and the usurper defeated and deposed from second place in the universe.

Having won the battle as a human being, Jesus has given us the same Holy Spirit who guided and empowered Him. This makes it possible for us ordinary humans, as we follow Jesus' example of obedience and intimacy with the Father, to return to the original place of authority for which we were created.

Jesus went behind enemy lines to defeat the enemy and begin to establish His own Kingdom in the middle of enemy territory. And as He set about establishing His Kingdom, He assumed the authority ("glory") He had with the Father before the creation of the world (John 17:5). And since this was behind enemy lines, it meant warfare—spiritual warfare aimed at taking back God's world from the usurper. Then Jesus recruited us to continue the operation in Satan's territory.

So the context in which we operate as soldiers in Jesus' army is one of spiritual warfare. It is on the battlefield that we assume our authority. And it is the enemy of our General, Jesus, that we challenge when we exercise that authority. Every time we assert our authority, we are cutting into the domain of the impostor king who took it away from our ancestor, Adam. According to Romans 16:20, it is God's desire that we press on with Jesus until that enemy is crushed under *our* feet.

Our redemption, then, is first a restoring of humanity to the possibility of the kind of relationship God intended when He created Adam and Eve, and then an empowering for victory over the evil one within the territory he stole from us. Redemption enables both our relationship with God and our victory over Satan. And the authority and power that come with the relationship enable us to participate in present victories over the usurper.

How Much Authority Does Satan Have Now?

John says, "The whole world is under the rule of the Evil One" (1 John 5:19). Exactly how much authority does Satan have? Can he do anything he wants or are there restrictions? What about differences between non-Christians and Christians? Can he hurt Christians, or only non-Christians?

First of all, we know what Satan wants to do. As John states, "The thief [Satan] comes only in order to steal, kill, and destroy" (John 10:10). And he does whatever he can within the parameters of his authority. This authority, according to Hebrews 2:14, may include the ability to bring about death—though still within the limits God sets for him.

Knowing what Satan intends for us, while noting the fact that there are many people still alive in the world, suggests that much of the time Satan does not get his way. The reason he cannot destroy those still alive must be because they are, at least for the present, protected

23

by a greater power, the power of God. All who are alive, whether Christian or non-Christian, are alive because they are protected by God.

Some people, however, seem to have greater protection than others. In the first chapter of Job, Satan complains that God has "always protected [Job] and his family and everything he owns" (Job 1:10), thus keeping enemy forces from doing what they wanted to do to him. God agrees to relax His protection, allowing Satan to do anything but take Job's life.

From Job's story we learn at least two things about authority. First, *Satan's authority is limited by God and, in some cases at least, very strictly limited.* Job seems to have been granted special protection beyond that available to the rest of mankind. Thus, in Job's case, and probably in many other cases down through history to this day, God sets even stricter limits than normal on Satan.

The second thing we learn is this: *Under certain circumstances, God grants greater authority to Satan than is ordinarily his.* Satan requested permission to launch a special attack on Job and was granted it. Or consider the apostle Paul. Whether it was in response to a request of Satan that God granted him the right to attack Paul, we cannot know. But we do know God allowed "Satan's messenger" (2 Corinthians 12:7) to afflict Paul to keep him from being puffed up with pride. It is not impossible that this is also what happened with King Saul, about whom it is recorded that "an evil spirit sent by the LORD" troubled him (1 Samuel 16:14; see verses 15–16, 23; 18:10; 19:9). We know God was fed up with Saul. He may, therefore, very well have given Satan extra permission to harass him.

From other Scriptures we derive a third principle concerning how much authority Satan has. In Exodus 1:8 we learn that an Egyptian pharaoh came to power who

24

did not know about Joseph and felt no obligation to keep the agreement of his predecessors to treat the Israelites kindly. As long as the pharaohs kept their agreement to treat Israel well, Satan could do nothing to the Israelites. But as soon as a pharaoh was willing to put aside that agreement, the enemy was given his chance to afflict them. It becomes clear, then, that *if Satan is to be able to exercise the authority he wants to, he needs human cooperation.*

At the time of Jesus' birth, it was the agreement of Herod to carry out Satan's plan that enabled the enemy to institute the slaughter of the babies. These and other examples suggest that the amount of authority Satan can exercise in any given situation may be calibrated to the amount of human cooperation he receives.

Another possible area of satanic authority is weather. It is not clear from the Gospels what Satan's attempt to kill Jesus in the storm (Matthew 8:23–27; Mark 4:35–41; Luke 8:22–25) indicates concerning his authority over weather. Is weather one of the areas Satan gained authority over at the Fall? Or did he gain authority in that case by special permission? I suspect God controls weather, but that He sometimes gives Satan special permission to interfere in the normal operation of things.

I heard recently, for example, about a man who had a son with a terminal illness. In his concern for his son, he vowed that he would be willing to give up his life if his son would thereby be healed. Sometime after the man made this vow, he and his son were walking together outside and were struck by lightning. The father was killed, and at the same moment the son was apparently healed. (At least, the doctors could find no trace of the disease in him after that event.) I assume that God did not cause the father to be killed. He did, however, allow the enemy to empower the vow, which resulted in death for the father and healing for the son. Satan could have that authority only with God's permission.

Another problematic area concerns death. Hebrews 2:14 speaks of Satan as the one who *"has* [present tense] the power over death." Does this mean Satan is the agent of death all the time? Or some of the time? Or are we being misled by the tense of the verb? We explore these and other principles relating to Satan's authority in chapter 5.

What Are the Implications for Christians?

On several occasions people have come saying something like this: "I had fewer problems in life before I became a Christian than I have had since. Can you tell me why?"

In return I ask, "If you were the enemy, whom would you attack—your friends, those who are on your side and doing your bidding; or your enemies, those committed to Jesus, who could hurt you?"

Other people ask whether, if they get into spiritual warfare, their families are in danger. I answer yes. Then I ask them how they prefer to lose a battle—running, hiding or fighting.

For we *are* at war, whether we like it or not. And in war, if we are not fighting—if we are simply standing around, or hiding from the reality of the war, or actually running away from it—we are being defeated. I would rather lose while fighting than in any other way. If we are fighting, though we may lose some of the time, we often win.

The point is, Satan has real authority to harass and even attack us. He is our enemy, according to 1 Peter 5:8 (a letter written to Christians), roaming around "like a roaring lion, looking for someone to devour." And since we are at war, we should expect harassment and attack.

Apparently Satan also has authority to blind people's minds to the truths of God. Paul says, with respect to unbelievers:

They do not believe, because their minds have been kept in the dark by the evil god of this world. He keeps them from seeing the light shining on them, the light that comes from the Good News about the glory of Christ.

2 Corinthians 4:4

And not only unbelievers. I am afraid Satan is able to blind certain Christians, too, leading them away from Christ and making it impossible for some of them to return. Hebrews 6:4–6 speaks of such people, stating that it is impossible to bring back to faith those who have once been believers and then abandoned Christ. The enemy also seems able to render many Christians ineffective. It is as if they came to Christ and got locked up almost immediately in a prisoner-of-war camp, headed for heaven but no threat to the enemy.

Satan definitely has the authority to hinder God's people and organizations, whether directly or indirectly, through people who (knowingly or unknowingly) serve him. In 1 Thessalonians 2:18, for example, Paul speaks of Satan as the one who prevented him from traveling back to Thessalonica to visit the church there. In 2 Corinthians 12:7 Paul refers to his "thorn in the flesh" (KJV) as "Satan's messenger to beat me and keep me from being proud," even though it was clear to him that God Himself had allowed the problem. And Satan was undoubtedly behind the imprisonments, whippings, stonings, shipwrecks and multiple dangers that Paul lists in 2 Corinthians 11:23–27.

Doesn't God protect us? Doesn't He send angels to look after us? Indeed He does. If He did not, none of us would be here, since the aim of the enemy is to kill and destroy us. Often dealing with demons makes us aware that God's angels are helping us. (Realizing this, one of my former ministry team members asked a demon how many angels were present. The demon answered that the room was filled with them.)

But if angels are always present to protect us, why do bad things often happen to Christians? I am afraid I do not know the answer. I assume, though, that we have the right to ask for more angels to protect us whenever we find ourselves in dangerous places. It is my practice to keep myself constantly aware (though in a calm frame of mind) that I am living in enemy territory. And although God is supreme and granting me a great deal of protection, I do not know all that is going on, so I ask regularly for more protection—for example, when I am driving or riding in a car, when I am walking on sidewalks or crosswalks, when I am traveling by plane, and at other times and places that seem dangerous. More on this in the next chapter.

Misunderstanding the Enemy's Authority

The activity of Satan in the world is so obvious that many assume he has more authority and power than is actually the case. Others, of course, ignore or deny his existence and blame human beings or our environment for all the trouble. Either of these extremes, as C. S. Lewis pointed out, is dangerous. And both positions leave us misunderstanding the enemy's authority and power.

Overestimating Him

For those who believe Satan is alive and active, most know in their heads that the power of God is greater

28

than that of Satan. But the box score of good and evil seems to indicate Satan is winning. So for those who simply look at surface-level phenomena, it looks as though there is a big Satan and a small God.

Unfortunately, many Christians fall into this category and, without meaning to, give Satan more honor than he is due. Even in Pentecostal and charismatic circles, where the power of both God and Satan are frequent topics, fear of the enemy is heightened beyond what it should be. Stories of violent deliverances, for example, often focus attention more on what the enemy did than on what God did. Seldom do such circles recognize that most of what demons do is bluff rather than power, or that by first taking authority over the strongholds within a person, the power of the demons can be greatly reduced before they are challenged. (See my *Defeating Dark Angels* for a complete treatment of this approach.) My colleagues in ministry and I have been able to perform literally thousands of deliverances without violence by using this approach.

Another unfortunate aspect of our Christian experience that gives the impression Satan has more power and authority than he does is irresponsible English translations of certain passages in the New Testament. There is absolutely no warrant in the Greek for the translation *demon-possessed* that appears in Matthew 4:24; 8:16, 28, 33; 9:32; 12:22; Mark 1:32; John 7:20; 8:48, 52; 10:20; and Acts 19:13 in the King James, New King James, American Standard, New American Standard, Revised Standard, New Revised Standard and New International Versions. The Greek term in these passages translated *demon-possessed* means simply "have a demon." (See the rendering in Today's English Version or *Good News Bible* of the above verses.) When the translations give the impression that someone who harbors a demon is "possessed" by that demon, people get a dis-

29

torted view of Satan's authority. The term exaggerates the amount of authority the enemy has—and, I am sure, puts a smile on his face.

The truth is, no one is controlled by a demon one hundred percent of the time, as is implied by the term *possessed*. There are, of course, shamans in the world who call on spirits to possess them for various purposes. But even in those cases, the possession lasts for only a short time. My ministry associates and I have found that, although demonization is common, comparatively few people who are involuntarily inhabited by demons are taken over to that extent. And the vast majority of those who have demons are seldom, if ever, under the total control of the demons. Even the Gerasene demoniac, the most severe case in the New Testament (Mark 5:1–20), had enough free will to run to meet Jesus and to fall on his knees in worship (verse 6). The demons would not have had him do that, even though they were able to control his behavior totally at other times.

In reality, the devil has little, if any, power or authority other than that granted him by those who obey him or their ancestors. Even most of those who harbor demons are able (often with difficulty) to thwart much of what they try to do. As Nigel Wright says in *The Satan Syndrome* (Zondervan, 1990):

> The vitality of the devil is parasitic and his strength substantially drawn from humanity. . . . The power that the devil has in himself is far less than we might imagine and far more dependent on that which mankind gives him.
>
> p. 48

Because of this, James can assume it is possible for humans to "resist the Devil," resulting in his (eventually) running away from us (James 4:7). And as Walter

Wink points out, the devil of James 4:7 "is not the devil of popular fantasy, that virtually omnipotent enemy of our race. This devil knows his place!" Wink goes on in his book *Unmasking the Powers* (Fortress, 1986) to quote Ignatius Loyola to the effect that this enemy by nature is given to flight as soon as someone spiritual stands against him, courageously doing just the opposite of what Satan has tempted him or her to do.

Underestimating Him

It is just as dangerous, on the other hand, to misunderstand the presence and power of Satan by ignoring or denying his existence. This is the fallacy millions of Western Christians have fallen into. By ignoring him, we have allowed the enemy to do his work unchecked. Many sincere Christians even deny his existence, preferring to see the evil of the world exclusively in humans or human structures. They think Jesus was simply accommodating Himself to the ideas of His day and culture by referring to psychological problems and other unexplained phenomena as demons, and by personifying evil and naming it Satan.

Soldiers who are on the battlefield but not fighting cannot expect to win. This is one reason so many Christians are living defeated lives.

Such inactive soldiers do, however, win occasionally—when they do the right thing inadvertently. Happily, some who ignore the enemy do win at least several battles by following some of the spiritual rules, even though they know nothing of the impact of their behavior in the spirit world. When a man loves God with all his heart, soul and mind, and his neighbors as himself (Matthew 22:37–39), he wages spiritual warfare whether he knows it or not. Likewise when a woman prays, worships and does deeds of mercy. But although occasional battles may be won even by bystanders, it takes active soldiers to win the war. If we do not assert our authority over Satan, he will assert his authority over us.

To misunderstand the position of the devil relative to that of the children of God is to misunderstand who we are and the authority we are given in that position. Unlike Satan, we bear the image of God and have been redeemed by God and made co-inheritors with Jesus of the riches of our Father God (Romans 8:17; Galatians 4:7). By virtue of our position, and the fact that God the Holy Spirit lives within us, we carry infinitely more power and authority than the whole satanic kingdom. This is what we need to understand as we probe the various dimensions of spiritual authority.

Recognizing the Cosmic Conflict

Many people object to the "two-kingdoms-in-conflict" teaching. They do not like this interpretation of Scripture, feeling it gives the enemy too much attention and does not put enough focus on God's great plan of redemption. Some are also bothered by the teaching that we are affected (as this approach contends) by the actions of our original parents. This does not seem fair, they say, since we were not there to have our say or to place our vote.

In answer to such positions, I point out that God has rules (see chapter 4), such as the rule that has established a mystical bonding between members of the same family and, indeed, between all of us as members of the human race. This means there is spiritual as well as biological inheritance, enabling the sin of our first parents to be passed down to all their descendants, and spiritual bondages and strongholds to be passed from generation to generation within families.

With regard to spiritual warfare, some claim that most of the Bible does not speak overtly to this theme. In a sense they are right, especially when the Bible is interpreted naturalistically rather than supernaturalistically. But I remind these people of the opening three chapters of Genesis that clearly introduce a spiritual and cosmic conflict between Satan and God, with humans as the intended prize; and about the book of Revelation, with its focus on the climax of the same struggle.

Those willing to listen usually open up to this perspective when I point to the glimpses of the interactions between God and Satan that are provided by Job, Daniel, the Gospels and Acts. Although not every page and verse of the Bible speak to the spiritual warfare theme, a good bit of Scripture does. And whether we understand or agree with it or not, the apostle Paul reminds us,

> We are not fighting against human beings but against the wicked spiritual forces in the heavenly world, the rulers, authorities, and cosmic powers of this dark age.
>
> Ephesians 6:12

Recognizing the cosmic conflict throughout the Bible, capped by these words from Paul, should help us view the entire biblical revelation *through spiritual warfare lenses*. When we begin to do so, both Scripture and the authority issues in focus here take on new significance. War between the two kingdoms is the essential backdrop from which to interpret the Bible and discover what spiritual authority is all about.

With this background, then, let's turn to a discussion of several basic issues concerning authority, including how it is transmitted.

2

Jesus' Credit Card

Dad, would you put my name on your Visa card? I'm going off to college fifteen hundred miles away, and the car might break down. You wouldn't want me to be stranded somewhere without being able to pay the bill, would you? I promise I won't misuse it."

The words were those of my son, Rick. And they all made sense to me, though I was a bit apprehensive about whether he would keep his word not to misuse the card. But he is *my son,* my own flesh and blood, and I was an important part of this, his latest adventure. I knew that, in addition to paying his tuition, my granting him this request made sense. My name would still appear first on the card as the one with ultimate responsibility. But Rick's name would appear immediately under it, giving him authority to spend whatever the company would allow me by way of credit.

When my son's name was added to my credit card, he gained all the financial authority that *my* name would bring. At that time, my son's name carried no authority, since he had no credit with any financial institution. But with my name to back him, he would be able to handle almost any emergency that might confront him far from home.

When I did this for my son, I made it clear that I expected him to not misuse the authority I was giving him. He was young and might well have misused it, and he needed to keep on good terms with me or his privilege might be revoked. But to his credit, he never misused the privilege.

Jesus' Authority under the Father

When Jesus came to earth, it was as if He carried a credit card from His Father with the Father's name at the top and His own name under it. He, like my son, *came with all the authority His Father's name would bring.* He had full authority to spend whatever was in the Father's account so long as He kept on good terms with the Father and spent it for purposes of which the Father approved. Jesus knew both that He had His Father's authority, and that His right to use it was contingent on His maintaining intimacy with His Father.

For as He stated in John 5:30, "I can do nothing on my own authority . . . because I am not trying to do what I want, but only what he who sent me wants." Earlier in the same chapter, He said that "the Son can do nothing on his own; he does only what he sees his Father doing" (John 5:19). And with reference to His teaching, He said, "I do nothing on my own authority, but I say only what the Father has instructed me to say" (John 8:28; see John 7:16–18).

Jesus was a Man under authority. He worked according to the guidelines He and the Father had agreed on before He came to earth. The major guideline, as we noted in the last chapter, was that *He would never use the power and rights of His divinity while on earth* (Philippians 2:6–8). He agreed to work only under the authority of the Father and the power of the Holy Spirit. Following the Father's instructions, Jesus did nothing miraculous until after His baptism.

Jesus' power came from being filled with the Holy Spirit. The source of His authority, however, was His intimacy with the Father. He spent hours and hours in prayer alone with the Father, keeping in close contact with Him and cultivating that most precious relationship. In this way, He kept His will lined up with the Father's, seeing to it that He always obeyed Him and that He did nothing except with the Father's agreement.

As Jesus ministered, His ears were always open to the voice of the Father. He was always listening for what the Father wanted to do. Because He listened, He could take authority confidently, knowing He was acting in God's purposes. Jesus' intimacy with the Father enabled Him both to maintain His authority and to get God's instructions concerning what the Father wanted Him to do each day.

It Was Surprising and Threatening

It was the authority in which Jesus worked that most surprised the people of His day, and that was most questioned by the Jewish leaders. We already observed that Jesus experienced a fairly normal childhood and young adulthood, during which the people of His hometown, Nazareth, apparently noticed little to predict what He would become. This is clear from the fact that they were amazed when He started to do miraculous things: "Where did he get such wisdom? . . . And what about his miracles? Isn't he [merely] the carpenter's son?" (Matthew 13:54–57; see Mark 6:1–6). They would not have asked these questions if they had seen any indication during Jesus' growing-up years of what He would become.

At about age thirty, Jesus went to John to be baptized (Luke 3:21–22), after which things took quite a different turn. The Holy Spirit came on Him at His baptism, and He started to minister in authority and power beyond anyone's expectations or understanding. He began to heal and cast out demons, causing amazement among the people: "What kind of words are these? With authority and power this man gives orders to the evil spirits, and they come out!" (Luke 4:36).

These people had seen demons cast out. The Pharisees had ways of getting at least some people free from demons. Jesus referred to this at one point when, in countering their claim that He worked in the power of Beelzebul, He asked by what power "do your followers drive [the demons] out?" (Luke 11:19). The people had not, however, seen demons approached in the authoritative way Jesus worked—and had not, of course, seen the demons respond as if they had no option but to obey.

If the people were amazed, the leaders were threatened by Jesus' authoritative way of going about His ministry. But in spite of the fact that He did things no one else could do, they refused to believe He had come from God. So they challenged His authority, asking, "What right do you have to do these things? Who gave you such right?" (Mark 11:28; see Luke 20:2). These were the religious leaders questioning His right to help, His right to heal and free people from the clutches of Satan. How ironic! Those appointed to serve God and demonstrate His care for His chosen people were opposing the One who was doing what they were supposed to be doing.

But their own power and authority were threatened. The extent of this perceived threat is seen in John 12:19, where they exclaim, "You see, we are not succeeding at all! Look, the whole world is following him!"

So the scribes, Pharisees and other Jewish leaders, instead of recognizing in Jesus the God they claimed to serve, played into Satan's hands and opposed Jesus. Thus, they used their authority to "lock the door to the Kingdom of heaven in people's faces," neither going in themselves nor allowing others to enter (Matthew 23:14).

Satan's temptations were his first direct challenge to Jesus' authority. The devil offered Jesus the authority he had won from Adam, showing Him "all the kingdoms of the world. 'I will give you all this power and all this wealth. . . . It has all been handed over to me, and I can give it to anyone I choose'" (Luke 4:5–6).

This being whom Jesus later referred to as "the ruler of this world" (John 14:30) was offering our Lord an easy way to the authority the Father planned to give Him through death and resurrection (Philippians 2:9–11).

At the end of Jesus' time on earth, we see a further confrontation between Jesus' authority and that of Rome represented by Pilate. This Roman official asserted his claim to authority over Jesus as he attempted to get Jesus to defend Himself, saying, "Remember, I have the authority to set you free and also to have you crucified" (John 19:10). In response Jesus pointed out the real source of Pilate's authority: "You have authority over me only because it was given to you by God" (verse 11).

Jesus Gives His Authority to Us

As One under authority yet exercising the authority of God, Jesus did the most amazing thing after His resurrection: He passed on the authority in which He worked to His followers.

During His ministry, He sent them out to heal and cast out demons in "power and authority" (Luke 9:1; see Luke 10:9, 17). The disciples had worked in Jesus' authority while He was on earth, and He had promised them that when He left, He would send them the Holy Spirit, the One who had empowered Him, to enable them to do all He had done and more (John 14:12). So, just before Jesus left, He instructed them to wait in Jerusalem "for the gift I told you about, the gift my Father promised . . . the Holy Spirit" (Acts 1:4–5). And He commissioned them to carry out certain tasks:

> "Go, then, to all peoples everywhere and make them my disciples: baptize them in the name of the Father, the Son, and the Holy Spirit, and teach them to obey everything I have commanded you."
>
> Matthew 28:19–20

This Great Commission, however, is prefaced by this statement:

> "I have been given all authority in heaven and on earth."
>
> Matthew 28:18

Thus, Jesus' final command to us, as well as our commission to represent Him, are grounded in the authority He won through obedience to the Father. His command—that we bring all peoples into a discipleship relationship to Him, initiating them into the family of God and teaching them to obey everything Jesus has commanded us—is made on the basis of the incredible authority given Him by His Father.

39

The Great Commission implies, I believe, that Jesus' authority will underlie ours as we obey.

Knowing Who We Are

Both Jesus and my son, Rick, knew who they were in relation to the one granting them authority. If we are to operate properly in Jesus' authority, we, too, need to understand who we are in the universe—our identity.

It was *my* son who asked to have his name put on my credit card, not someone else's son. Our relationship is very special. This made it possible for Rick to ask such a favor with confidence, knowing I would grant his request because of who he is in relationship to me. He was (and is) proud to bear my name and be identified with me. And I am proud to have him bear my name and be identified with him. So he could come to me without fear of being rejected, knowing and trusting both our relationship and my positive attitude toward him. As my son, he has certain rights stemming from his relationship with me.

I have become convinced, through working in inner healing and deliverance, that the enemy's primary area of attack is our self-image. *He does not want us to discover who we are.* I work with victimized, abused and defeated people whose lives are often characterized by severe hopelessness or depression. Yet they are often brimming with hidden talents and untapped spiritual gifts given to them by God at conception. The enemy, knowing what these gifts and talents are, has done his best to keep these people from knowing their abilities. And he has destroyed or nearly destroyed their perception of who they are intended to be.

My aim is to get them cleaned up from their emotional problems and any demons they may be carrying, and to bring them to a new understanding of who God made them to be. What a joy it is to watch people come to know who they are!

If we are to live and minister effectively for Christ, we need to know who we are and what that means. As Dean Sherman says in *Spiritual Warfare for Every Christian* (Frontline, 1990), "If we are unsure of ourselves, it is because we do not yet know who we are, or in whose authority we operate."

Let me summarize eight important points relative to who we are.

1. *We are created "only a little lower than God"* (Psalm 8:5, NLT) and in the image of God Himself (Genesis 1:26). Our position at creation (as we saw in the last chapter) was far above all created beings, including the angels—in second place in the universe. We must never forget this, for the enemy will not be content until he has blotted it out of our minds.

2. *Although in Adam we gave it all away, God has stepped in and redeemed us.* Through the Fall we dropped to a position below the angel Satan. But God did not leave things that way. He made it possible through Jesus, the second Adam (1 Corinthians 15:45–47), for us to be reestablished in our rightful position just under God, on the basis of our faith. I think it is significant that God did this for us but not for the angels. We, not the angels nor any other part of God's creation, are His masterpieces. And only we have been offered redemption.

3. So now, as John says, *we who have committed ourselves to Christ are the children of God:* "See how much the Father has loved us! His love is so great that we are called God's children—and so, in fact, we are" (1 John 3:1). As God's beloved children, we even inherit with Christ (Romans 8:17; Galatians 4:7). God has adopted us, chosen us (Ephesians 1:4), much as a childless couple chooses and adopts a child into their family. By His

41

choice we are part of God's family, restored through redemption to our original position above Satan. And the universe, including Satan's hosts, have to recognize this fact.

4. As family members, *God gives us the Holy Spirit to live within us.* Thus we get to carry infinitely more power than all the satanic kingdom put together! Within us lives God Himself, the Creator and Sustainer of the universe and of all the angels, including Satan. When we realize this, we are different persons in relation to the enemy and the universe. For we know this really is our Father's world, even though Satan has control of it for the present (1 John 5:19).

It was difficult for the disciples to understand why Jesus needed to go away so that the Holy Spirit could come (John 16:7). The disciples (and we) may wonder how anything could be better than Jesus' presence. But I believe Jesus was pointing to the time when the Holy Spirit would not simply be *with* them but *in* them (John 14:17).

For up to the coming of the Holy Spirit in Acts 2, the relationship between the followers of Jesus and the Holy Spirit seemed to be an external one. Jesus was with them and, on occasion, guiding, giving them authority and empowering them (see, for example, Luke 9:1–6). But since the Holy Spirit came on all of them in Acts 2, God Himself has come to live *in* us, bringing with Him power (Acts 1:8), gifting (1 Corinthians 12:1), fruit (Galatians 5:22–23) and *the very presence of God permanently from within.*

5. Our position has been further dignified by the fact that *God in Jesus has united with us for eternity.* He could not have united with an angel or animal, only with one who bears His image. So God in Jesus joined Himself to us, forever becoming the union between Creator and creature. In His ascension Jesus never went back to simply being God. He is still one of us and will be for eter-

nity! And because of this, we get to share with Him the inheritance reserved for the siblings of the King.

6. *We are children of the King.* This is our true identity, giving us special rights and privileges with our famous Father. We have, among other things, special permission as His princes and princesses to come into the King's presence at any time. Someone has written a book about life with a famous father entitled, *I Called Him "Dad."* Though many would have given their right arms to spend time with this person's famous father, only the son, the author of the book, got to come into that man's presence at any time, without an appointment.

That is the way it is with us and God. The awesome Creator of the universe, the One whose name strikes fear into the hearts of those who have offended Him—this God, this fearsome One, is our Father. We need have no fear in His presence as Isaiah did (Isaiah 6:5) or uncertainty as Esther did (Esther 4:11) over whether the King will extend His favor to us. We have been invited to come boldly and confidently into His presence (Hebrews 4:16), running even into His throne room, knowing we are welcome because we are His children. And we call Him *Abba,* our dad (Romans 8:15; Galatians 4:6). So to exercise our authority properly, we need to know experientially just who we are and, as with my son and the credit card, just who our Father is.

Allowing this truth to penetrate the deepest parts of me has transformed me. It has destroyed my negative self-image. I have lived most of my life with a Charlie Brown or Murphy's Law attitude that says, "It's normal for things to go wrong, so if anything goes right, it must be a mistake." With this attitude, I felt God must have made a mistake by linking up with me. What freedom I have found in allowing myself to accept and bask in the truth of what God thinks of me! And what confidence in operating in the authority and power He has entrusted to us!

We are saved by God's grace (Ephesians 2:8). We are also adopted, given position and empowered by that grace. All this is incredible—totally beyond anything we deserve. Yet God Himself has chosen to arrange things this way. So we stand in the universe as the adopted children of God Himself, given all the rights and privileges of family members, including the right to operate in the power and authority of the Maker and Sustainer of the universe.

7. *By His grace God actually trusts us!* Something within me says, *He should have known better than to entrust His work to us.* But just as Jesus forgave and trusted the adulteress (John 8:1–11); forgave, reinstated and trusted Peter (John 21:15–19); and trusted His disciples enough to turn the Kingdom over to them; so He trusts us. When Jesus left the earth, He entrusted us with the Holy Spirit and predicted that with Him we "will do what [He did]—yes, [we] will do even greater things" than He did (John 14:12). Jesus trusted the disciples and us so much that He calls us His friends—those entrusted with "everything I heard from my Father" (John 15:15). It is, therefore, our Kingdom as well as His (Luke 12:32; 22:29–30). Knowing who we are enables us to work in unison with the Lord, tapping into the riches of our position in Christ.

Back when there were genuine kings and queens, their rule was absolute. The princes and princesses had authority as well, and all the subjects of the kingdom had to yield to their authority. In the spiritual realm we carry the same authority as God's princes and princesses. When we understand that identity and use the power of Jesus' name appropriately, the spiritual realm has to obey. We have "every spiritual blessing in the heavenly world" available to us (Ephesians 1:3). If

44

only we could grasp how much God wants us to appropriate the authority and power that rightly belongs to
us, based on our position in Christ! The satanic kingdom trembles to think what that would mean.

The position God has given us is awesome. We are in
such an elevated place that the angels watch us curiously
(1 Corinthians 4:9; 11:10; 1 Timothy 5:21; 1 Peter 1:12)
and serve us (Hebrews 1:14). Furthermore, we will get to
judge them (1 Corinthians 6:3). Again, God did not think
highly enough of the angels to redeem those who followed
Satan; He redeemed only us. What grace and love! What
a privilege is ours to belong to God's family! We must never
forget who we are, even when we do not feel like it.

8. *Spiritual authority, then, is part of who we are.* It is
recognized by God and by the enemy world as *flowing
from our very beings.* As Michael Crow has written, spiritual authority

> is the activity of God which occurs in and through a per-
> son's life, not simply because of his or her position or
> competency. It is the operation of the Spirit of God which
> emanates out of a leader's personality, gifting, charac-
> ter and intimacy before God, and influences others
> toward a similar commitment to the purposes of God.

As Christians we have no choice as to whether or not
we possess this authority. It comes in the package when
the Holy Spirit is given to us. Our only choice is whether
we learn how to use this authority, and then actually
make use of it. Like a credit card.

Our Authority under Jesus

We have seen that, on what was probably Jesus' last
day on earth, He stated, "I have been given *all* author-

ity in heaven and on earth" (Matthew 28:18, italics added). On the basis of that authority, He commissioned His followers with the authority to make disciples of "all peoples everywhere," and promised to be with them "to the end of the age" (verses 19–20).

What a great day when He was able to claim "all authority"! It meant He had fulfilled His mission, successfully completed the task assigned Him by His Father. He had refrained from claiming this authority during His pre-resurrection time on earth since He had agreed with the Father to work only under His authority. But now the Father had chosen to turn over all heavenly and earthly authority to His Son in repayment for Jesus' obedience. As He did so, "God raised him to the highest place above and gave him the name that is greater than any other name" (Philippians 2:9).

One of Jesus' first uses of that authority was to give us the Holy Spirit, as He had promised in John 16:7. In anticipation of this empowerment of His followers, Jesus had told them, "As the Father sent me, so I send you" (John 20:21), and, "Whoever believes in me will do what I do—yes, he will do even greater things, because I am going to the Father" (John 14:12). This means we get the credit card! Now, though, it has Jesus' name, the name above all names, on the top, with our names under it.

With the credit card, we go into the world with Jesus' authority to spend whatever is in His account so long as it is for purposes of which He approves. And He says, "I will do whatever you ask for in my name" (John 14:13), meaning, "I will back up with My authority whatever you say and do that is in accord with My will and the Father's purposes."

So we are to imitate our Master. And we have the ability to do so with the same power of the Holy Spirit under which He worked, and the authority He has given us to use that power. As Jesus obeyed the Father, receiving the Holy Spirit and launching out into ministry, so we are to obey Jesus' command by being filled with the same Holy Spirit who empowered our Lord (Luke 24:49; Acts 1:4–5, 8). Then we, too, can be launched into a ministry of love, power and authority like His and actually do what He did. What He did we are to do, and even more.

Many Christians think they have no right to even think such a thing. After all, they say, "He was God and we are not. He had the power and authority of God; we are merely human." But it is clear from Scripture, as I have pointed out, that Jesus laid aside His divine prerogatives to become human. Though in some mysterious way He continued to be fully God, He compartmentalized His deity and never used it while on earth. So He, like us, lived in a state of powerlessness, except for what the Father entrusted to Him (John 5:19).

One of the things God promises us is the right to use our authority to bring about whatever is in accord with His will (1 John 5:14). Our task is to get our wills lined up with the will of Jesus and the Father, and on that basis to exercise the authority they have given us. This comes for us, as it did with Jesus, from spending time in prayer and fellowship with God in private, listening to Him to get His instructions and to line up our wills with His. Then we receive from God the necessary power and authority for the specific task ahead of us. Our aim in our relationship with God should be nothing short of total intimacy. Again, Jesus is our model.

When seeking to heal or release people from demons, there is no doubt that, through our filling, we have enough power to accomplish what is needed. But we must ask ourselves, *Does what I am seeking to do line up with God's will? Is this what the Father wants?* Jesus' success rate in ministry was one hundred percent, since He always lined up His will with that of His Father. He

47

obeyed continually, and in that obedience attained perfection. What we are able to do in His name may be considerably less than He could do. The difference, I believe, lies in our ability to hear and follow the Father's will.

We know certain things already, however, about the Father's will. We know He wants people to be blessed, to be free from satanic captivity (Luke 4:18), to be joyful and to experience love. Jesus never left the people He ministered to with such problems. He never said things like, "Hang onto your problem. Through it God wants to teach you patience." So to bring release to a given person at any time from illness, brokenness or demonization is likely to be in line with God's purposes; and we can minister confidently in such a way as to expect God to work in at least these key areas. Whether He desires to relieve a person of a particular disability at precisely this time is not as easy to determine. So we are to pray to find out.

For me the biggest challenge in ministering to others is not in the area of power, but in the area of the intimacy of my relationship with the Father—a relationship that is essential to coordinate my will with His. Apart from an intimate relationship with God and an ear tuned to what He desires to do, our own authority-taking can be powerless. What seems to put the power in our authority-taking, as it did with Jesus, is intimacy and hearing God. Together these enable believers to (like Jesus) do the works we see our Father doing. Discerning God's purposes packs our authority with God's power.

During ministry, prayer is crucial. Throughout any given ministry session, we are to pray continually for guidance. But the ministry itself is a time not of asking God for something we have not yet received, but of exercising authority He has already given us. We are to minister as Jesus did—with and in authority. Jesus commanded things to happen as if He was in charge. He spoke to diseases, to demons, even to people as One who knew both who He was and the authority He had been given. This is our privilege and mandate as those who carry His name.

When Jesus sent out the Twelve in Luke 9, and the 72 in Luke 10, He "gave them power and authority to drive out all demons and to cure diseases" (Luke 9:1). Some contend that this empowerment was just for the disciples, but I believe the Master intended for His followers to teach their followers this authority-taking, along with the other things He included when He said, "Teach them to obey *everything* I have commanded you" (Matthew 28:20, italics added). And again, Jesus' promise in John 14:12 holds that "whoever believes in me will do what I do."

On this basis, we are to exercise our authority in the same areas in which Jesus ministered—in sickness, death, blessing, deliverance from demons, forgiveness (John 20:23), teaching and above all loving. In order to equip us for these tasks, when Jesus ascended to heaven, "he gave gifts to mankind" (Ephesians 4:8). And the extent of our authority in any given area, as we will discuss in chapter 5, is calibrated to our gifting.

Authority "Praying"

When we are speaking to God, we usually call what we are doing *prayer.* Jesus believed in prayer and practiced it frequently. But prayer, at least in the usual sense of the word, was not His central activity when He was healing people or delivering them from demons.

There are at least six kinds of activity we may call prayer. The most common of these, the one we usually think of first, is what I will call *asking prayer*. In this kind of prayer, we ask for what we would like or need, as Jesus has invited us to do. As He said in John 16:24: "Until now you have not asked for anything in my name; ask and you will receive, so that your happiness may be complete."

Another familiar kind of praying is *confession praying*. We are told that "if we confess our sins to God, he will keep his promise and do what is right: he will forgive us our sins and purify us from all our wrongdoing" (1 John 1:9). So we pray to confess and receive forgiveness.

A third kind of prayer that may be performed as either prayer or worship is *thanksgiving prayer*, in which we express our gratitude to God without requesting anything from Him.

Then there is *intercession*, an intense kind of praying in which we lay hold of God concerning something we feel especially troubled about. Some with the gift of intercession agonize over a given situation, much like a woman going through labor to bring a child into the world.

The two kinds of prayer most relevant to the present discussion are what I will call *intimacy praying* and *authority praying*. The first of these is the most basic of all the kinds of prayer. It involves simply being in God's presence. We have already spoken of the need for intimacy with God if we are to exercise the authority He expects of us. Jesus modeled this kind of praying by going up a mountain or out into the wilderness to be alone with the Father, and during these times He was refreshed and enabled to meet the challenges of the day. It was also at these times that He received His instructions from the Father as to what He should do next. Jesus could then teach and minister with authority.

Although we often use the expression *praying for healing,* and refer to this activity as "authority praying," I do not believe this is a form of prayer. It is, rather, the activity appropriate immediately *after* prayer when we are ministering to someone.

Jesus certainly prayed before ministering (John 11:41–42) to get His directions from the Father. Sometimes He prayed all night. But while ministering He did not ask the Father to do the job, as I have heard many do when they want someone healed or delivered. With His Father's authority He simply spoke and it was done, because He submitted to the Father's will and always obeyed Him. He knew who He was and what His authority was, so He had no need while ministering to pray in the "asking" sense.

Jesus took the authority the Father had given Him and acted on His behalf. He usually *commanded* the person to be well (Luke 4:39; 5:13; implied in 7:6–10), or the spirit to leave (Luke 4:35), or the winds and waves to be still (Luke 8:24), or the person being healed to do something in faith (Luke 5:24; 6:10; 7:14). Sometimes He touched the person (Luke 5:13). At other times people touched Him and were healed (Luke 8:44; Matthew 14:36).

Yes, Jesus prayed before He did His deeds. But what He did *during* them should not be called prayer. So referring to the part we are to play in God's healing ministry as "praying for healing" may be misleading. We are to imitate Jesus and take authority as He did. When Jesus said that whoever believes in Him will do what He did, I believe He meant to include the *way* He did things in the *what* of that verse. Like Him, we are not to ask God to do the works, but to line up our wills with His and talk not *to* the Father, but *on His behalf,* speaking authoritatively to correct the situation.

51

An overview of this perspective on prayer might be described as follows:

We are to pursue intimacy with God (as Jesus did).

1. Flowing from this intimacy, we are expected to
   - ask;
   - confess;
   - praise and give thanks;
   - intercede.

2. In this intimacy we hear God and receive His instructions.
   - On the basis of these instructions, we operate in the authority God gives to His servants.

Exercising the Authority We Have Been Given

In this section we will review areas (which we will treat in more detail later in the book) in which we are to assert the authority we have been given.

When we assert authority over children or animals, we usually do it vocally. We command what we expect to happen. It is important that we realize, in dealing with spiritual authority, that the spirit world is always listening. So we can speak out what we expect to that listening world, and know we are heard. A useful way of asserting our authority is simply to say something like this: "I speak [protection, blessing, healing, etc.] in the name of Jesus Christ."

Asserting our authority vocally is easiest with demons. They can answer back. But when we command illness to stop or weather to change, it is much less obvious that our words have been heard, especially when the change we have commanded does not take place immediately. Among the reasons for the apparent lack of response might be: We have not really heard from God;

or it is not God's timing yet for the change to take place; or we do not have the right amount of authority to effect this change; or the problem may not be under the control of enemy spirits.

The spirit world cannot turn a deaf ear, however, to the commands of God's servants. Just as we know God hears us when we speak to Him (1 John 5:15), so we can be sure that the entire invisible world is listening when we direct our words its way. Any command we utter, therefore, that relates to the activity of enemy spirits will be heard loud and clear by them. And if our command is in accord with what God wants to do, it will be done.

With our wills lined up with God's, we can and should assert our authority in at least three areas: to protect, to prevent and to attack.

1. To Protect

With regard to protection, we have no need to fear or be the least insecure. As the psalmist states,

> The LORD will not abandon his people; he will not desert those who belong to him. . . . The LORD defends me; my God protects me.
>
> Psalm 94:14, 22

If the Lord were not protecting us from the enemy, we would all be goners. It is clear what the enemy wants to do to us—"steal, kill, and destroy" (John 10:10). It is because of the high level of protection God grants us as His children that the enemy cannot carry out his will.

So we need not be insecure with regard to God's protecting activity. He is always guarding us at a high level.

Yet there are things going on in the universe that we may be quite unaware of. We might not know, for example, if God loosened His protection of us as He did when He allowed Satan to attack Job. And there are rules in the universe (see chapter 5) of which we might be unaware that could allow the enemy to get at us from time to time. Just before His arrest, Jesus advised His disciples to increase their protection by praying that they "will not fall into temptation" (Luke 22:40), and, in the end times, by being "on watch," praying "always that [they] will have the strength to go safely through" the end-time troubles (Luke 21:36).

So, on the one hand, we can assume a high level of protection. But, on the other hand, we need to be alert to vulnerabilities that require more prayer—including, I believe, more authority-taking for protection. For there may be areas in our lives that are not healed (even if we are not aware of what they are) that give the enemy a right to interfere in our lives. If so, we need to claim as much protection as possible.

By learning more of what is going on in the spirit world, however, and more about who we are, I believe it is possible to gain more protection than God grants automatically. For in spite of whatever is going on, there is good news! We have the authority to counter the enemy's devices. We simply need to be aware constantly of who we are and the fact that Satan is less powerful than we are (with the Holy Spirit within us). He can have only the rights that we do not challenge. But it is up to us to ferret out all the authority he has been given and to cancel it.

The world is a dangerous place. I am sure I do not know all the rules that could result in problems for myself and those dear to me. So, without being fanatic or fearful, I claim God's special protection regularly as I go about my daily activities. Much of this is experimental, since I am not always sure whether I need more protection than I would receive if I did not claim more.

I call on God's protection and safety, for example, whenever I am driving, by saying something like this: "I claim safety and protection, in the name of Jesus Christ, as I drive." I also claim protection over myself when I am in a potentially dangerous place. One place I sometimes go that could be dangerous is the health food store, since some of these are run by people into New Age spirituality. So, knowing my authority, I simply claim protection before I go in, saying, "I claim the protection of Jesus Christ over any enemy power that may be operative in this place." If I forget to say this, and notice later that something strange seems to be going on, I cancel any rights the enemy may have gained over me in that place.

I claim God's protection regularly over our home and family. And when I am on the road and staying at a motel, I claim Jesus' protection over the room I am staying in—although I often forget to do this, and on only a few occasions did it seem to matter. At such times, when there seemed to be some hindering power in the motel room, I claimed God's presence and protection after the fact, and things changed.

2. *To Prevent*

Much of the discussion on asserting our authority to protect also applies to using it to prevent things from happening. Often we can see something about to happen and, by taking authority over the situation, prevent it.

On several occasions teachers have described for me the change that has taken place in the behavior of their children after they asserted their spiritual authority over the classroom. They have learned to go into the room before the children arrive and claim it for Jesus Christ. Once I even heard about a person who, concerned over the dangerous way children were running around a motel swimming pool, took authority over the pool area and found that the children's behavior improved.

One of the most effective preventive strategies, I have learned, is when I see a potential disagreement coming, to say, "If this is the enemy, stop it!" I am seldom sure in such a situation that it actually is the enemy. But enough potential problems have not happened when I have used this strategy that I have come to believe in it. On several occasions, when I saw an argument with my wife coming, I said these words under my breath, and our mood changed immediately.

On learning about this aspect of authority about seven years ago, a young woman who was then a student of mine decided to experiment with it. Her sister was coming to visit that evening, which usually meant some kind of difficulty or argument. Just prior to her sister's arrival, my student took authority over her sister, their time together and whatever passed between them. For the very first time in their recent relationship, the sisters spent an enjoyable evening together with no problems.

Regarding my family, I regularly state to the spirit world that "if you [the enemy spirits] want to attack my wife, children, their spouses or our grandchildren, you must go through me, because I am the gateway into this family. But on the authority of Jesus Christ, you will not get through me." I believe this activity has had a lot to do with the prevention of attacks on our family.

I will give further illustrations later of people who have seen situations change by using this preventive strategy.

Another area in which we can prevent enemy activity is in dealing with any artifacts purchased overseas or in New Age or Native American contexts. In many societies such items are dedicated routinely to evil spirits—often as they are made. When dedicated objects are in our possession, they give the enemy rights. But these rights can be taken away when we claim the power of Christ to break Satan's power over the item.

My practice is to speak the breaking of enemy power over anything I buy in a "suspicious" place (even medicines or food supplements bought at health food stores), and then to bless the item with the power of God, so it becomes a source of blessing rather than of danger. I make one exception to this cleansing rule: If something has no purpose other than a religious or occult one, I destroy it after praying over it. A few years ago I was asked to help a friend deal with his Freemasonry books and paraphernalia. He had turned to Christ and knew those objects carried satanic power. So we took authority over them to break all enemy power, burned whatever was burnable and threw the rest in the trash.

3. *To Attack*

Finally, we should assert our authority to attack. When we minister healing or deliverance to people, we are attacking the enemy's grip on them.

Because much in the following chapters has to do with attacking the enemy, joining with Jesus to take away his rights in people and places, we will not deal with this subject thoroughly here. Suffice it to say that since Satan is "the ruler of this world" (John 14:30), we are attacking him whenever we assert the authority given us to hinder his plans. Thus, preventing and protecting are also forms of attack. Our task in any use of this authority is to capture as much as possible of what the enemy has asserted his authority over.

Even witnessing for Jesus is a form of attack. The result, I believe, depends on the will of the person we are witnessing to. But people have reported to me that things changed dramatically when they claimed the authority of Jesus to break through the blinding spoken of in 2 Corinthians 4:4, where it is recorded that "the evil god of this world" keeps people's minds darkened so they cannot respond to the Gospel. Believers are especially able to assert our spiritual authority to bring about change in those over whom we have human authority (for example, our children, other family members, our students). As those who belong to Christ, we have the right to claim our authority to open them up to the light of God.

I am often asked if our authority to attack works at a distance. If we look at the account of Jesus' healing of the Roman officer's "very dear" servant (Luke 7:1–10; Matthew 8:5–13), I have to answer yes, although some of the details of that situation probably indicate that certain conditions have to be met in order for authority to be exercised effectively at a distance.

The first thing to note: Jesus had heard from the Father that He was to heal the servant, for He was already on His way to minister to him. Second, a great amount of faith was exercised by the Roman officer, probably paralleled by great willingness and faith on the part of his servant. Third, the officer showed profound understanding of the spirit world and Jesus' position in relation to it.

We might infer, then, that when we find willingness and faith on the part of the recipient, and a go-ahead from the Father, the enemy can be attacked successfully even at a distance. I do not know if ministering over the telephone counts as attacking at a distance, but I have often ministered effectively over the phone, both in deep-level healing and in casting out demons.

Authority to Bless and Curse

We will deal with blessing and cursing again in chapter 8, but they are such an important aspect of our authority that I will begin to treat them here.

If we can judge by Jesus' behavior after the resurrection (John 20:19, 26), He blessed people regularly, when He came into their presence, with the lovely Hebrew greeting *Shalom,* "peace." He commanded His followers to bless people's households in the same way when He sent them out to minister (Luke 10:5).

We learn from Luke 10 that we are to bless freely, before we even know how our recipients will react. But not everyone will accept us (verses 6, 10–11). When this happens, we are justified in taking back our blessing (verse 6), since the person who declares a blessing "owns" that blessing. Indeed, if we are rejected, we can go further and publicly shake the dust of the unreceptive town off our feet (verse 11).

We are not authorized, however, to curse those who reject or offend us, although with the authority to use words to bless others comes the authority to curse. Instead we are commanded to bless and pray for others, even those who curse us (Luke 6:28; see Romans 12:14; 1 Corinthians 4:12). And according to 2 John 9–11, we are not to bless heretics—"anyone who does not stay with the teaching of Christ, but goes beyond it." A heretic, says John, "does not have God." So we are not to "welcome him in [our] homes" or "even say, 'Peace be with you.' For anyone who wishes him peace becomes his partner in the evil things he does."

The authority to bless and curse is an incredible endowment. God empowers our words, so we need to watch them and use them only as He directs us. I doubt He wants us to use them indiscriminately to bless everyone. We should listen to Him, therefore, blessing only those He tells us to bless. It is from listening to Him, furthermore, that we hear what we are to bless them with.

Things happen when we bless. I have heard many people remark that they felt a pleasant charge like electricity flow through them when I spoke a blessing over them. I believe it was Agnes Sanford who reported an experience in an elevator in which she blessed a woman silently who was complaining about everything. By the time the woman got off the elevator, she had become positive about the day and about life in general! I have had similar experiences with people to whom I have ministered.

In addition, the protection we discussed in the previous section can be brought about by blessing whatever it is we seek to protect. Besides protecting cars, computers, homes and family members, I have been experimenting with blessing myself with protection from disease and accident. I think it has been working.

There is a kind of passing along of blessing that seems to happen when we take authority over places and things that are then used by others. The power of God through blessing apparently extends even to influencing people who use objects that have been blessed. This happens (as I suggested) when teachers take authority over their classrooms. It also happens when we bless churches, sacred objects, our homes, specific rooms within our homes, the furniture on which people sit, our offices or other workplaces, computers and other objects people use. The blessing carries over to the people who use the items or places.

With this in mind, we should take seriously the blessing of our food before we eat. We have the authority to empower food and drink to bring blessing to those who eat and drink it.

A scriptural example is the use of Paul's handkerchiefs and aprons to bring healing and deliverance (Acts

19:12). People have told me things changed when they blessed letters and sent them to people. I am not sure what the rules are in this area, but it cannot hurt to experiment with using our authority to bless things used by or given to others. We can bless places and buildings with freedom from enemy activity, and with protection against any plans he might have for them in the future.

Things also happen when we curse by directing negative words toward people or objects. Many who have spoken such negative words toward themselves have found themselves, or parts of themselves, cursed. Often people who are sexually abused, for example, curse their sexual organs or their ability to enjoy sex. Such directing of spiritual power toward oneself is likely to develop into disease in one's sexual organs or dysfunction in one's sexual experience. I have seen dramatic changes in people who have asserted their authority to renounce the curses they put on themselves or parts of themselves. Once they have renounced the curses, I usually ask them to go on and begin blessing those parts of themselves that are now freed from the curses. We can do this with the authority God gives us.

A helpful use of cursing is in praying for people who are ill. Often I curse the germs and viruses (never the people) that are causing the illness. Frequently things change, probably due, at least in part, to the cursing of the germs and viruses. Since we do several other things when we minister to people, however, it is impossible to know just how big a part the cursing of germs and viruses plays in our healing experiences.

Authority to Bind and Loose

In Matthew 16:19, just after Peter's great acknowledgment of Jesus as the Messiah, and again in Matthew

18:18, the Lord makes an amazing statement: "What you prohibit on earth will be prohibited in heaven, and what you permit on earth will be permitted in heaven." When Jesus says this to Peter, He uses the singular *you*. But when He repeats it in Matthew 18, He uses the plural *you*, extending this authority to the whole group, and to all His followers down through the centuries.

Older translations use the word *bind* rather than *prohibit* or *forbid* (Phillips), and *loose* rather than *permit* or *allow* (New English Bible). Whatever terms are used, the focus is on the close relationship between what happens on earth and what goes on in heaven. Jesus' statement would seem to confer great authority on us to do *something*. Just what that something is, though, is hard to figure out with any high degree of certainty.

The Aramaic terms that underlie the Greek words were used technically to relate to the excommunication and reinstatement of people. The original hearers, in the view of Herman C. Waetjen in *The Evangelical Dictionary of Theology* (Baker, 1984), would probably have assumed that Jesus was giving His followers "the authority to exclude from, as well as to reinstate in, the community of believers." This is an incredible authority to have. But the question is, did Jesus intend something broader than simply including or excluding people from the Christian community?

Many people speak of "binding Satan" and often say things like, "I bind you, Satan," when they want to stop something he seems to be doing. Some who speak like that, I am afraid, regard these words as almost magical, as if by their simple utterance, the enemy will be stopped. We do have authority over Satan, but it is questionable that is what Jesus had in mind when He made those statements. So I would rather say things like, "Stop it!" or "I forbid you to do that!" to make the point in more understandable terms.

But there is probably a relationship between those statements and the one in John 20:23 where Jesus says, "If you forgive people's sins, they are forgiven; if you do not forgive them, they are not forgiven." If so, one of the things we have authority to do that is honored in heaven is to forgive. Again, we will explore this further in chapter 8.

In whatever sense we take binding and loosing, Jesus has given us great authority. This authority is wielded ordinarily through words, whether they be words of commitment, vows, blessing/cursing, accepting/rejecting or forgiving/not forgiving. It is important that we use this authority, as Jesus used His, with wisdom.

If Only We Realized How Much Power We Carry!

Our authority gives us the ability to use the power God gives us through the indwelling of the Holy Spirit. Most of us, however, seem only vaguely aware of how much power that is. We would do well to consider that when the Holy Spirit dwells within us, we are invested with the power of God Himself, and with the full authority of Jesus to use it. What a tragedy that many of God's choice people, although given both His power and the authority of His credit card, either do not realize what is theirs or else refuse to exercise those rights!

A friend told me once about an acquaintance who had been converted to Christianity out of a New Age group. While in bondage to Satan, this woman had the ability to "see" the amount of spiritual power different people carry with them, and could spot Christians "a mile off" by simply noting the amount of power they carried. Although she knew Christians wield more power than New Agers, she also knew that most Christians have no idea

63

what to do with that power. So the Christians were no threat, except the occasional one who knew how to use the power of Christ. She and her fellow New Agers tried to keep well away from such people.

How different their experience might have been, the convert remarked, if the Christians they met had only realized how much power they carried, and had exercised their God-given authority to use it.

So that we ourselves may better realize our own God-given authority, let's turn to a discussion of the nature of that authority.

3

What Is This Authority?

Several people in New Testament days apparently went around casting out demons. Like anyone in a deliverance ministry, they were always open to learning new techniques. They probably attempted to coax out the demons, as was the custom among the Pharisees of Jesus' day. Then they heard that some were having success driving out demons by using the name of Jesus, a prophet about whom a Jew named Paul spoke. So they decided to try this new approach. We are not told how many used it, nor how often they were successful. But the impression given in Acts 19 is that there were a number of these deliverance specialists, and that the new approach worked for a period of time.

Seven sons of a Jewish high priest named Sceva, however, tried the technique on the wrong demon. This demon was not buying their approach. He was apparently a powerful demon, and knew who had authority over him and who did not. So he responded to their command to leave by saying, "I know Jesus, and I know about Paul; but you—who are you?" (Acts 19:15). Then he proceeded to beat up all seven of the brothers, attacking them "with such violence that he overpowered them all" (verse 16). These seasoned deliverance specialists "ran away from his house, wounded and with their clothes torn off," never to try that approach again!

There is a big difference between having the authority of Jesus and not having it. These men did not have that authority. But we do. That should change things for us.

Defining Authority

We have already noted Jesus' words, "I have been given all authority in heaven and on earth" (Matthew 28:18), and, "I have given you [the disciples] authority, so that you can . . . overcome all the power of the Enemy" (Luke 10:19). Earlier, as Jesus sent the disciples out "to preach the Kingdom of God and to heal the sick" (Luke 9:2), He gave them "power and authority to drive out all demons and to cure diseases" (verse 1). If Jesus meant what He said to apply to us, and I believe with all my heart that He did, we have been given a truly awesome privilege and responsibility.

The concept of authority is closely connected in the Scriptures with the concept of power. The Greek words representing what Jesus gave His followers are *dunamis,* power, and *exousia,* authority.

Dunamis occurs some 118 times in the New Testament. Paul uses the word frequently, as do the writers of the first three Gospels. It is the normal word for power, might, strength or force, and is often used in the plural to refer to miracles ("wonders") in the phrase *miracles and wonders,* as in Acts 2:22, 2 Corinthians 12:12 and Hebrews 2:4; or to supernatural beings ("powers"), as in Romans 8:38, 1 Corinthians 15:24, Ephesians 1:21 and 1 Peter 3:22.

The power of God is ordinarily referred to as *dunamis,* as is the power Jesus gives us (Luke 9:1). But earthly power, whether of rulers, of armies or of weather, was also labeled *dunamis.* So the English word *power* is usually an adequate translation of this word.

Exousia, though often referring to power, focuses on the right to use power rather than on the power itself. This word occurs 108 times in the New Testament, always related to people. It is a personal right, either because of status or by delegation, to assert power, whether in legal, political, social or moral ways in the human world or in the spiritual realm.

In the New Testament, both power *(dunamis)* and authority *(exousia)* flow from the work of Christ, first as He employed them and then as He empowers His followers to do His works. As we have noted, Jesus received His power from the Holy Spirit, and His authority from maintaining His intimacy with the Father. At the end of His ministry, then, He gave His followers the Holy Spirit (Luke 24:49), the source of His power, and advised them to keep close to Him (John 15:1–17).

Thus, the authority we participate in is that modeled by Jesus Himself and grounded, as it was with Jesus, in the same power of the Holy Spirit. It is the God-given right to receive and use God's power that flows from the indwelling Holy Spirit.

What Our Authority Is Not

If we are to understand properly what our authority is, we need to consider what it is not. We need to know, first of all, that the basis of our authority is our position in Christ, and certainly not our feelings. We may not always *feel* authoritative, any more than we always feel married or even accepted by God. Our feelings are just not good indicators of the truth.

A missionary I will call Lisa is a case in point. Lisa and her husband were students at the School of World Mission where I teach and were learning a lot about spiritual warfare. When Lisa came for ministry, one of her main concerns was her inability to exercise her spiritual authority in Christ. Every other Christian was worthy of the privilege, she felt, except her.

Lisa was believing a lie, and her feelings supported the lie. But as she began to practice using her authority, she learned just how crippled she had been by the lie. To escape her dilemma, she began to choose to go against her feelings and believe the truth. She found that by accepting and choosing to believe the truth of her authority, and then by acting on it, she was as worthy as anyone.

Lisa has now become a powerful spiritual warrior and a real threat to the enemy's kingdom.

Nor should we see Christian authority as a kind of gifting or personality type. We may regard certain people around us as "persons of authority" because they have an authoritative manner about them. The Christian's authority truly is a gift, but it is given to *everyone* in God's family and is not related to personality.

Several members of my ministry teams over the years have had meek and mild personalities, but it is exciting to see how obediently demons respond to their authority. Those who attempt to command demons purely on the basis of their own personal authority, on the other hand, do not (like the sons of Sceva) get very far.

Our spiritual authority is rooted in our position as members of God's family. It is ours whether or not we feel it, whether or not we have a special gift or personality type. Although there is a relationship between gifting and the authority to minister in any given area (as we will see in chapter 6), that relationship is secondary. All Christians have the right to both pray and relate to enemy forces in Jesus' name. This authority has been won for us legally by Jesus through His victory on the cross and from the tomb, where, according to Dean Sherman in *Spiritual Warfare for Every Christian*, "Jesus took from the devil the legal right to the balance of power on this planet."

But it is scary to have the authority of God and to use His power. It would be easy to misuse it. Indeed, the amount of spiritual abuse occurring in churches today should warn all of us to be careful lest we misuse the authority that has been delegated to us. Perhaps the following considerations will help.

1. We Do Not Own It

First and foremost, *the authority should not be seen as something that belongs to us.* It is entrusted to us by God and we are to manage it. Our first responsibility, then, is to be faithful to our Master in the way we use what He has trusted us with. "A person who is put in charge as a manager must be faithful" (1 Corinthians 4:2, NLT). We are to treat this authority as something precious, something we do not own but are trusted to manage, lent us by the One to whom we have committed our lives. We dare not consider it a right or legacy with which we can do anything we want.

2. We Must Use It Rightly

Since we are stewards or managers of something we do not own, *we need to be careful to use the authority for the purposes for which it was given to us.* Happily we

69

have Jesus to model ourselves after. We are never to use spiritual authority to show off or simply to enhance our own reputations. Such use of authority and power was refused by Jesus (Matthew 12:38; 16:1; Mark 8:11; Luke 11:16).

When someone is in need, however, especially if that person is being tormented by the enemy, we are to show the same kind of compassion that motivated our Master.

3. We Must Not Presume

Third, *we must be on our guard to fight any tendency to presumption.* There are several dimensions to this problem.

a. *We must never assume that our authority gives us the right to command God to do our will.* This is one of the errors Satan made when he "put the Lord . . . to the test" (Matthew 4:7) by seeking to control when Jesus would do miraculous things. Although God in His mercy sometimes gives us our way, we should be careful not to try to force His hand. As usual, it is Jesus who showed us how it should be done. For He did nothing on His own authority, as we have seen; He said and did only what the Father instructed Him to do (John 5:19; 8:28).

We fall into the error of trying to force God's hand, I am afraid, when we try to bargain with Him over someone's healing. "This person has done so much for You; surely he deserves to be healed," we say, or, "It would be such a great testimony to all the unbelievers for her to be healed."

b. Even worse is the idea that we should simply name what we want and claim it. People who teach this are, perhaps without realizing it, leading us to believe we can coerce God into doing our will. "God wants us to be happy," they say. "So if we simply exercise our faith by picturing what we want and claiming it, He will give it to us, if our faith is strong enough." Then, if we do not receive our desire, it is ostensibly because we do not have enough faith, or else there is sin in our lives. This is not a proper use of authority. It is presumption and deceit. And this kind of teaching leaves many Christians confused about the nature of God and feeling guilty about their lack of faith.

A friend of mine who has used a wheelchair all her life told me of something that happened to her at a church picnic. During the prayer and worship time, an athletic young man came to ask if he could pray with her. Of course, she accepted. Much to her surprise and dismay, after the young man prayed for a few seconds, he attempted to yank her out of her chair. When it was obvious she was not healed, he turned to her and asked, "Where's your faith, sister?" Later on, her pastor suggested that she should have replied, "Not in you, brother!"

Faith is not refusing to accept or believe reality. It is pressing on with God despite a reality that is sometimes not of our choosing.

c. Another presumptuous way of trying to get God to do our will is by *making our plans first and then expecting God to bless them.* I am afraid I make this mistake often. I am used to being in charge, and have long had the habit of working things out pretty well on my own before I think to consult God. I am trying to break this habit by remembering to consult God first. But it is easy to assume that we know in advance exactly what to do, and then simply to go ahead and do it. In this way we abuse the privilege God gives us of working *with Him* in His authority.

d. A related presumption is that *we alone know the mind of God* on any given issue and can therefore assert His authority without reference to what others are thinking. This error leads us to use our authority to promote a personal agenda. We may be ambitious to achieve prominence or a certain position and assert the authority God has given us for selfish ends. But just as prophecy is not to be interpreted individualistically (2 Peter 1:20), so any plans for the use of authority should be made in consultation with others who hear God's voice, especially if that authority is to be applied in a church or community setting.

e. Then there is the presumption that leads to *wrong timing*. We may discern correctly what God wants but run ahead of Him, using our authority to implement some plan or tackle some problem before the time is ripe. God tends to work slowly. We tend to be impatient, even to the point of wanting to force God's hand. We must resist this presumption.

f. Finally there is the presumption that leads to *defiance or rebellion*. Unfortunately there are people once committed to God who, like Satan, use the authority God gives them to resist Him. They are like King Saul, who could not wait for the prophet Samuel to arrive to offer the appropriate sacrifice (1 Samuel 13:7–14), or who, on a later occasion, took the attitude that "there's no time to consult the LORD!" (1 Samuel 14:19). God is very patient, however, and often allows even those who are disobedient to Him to continue to operate in His authority, at least for a time.

4. We Are Not Indispensable

The fourth misuse of authority *results in spiritual pride*. It is important not to get so focused on the results of ministry (many of which are truly spectacular) that we begin to feel we are especially gifted or, worse, indispensable to God. If we fall into these errors, spiritual pride develops, and our ability to love and serve as Jesus wants us to suffers. Our relationship to the Giver of our authority must always take priority over the results.

Remember the reactions of the twelve disciples, and then the 72, after Jesus gave them power and authority over demons and to heal diseases. They came back rejoicing, astonished at the results of their authority (Luke 10:17). They marveled at what they had been able to do in spiritual power. But Jesus quickly put the issue of spiritual authority back into perspective for them by reminding them that it is our relationship to God that is most important, not our ability to do spectacular things. He said, "Don't be glad because the evil spirits obey you; rather be glad because your names are written in heaven" (verse 20).

So let these misuses of the authority God gives us warn us to be careful to use it rightly—in submission and obedience to our Lord. We must always remember that our authority is not a license to do whatever we want, whenever we want to do it. Our motivation for using God's authority needs to be as pure as possible. We must not be seeking our own gratification, but rather the glory of God. We must be attempting to fit in with His purposes when we take His authority, so that through faith our wills are aligned with His will.

When there is success, then, we can rejoice over what God has done and over the fact that we were submissive and obedient.

Accountability to God

A critical concern in the exercise of power is our *accountability*. In the Kingdom of God, the one who has authority is accountable to God to discover and follow His will, rather than to simply implement his own desires. As Watchman Nee has well put it in *Spiritual Authority* (Christian Fellowship, 1972):

> For one to be in authority does not depend on his having ideas and thoughts; rather does it hinge on knowing the will of God. The measure of one's knowledge of God's will is the measure of his delegated authority. God establishes a person to be His delegated authority entirely on the basis of that person's knowledge of God's will. It has nothing at all to do with having many ideas, strong opinions, or noble thoughts. Indeed, such persons who are strong in themselves are greatly to be feared in the church.
>
> p. 116

Conformity to the will of the One who grants the authority is, then, a major requirement. And indeed, whenever we assert the authority given us, it is up to God whether or not He will carry it out. But as 1 John 5:14 tells us, "We are sure that he hears us if we ask him for anything that is according to his will."

We are to use the authority delegated to us, wrote Nee, to represent God and His will, not to substitute our desires for His. *Our authority is a delegated authority*—delegated by God. We are simply stewards of what He has entrusted us with. We are never to assume that our authority comes from any quality or worth inherent in us. Whether our authority is greater or smaller, we are all of equal value to God.

Take a husband's authority over his wife. It is based not on any greater value of a man (there is none), but solely on the fact that God has delegated authority in this way. Likewise with the authority of parents over children, or of pastors over their congregations. The authority God delegates to each of us may differ, for it is not inherently ours. It is something granted to us, as

Nee points out, *for the purpose of representing the God who gave it to us.*

In Obedience

Since this is a delegated authority, it is crucial that we exercise it in obedience. We must be conscious at all times that big mistakes have been made in this dimension of the relationship between God and humans, and to try not to make any more. The sin of Adam, the one that gave away our human authority over creation, was the sin of disobedience. And it was through obedience that Jesus, the second Adam (1 Corinthians 15:47), won back our right to assert authority over the universe.

Practicing obedience to the One under whose authority we operate teaches us how to exercise the authority He delegates to us. As we obey, we become more like Him, both in character and in our relationships with those under our authority. We learn, for example, to focus on Him, the Giver of the authority and power (as well as of all other gifts of the Spirit), not on the gifts themselves. Assuming obedience and submission to God, then, we take a stand for the same things that the One we obey stands for.

To Other Believers

In addition to our accountability to God, we need to relate to mature, dedicated people who will hold us accountable. We have seen over and over in public life what happens when people in authority are not accountable to others in the way they exercise their authority. The founders of our country set up our government with three branches to give it a system of checks and balances, so that, theoretically, no one branch has more influence than another. Temptations to misuse our authority proliferate in the exercise of spiritual authority. It is important, therefore, to make sure there are safeguards to prevent that from happening.

We need to solicit the help of others to constantly monitor our submission and obedience to God in the way we exercise our authority. It is important that each Christian belong to a group of respected, mature believers who can give feedback in the wisdom of God. Too often those in Christian ministry isolate themselves from fellow believers who can advise and, if necessary, correct them. We tend to be lone rangers, consulting only ourselves. But God wants us to function as a body, not as isolated body parts.

One of the best decisions I have made is to join between five and ten men weekly for fellowship and counsel. We have different gifts but the common purpose to live for and serve our Master as faithfully as possible. We seek to hold one another accountable, both in personal matters and in ministry.

Every Christian needs, with the help of such a group, to conduct regular reality checks on ourselves, by comparing what we are doing to the ways in which Jesus carried out His activities.

In Examining Fruit

An important but often slower measure of accountability is the fruit a ministry produces. Jesus said that if we are connected to Him, the Vine, we "will bear much fruit" (John 15:5). If the authority we exercise results in people being helped, healed, freed and growing in the Lord, it should be continued. If there are constantly negative results, on the other hand, with people being damaged and the name of the Lord being dishonored, the activity should be discontinued. Any accountability group needs to be vigilant and bold in alerting us to negative fruit.

The nature of our authority demands that we keep ourselves aligned with the character of the One who grants us our authority. We are accountable to be true to the nature and character of God. One of the common pitfalls is behaving as if we can wear our authority as a lawman wears a badge, and commanding authority because of the power it represents. What we hear about police abusing their authority is true in the Christian realm as well.

Authority is an awesome responsibility and privilege. The power of that authority can be used to bear much fruit. It can also be mishandled and abusive. To remain submissive and obedient to the One who grants authority, we need to understand the character of God and, by holding ourselves accountable to live by that standard, to see to it that we do not overstep the boundaries.

In Healthy Fear

Another incentive to accountability is healthy fear. Fear can keep us accountable. Though fear of the enemy can be crippling, a healthy fear of misusing our God-given authority can be very freeing. Knowing how easy it is to overstep our boundaries and to misuse the authority God has granted us should raise within us a constructive kind of fear.

It is said that if we fear God, we need fear nothing else. Let that fear of displeasing God keep us accountable and able to work in freedom. It was this fear that guided Joshua and kept him faithful while he was conquering the Promised Land. He was told by God to "be determined, be confident" (Joshua 1:7). Out of fear of disobedience, then, Joshua could exercise his God-given authority boldly.

Power Wrapped in Love

The model for us to imitate, as always, is Jesus. With all the power of the Holy Spirit within His authority, He was remarkably controlled in His use of that power. He used His power only in a context of love. In fact, *He used His power specifically to show His love.*

So the preeminent rule in exercising the authority God has given us is to operate in His authority *lovingly.* Those with authority are tempted to behave harshly. This is not God's way. Jesus, while working in great authority, also recognized He was under authority, so His responsibility was to do His Father's works *in His Father's way.* Our responsibility is likewise to exhibit the character of Jesus as we assert the authority He gives us. We are to manifest the fruits of the Spirit (Galatians 5:22–23) as we operate in the gifts of the Spirit and to *wrap all authority in love.*

Throughout Scripture we see God's concern for those in difficult circumstances: orphans and widows (Deuteronomy 14:29; 24:17, 19; 27:19; Psalm 10:18; 68:5; 146:9; Isaiah 1:17; Jeremiah 22:3; Zechariah 7:10; James 1:27); the poor (Exodus 23:6; Deuteronomy 15:11; Psalm 35:10; 82:3; Isaiah 11:4; Zechariah 7:10); the oppressed (Psalm 10:18; Isaiah 1:17). God wants His power used for the sake of the powerless. This is why He was so angry with David for stealing Bathsheba from her husband. David, with all the power of his kingship and all the wives his position entitled him to, had used that power to defraud Uriah of his only wife.

Jesus, with this God-ordained concept of how power is to be used, resisted the temptation to do power demonstrations on demand or to show off. When asked to demonstrate His power in order to prove Himself, He refused. He would not use His power even to prove Himself to the skeptics (Matthew 12:38–39; 16:4; Mark 8:11–12; Luke 23:8–9). But when He saw someone in need, it is recorded over and over again that "his heart was filled with pity for them," or, as the older translations have it, He was "moved with compassion" (Matthew 9:36; 14:14; Mark 6:34; see Matthew 15:32; 20:34; Mark 1:41; Luke 7:13).

Likewise His heart was filled with compassion when He encountered demonization. But, although He could have made a big deal of delivering people from the power of the enemy, He chose to do it quietly. Jesus even shut the demons down when they tried to broadcast who He was (Mark 1:25; Luke 4:35), thus using His authority to keep control over the source and timing of the revelation of His Messiahship.

In all of this, Jesus used His authority and power to show God's love. *Jesus always wrapped His power in His love.*

So we must not lose sight of the fact that the authority God gives us is to be used only for His purposes and in His way. This is implied in the ideas of obedience and submission to Him. It is agonizing to me to see the apparent pride of some who conduct "miracle healing campaigns" or even local church healing services. They often seem more concerned to parade their own gifts than to honor the Giver of those gifts. I do not understand the graciousness of God in allowing those who seem to be misusing their gifts to continue to operate in them (though I am happy to claim that grace for myself when I overstep my bounds).

I was watching such a healer on television one evening (though I cannot stand to do it very often) and thought, *How different this must be from the way Jesus did things!*

This man was a showman, his every move timed for dramatic effect. He strutted. He swaggered as he moved from place to place on the stage to touch the people who had been brought to him. They usually fell backwards as he touched them—a behavior he expected and milked for dramatic effect. He lifted his head, touched his forehead and closed his eyes dramatically as he spoke his words of knowledge, as if he were dragging them out of the Master's mind.

Although God in His love and mercy uses this man and often brings blessing and healing through him, I doubt He approves of the way he goes about ministry. The man's performance made me angry because he was making a public spectacle out of the right Jesus has given us to assert authority over the results of illness and accident. Since showing off is so unlike our Lord, I feel this man was using his authority irresponsibly. My own conviction is that we are to use His authority in a way that demonstrates the character of Jesus.

Isn't it interesting that *the only characteristic Jesus mentions as designating a true disciple is love?* Although spirituality, intimacy, righteousness, authority, power and a number of other things are important marks of a disciple, love is the distinguishing characteristic. We are to imitate Jesus, therefore, by living lives of love; and all that we do with the authority and power God gives us is to be wrapped in love.

My rule is, if something is not loving, it is not Jesus' way, even if it is spectacular. Anything we do that is unloving, even if it is powerful, is not from God. The gifts of the Spirit (1 Corinthians 12:8–11, 28–31) are to be accompanied by the fruits of the Spirit (Galatians 5:22–23), especially love. I contend that people like the man I saw on television, even if they are marvelously gifted, abuse others even while they are trying to help them. This is not God's way of doing things, and it is not to be our way.

The first rule for each of us as we minister in the authority God has given us, then, is to *wrap God's power in God's love, as Jesus did.* Only if what we do is truly loving is it truly healing.

Other Ways to Exercise Authority

There are four other ways, in addition to being accountable to God and others, and bathing all use of authority in love, in which we are to exercise the authority we have been given.

1. *We are to exercise this authority in humility.*

I find the fact that God trusts us with His power and authority deeply humbling. Indeed, I have found nothing so humbling in my life as the experience of using the authority granted me by God to be doing things I know I cannot do in myself. As Nee says in *Spiritual Authority,* "The nearer one is to the Lord, the clearer he sees his own faults" and limitations. When we assert authority to minister healing and the Holy Spirit does not come to bring it about, nothing happens. But the fact that He comes so regularly—in spite of our weakness, unworthiness, sinfulness and just plain inadequacy— produces humility in anyone who thinks deeply about what is going on.

2. Second, *we need to exercise this delegated authority in the same kind of security that characterized Jesus.*

We can be as secure as Jesus was because, like Him, we know who we are, who God is and that He is the source of our authority. On this basis we can be free from insisting that others listen to us or submit to us. "The more God entrusts to us," wrote Nee in *Spiritual Authority,* "the more liberty we grant to people." Secure husbands are intent on enabling their wives to live in freedom. Pity the wife of an insecure, authority-abusing husband who is threatened by freedom. Secure parents allow their children a lot of room to grow in. Secure pastors and other leaders exercise their authority by encouraging freedom and growth, not by restricting it. Jesus was secure enough to reinstate Peter after his denials and to trust him with His sheep (John 21:15–17).

3. In the third place, *truly God-ordained authority always issues in service.*

Since Jesus is our model, His commitment to serving is the example we are to follow in the exercise of the authority He gives. As Richard Foster said in *Celebration of Discipline:*

> The most radical social teaching of Jesus was His total reversal of the contemporary notion of greatness. Leadership is found in becoming the servant of all. Power is discovered in submission. The foremost symbol of this radical servanthood is the cross. . . . Christ not only died a cross-death, He lived a cross-life. . . . He lived the cross-life when He took a towel and washed the feet of His disciples. . . . Jesus' life was the cross-life of submission and service. . . . The cross-life of Jesus undermined all social orders based on power and self-interest. . . . The cross-life is the life of voluntary submission. The cross-life is the life of freely accepted servanthood.
>
> pp. 101–102

As Paul taught in Ephesians 5:23, 25, a husband is to exercise his authority over his wife by giving himself for her, just as Jesus gave Himself for the Church. Jesus, our model for how to exercise authority, stated that He "did not come to be served; he came to serve and to give his life to redeem many people" (Mark 10:45). Authority is to be exercised in service.

4. *And all this adds up to maturity.*

The Christian is to exercise authority in as mature a fashion as possible. Though maturity is often difficult to define, any person who operates as a faithful steward in love, humility, accountability, obedience, security and service qualifies as mature. The proper practice of the authority God entrusts us with requires nothing less.

When and Where Are We to Exercise Authority?

Again Jesus has shown us the way. As we have pointed out, He did no mighty works on demand. When He was approached by one or more needy persons, however, the Scriptures note that He felt compassion or pity and healed them (Matthew 9:36; 14:14; 20:34; Mark 1:41; Luke 7:13). Most of Jesus' healings seemed to be in public (Luke 4:40; 5:18–20; 7:12–15; 8:42–48; 9:42–43; 18:35–43; 22:50–51), though sometimes He seems to have worked in private or semiprivate settings (Luke 5:12–14; 8:26–39). When crowds converged on Him, there is no record of His turning them away. Usually the Bible says He healed many or all of them (Luke 4:40; 5:15; 6:19; 7:21; 9:11). Sometimes He went to a home (Luke 4:38–39; 8:51–56; 14:1–4); at other times He healed in the Temple or a synagogue (Matthew 21:14; Luke 4:33; 6:6; 13:10–13); and once it is recorded that He healed from a long distance (Luke 7:2–10). Though there was much to do, Jesus never seemed to get frantic or even hurried.

An interesting thing about Jesus' use of His authority is that He seldom went looking for people to minister to. Perhaps this was because He did not have to. People knew He could heal and sought Him out. We do know of one time, however, when Jesus chose someone to minister to—the man who had been lying beside the pool of Bethzatha for 38 years seeking healing (John 5:1–9). The Master, undoubtedly on instructions from the Father, went to the pool specifically to seek and heal one person out of what may have been hundreds at the poolside.

The message in this for us would seem to be that if we follow Jesus' example, we should be prepared to minister in power and authority at any time, anywhere and to anyone. Although we, like Jesus, should rarely, if ever, set out to find those to heal, we should be open to pray with anyone who comes our way.

To get started, so that people know we are able and willing to minister in power and authority, we may have to keep our eyes open for those who need prayer. Americans today, even Christians, are so reticent to seek God's power for healing that I have found it important, especially when taking my first steps in a healing ministry, to ask people suffering from some ailment if they would like to be prayed for. Even the disappearance after prayer of such comparatively minor ailments as colds or headaches makes quite an impression. And once it becomes known that God uses you to heal, people will come to you.

So use your authority everywhere. The world is waiting for those who will be faithful to the One who has called us to do His works. It is up to God to bring results.

The Relationship of Spiritual Authority to Human Authority

All authority is from God, whether it is granted by Him directly, or indirectly through human means. Our primary concern here is for authority granted directly by God. It is important, however, to survey the varieties of human authority and the ways in which spiritual authority is (or should be) expressed in relation to them. For there are distinctions between the ways in which any given authority is granted and the ways in which it is exercised.

1. First, there is what we might call *status authority*. Positions such as head of family, head of church, head of state and even teacher (James 3:1) carry with them God-given authority commensurate with the responsibility that those in such positions bear for carrying out their duties. Often we also grant authority to people who have wealth, schooling or high status, such as those prominent in business, education, science, athletics, music, theater, media, politics and the like. We grant such people, for better or worse, the authority to set standards and influence us in a multitude of ways. A certain amount of authority and responsibility is given automatically by God to those in such positions.

In addition, Genesis 1:28 seems to indicate that every human has been given a certain authority over creation. Though we tend to think of these kinds of authority in human terms, I believe they have a spiritual dimension to them as well, springing from the fact that each such position is given by God as well as by humans.

2. Second, although we are conscious of these forms of status authority, there is a more direct form of spiritual authority that is, as Richard Foster says in *Celebration of Discipline*, "God-ordained and God-sustained." I will call this *personal intimacy authority*. This kind of authority may or may not have any relationship to the authority granted by human society or institutions. Personal intimacy authority is direct from God and unrelated to status. Foster elaborates:

> When people begin to move into the spiritual realm they see that Jesus is teaching a concept of authority

85

that runs completely counter to the thinking of the systems of this world. They come to perceive that authority does not reside in positions, or degrees, or titles, or tenure, or *any* outward symbol. The way of Christ is in another direction altogether: the way of spiritual authority. Spiritual authority is God-ordained and God-sustained. Human institutions may acknowledge this authority or they may not; it makes no difference. The person with spiritual authority may have an outward position of authority or may not; again, it makes no difference. Spiritual authority is marked by both compassion and power. Those who walk in the Spirit can identify it immediately. They know without question that submission is due the word that has been given in spiritual authority.

p. 108

Unfortunately, many in positions of human status authority have little, if any, personal intimacy authority. It is tragic for a church, a theological institution or even a nation or family if the person with human authority lacks real intimacy authority. Pastoral training institutions graduate people regularly who have learned to function in the classroom but have not been led close enough to Christ to gain either the intimacy authority or the personal capabilities to function adequately in church leadership. Countless churches and other Christian organizations are being led by people operating solely in human status authority.

But fellowship with God is crucial. We need (as Nee points out) to be in constant communion with Him, because there is an important intimacy requirement for those who carry another's authority. And there is a close connection, as we discussed in the last chapter, between "intimacy praying" (defined as spending time alone with God, as Jesus frequently did) and "authority praying" (defined as speaking in power and authority to bring about healing or deliverance, as Jesus did traveling around Palestine doing the will of His Father). Like Jesus, we need to learn, during times of intimacy with God, what He wants us to do with His authority, and then go out as Jesus did to exercise that authority in the world.

3. A third important consideration in any discussion of the relationship between human and spiritual authority is *the need to distinguish between the authority inherent in the position, and the presence or absence of this special God-given dimension* that Foster is describing. I believe (as I have indicated) that the head of a home and the head of a church are automatically given a kind of spiritual authority by God as an inherent part of their status. This is what young David recognized when he refused to attack King Saul, saying, "I must not harm him in the least, because he is the king chosen by the LORD!" (1 Samuel 24:6). Saul had the God-ordained authority of the position so long as he remained in that position, even though his behavior showed that he neither deserved the position nor retained the special spiritual authority that comes from closeness to God. He continued to have status authority, but not the personal intimacy authority that servants of God are meant to exercise. David, on the other hand, possessed the personal intimacy authority but not yet the status authority of the position of king.

Personal intimacy authority comes from spending time with Jesus. The only requisite is to be in an intimate relationship with the source of authority. This is the relationship Jesus spoke of in John 15: "I am the vine, and you are the branches. Whoever remains in me, and I in him, will bear much fruit; for you can do nothing without me" (verse 5). As we stay connected to the Lord, we gain the authority that personal intimacy brings, and we learn to use that authority in the right manner.

With regard to the latter, as Foster points out, the spiritual authority Jesus demonstrated "was an authority not found in a position or a title but in a towel," the towel He used when He washed His disciples' feet. The intimacy with the Father that gave Jesus this authority was matched by His use of the authority "not . . . to be served, but to serve" (Matthew 20:28).

The Paradox of Submission

Any discussion of spiritual authority needs to deal with submission, because the authority, as we have indicated, is not really ours, it is God's, and we gain the right to use it through submission to Him.

But, you may ask, if we submit, aren't we giving up our personal rights and autonomy? If we are working with people in the world, the answer is usually yes, since "the whole world is under the rule of the Evil One" (1 John 5:19) and tends, therefore, to go by his rules.

The governing principle is, submission puts one under the authority of the one to whom we submit, and we get whatever the character of that one dictates. If we submit to Satan, or to a human serving him, the result of our submission is captivity. But if the one submitted to is God, our submission results in freedom, since it is the character of God to set people free. What seems like a contradiction, then, is not, if it is to the freedom-giver that we submit.

The apostle Paul learned this lesson well, probably from Jesus. For he stated, "I am a free man, nobody's slave" (1 Corinthians 9:19), yet he represented himself in Romans 1:1 as a bondservant of Jesus Christ. This chosen designation reminds us of the statement made about Jesus in Philippians 2:7 that He "gave up all he had, and took the nature of a servant" in order to carry out the will of His Father. So by yielding to God, we actually become liberated. Submission is not about humiliation, although submission is based on humility. Nor is submission to God about bondage; it is about freedom—spiritual freedom.

We are expected, then, to use our freedom to clothe ourselves with humility (1 Peter 5:5), and thus to fight the pride that can floor us. For "'God resists the proud, but shows favor to the humble.' Humble yourselves, then, under God's mighty hand, so that he will lift you up in his own good time" (1 Peter 5:6). True biblical submission is humiliating only if it is done in pride. Surrender without grace is bondage. But as we exercise humility, God gives us the grace that enables us to submit. Surrender with grace is empowerment.

The Ten Commandments of Spiritual Authority

Dr. J. Robert Clinton, Professor of Leadership in Fuller's School of World Mission, has, in two books on Christian leadership, helpfully summarized and elaborated on much of what I have been presenting here. He calls his summary "The Ten Commandments of Spiritual Authority."

Throughout his books and teaching, Clinton connects the development of a Christian leader with an increase in spiritual authority. As Christian leaders mature, Clinton contends in *Leadership Emergence Theory* (Barnabas Resources, 1989), they find a distinct increase in their use of spiritual authority replacing mere human authority as "the primary authority used in leadership influence."

Clinton also points out that spiritual authority can be developed and exercised only in an experiential context.

It is neither given nor achieved by "armchair" Christians. It comes, rather, "from a life and a ministry which demonstrates the presence of God. . . . A leader with spiritual authority knows God and His ways and demonstrates this in life."

Furthermore, in an important addition to what we have discussed so far, Clinton asserts that spiritual authority is always a *byproduct,* never something to be sought for its own sake. In *The Making of a Leader* (NavPress, 1988) he writes, "A leader does not seek spiritual authority; a leader seeks to know God." As we grow in our experience with and obedience to the living God, the only true source of spiritual authority, we find our own spiritual authority growing right alongside.

With this introduction to Clinton's emphases, I present my version of his ten basic principles that he calls the "Ten Commandments of Spiritual Authority":

---

1. The ultimate source of authority is God. He it is who provides this "power base" to undergird ministry.
2. This authority is delegated by God. We are only channels for it, not owners of it.
3. We are responsible to God for how we exercise the authority He gives us.
4. True Christian leaders will recognize God's authority whenever it is manifested in life situations, whether through themselves or through others.
5. Persons in authority are subject directly to God, not indirectly through other authority figures.
6. Refusal to obey others in authority over us is actually rebellion against God, not just against the human instruments of that authority (Romans 13:2).
7. If we are rightly subject to God's authority, we will seek and recognize other spiritual authority and be willing to be subject to it.
8. We are never to exercise spiritual authority merely for our own benefit.
9. If we are truly working in spiritual authority, we do not need to insist that others obey us. That is their responsibility before God.
10. God Himself can be depended on to defend our spiritual authority. We do not need to assert it in such a way that we are defending ourselves.

Let these "commandments" or principles serve to summarize and amplify what we have been trying to say in this chapter. Now we can go on to a discussion of responsible versus irresponsible uses of the authority God has given us.

4

Using Our Authority Responsibly

What if our master, in anticipation of a journey, gave us the equivalent of five thousand days' wages, or even of one or two thousand days', and told us to use it on his behalf while he was away? That money is like the power God gives us. His command to use it wisely is our authority. What are we to do with it?

We know from Jesus' parable (Matthew 25:14–30) that two of the servants did the right thing with the money they had been given. They put it to use and were commended by the master, when he returned, for handling it well and doubling the amounts given them. But the third servant buried his money, refusing to use it out of fear of the master's shrewdness. He was condemned for not handling rightly what he had been put in charge of. The master took the money from him, called him "lazy" (verse 26) and had him cast out into "the darkness" (verse 30).

This was pretty harsh treatment for what might seem to us a fairly small mistake. The servant was afraid to risk. But apparently God does not take it kindly when we do not use, even risk what He has given us.

Jesus had a lot to say about stewardship. He spoke often, as He did in this parable, of the custom among wealthy people of going away and leaving someone else in charge of their goods. In Luke 12:41–48 Jesus described a servant who runs the household while his master is away, and who is happy and rewarded if he is found faithful when the master returns, or sad and punished if he has done an incompetent job. At another point Jesus even seemed to be praising a dishonest servant because of his shrewdness in using his authority to collect from his master's debtors (Luke 16:1–8).

In these and other stories, Jesus advocated what Paul states in 1 Corinthians 4:2: "The one thing required of . . . a servant is that he be faithful to his master." Peter adds, "Each one, as a good manager of God's different gifts, must use for the good of others the special gift he has received from God" (1 Peter 4:10).

Think of the gifting He has invested in each one of us. Think, too, of the authority and power—the authority of the Father and the power of the Holy Spirit—that He has put within us. What happens if we refuse to use these gifts? Does the message of this parable apply to us?

I believe it does. And I am frightened lest I be found to be like the lazy servant.

We can take these gifts and ignore those around us who are hurting. We can even ignore our families. Those of us in leadership positions can ignore our students, our parishioners, our employees. We, whom God in-

93

tended to be conduits of His love and power, can easily become blockers of that love and power if we do not take the authority we have been given to use the credit card on behalf of others. As Dean Sherman points out in *Spiritual Warfare for Every Christian:*

> With our authority comes the responsibility to use it for God's purposes. If we don't rebuke the devil, he will not be rebuked. If we don't drive him back, he will not leave. It is up to us. Satan knows of our authority, but hopes we will stay ignorant. We must be as convinced of our authority as the devil is.
>
> p. 123

Sherman goes on to illustrate irresponsibility by pointing to policemen who have been given legal authority to protect people and apprehend those who are breaking the law. He asks:

> What if I were to arrive home and find people stealing my possessions? I call the police from my car phone and they rush over to my house. But to my surprise, they line up along the sidewalk and begin to sing about their authority, declaring it to one another. All the while, intruders finish cleaning out my house! This may seem ridiculous, yet that is often an accurate picture of what we do. We talk about our authority. We sing about it. We even proclaim it loudly. But we don't exercise it. We must recognize that there is a difference between having authority and exercising it.
>
> pp. 123–124

We who are heads of families (as we will see in a later chapter) have the responsibility to use our authority to free and protect those under our care. Those of us with authority in churches are responsible to use it to free and protect the flock that has been entrusted to us. Those of us in administrative positions, in whatever organization we serve, have the same responsibility for those under us.

We have the responsibility *and* authority to rid ourselves, our homes, our families, our workplaces and our churches of demonic intruders and influences. Are we doing this? We are not simply to sit back and drift into glory. We are to use the gifts, including the great gift of authority, that the Master has given us. This book is an attempt to help us know how to do this.

Furthermore, we are responsible to learn the rules for using our authority in the spirit realm. (In the next chapter we will discuss some of the rules at work in the relationships between humans and the spirit world.) Our ignorance of these rules, as with physical laws like the law of gravity, does not keep them from affecting us. Whether we understand what the enemy is doing or not, he will keep doing it until we take the authority God has given us and stop him.

Misuse of Authority

Responsible use of authority is one of the biggest issues in our society. Almost daily we hear of politicians, law enforcement officials, CEOs of large corporations and even popular Christian leaders who have blatantly misused authority. This is bad enough when secular authority is being misused, but it is tragic when it involves spiritual authority.

Misuse of authority is one of the things God risked when He gave us both authority and freedom, for we can use our freedom (as we have seen) to misuse our spiritual authority. Parents can use their authority to dominate their children and stamp out freedom and creativity. A pastor can use his authority to gain perks and prestige for himself rather than to help his people. He can even use a church to enhance his own social position in a community or denomination. Christian healers can produce spectacles, with themselves at the center, so that God is hardly noticed, no matter how often they give Him credit. Or, like Adam, we can use our spiritual authority and freedom to sin.

It is easy to misuse authority, whether human or spiritual. Let's look at six ways it is misused in the spiritual realm.

1. When the Person Given Authority Is Exalted

Authority is misused whenever it exalts the person to whom the authority is given, rather than the Lord, the source and giver of the authority. Unfortunately, many who have been exalted by God turn aside from His ways and misuse the authority they have been given, turning that authority into a counterfeit. King Saul is an obvious case. Even though Saul's authority had been legitimately given to him, he misused it to the extent that he attempted to kill God's chosen one, David (1 Samuel 18–21), to whom God had given the authority that had been Saul's.

At least two of the apostles, James and John, tried to exert their authority to gain position for themselves (Mark 10:35–45). But, as Jesus said, it is not to be this way in the Kingdom. Our authority is used rightly only when we imitate Jesus by serving others.

2. When Those without Power Are Hurt

Authority is misused and God is angered when those with authority use it to hurt the powerless. Guidelines are given throughout the Bible concerning how those in power are to treat those without it. The story of David and Bathsheba is a case in point. Though David was guilty of both adultery and murder, it was the misuse of his authority and power as king on which the prophet Nathan focused in his parable (2 Samuel 12:1–15). God speaks the harshest condemnation against "those who cheat employees out of their wages, and those who take advantage of widows, orphans, and foreigners" (Malachi 3:5). And it was the misuse of the Jewish religious leaders' authority and power that aroused Jesus' wrath. He condemned the teachers of the Law, for example, for "[taking] advantage of widows and [robbing] them of their homes" and then making long, pious prayers (Mark 12:40).

Those of us in positions of power are especially vulnerable to the possibility of misusing our authority. As James said, we should not all want to be teachers (or other leaders) since "teachers will be judged with greater strictness than others" (James 3:1). When you are a leader, it is easy to step on other people's toes without noticing it. We need to train ourselves to be careful in the way we use our authority, and to be especially sharp in noticing reactions that may indicate we have misused someone or encroached on his or her territory.

It is easy to misuse words. Several years ago a student of mine who had gotten to know me well asked one day, "Have you ever noticed how you put people down in class when you answer their questions?"

I denied that this was happening.

She said simply, "Watch yourself."

So I started to notice how I answered students' questions. And to my surprise, I discovered she was right. I had been misusing my authority as a teacher by responding cleverly to student questions in such a way as to intimidate them. Out of my own insecurities, I had been using their questions to parade my knowledge in contrast to theirs. Because I had heard most of their questions before, I had opportunity to develop clever answers to them. So sometimes, anticipating what the question would be, I would not even wait for the student to finish the question before giving my answer. I was able in this way to show my intelligence at the expense of those over whom I had authority.

Now I work hard in these situations to use my authority lovingly rather than to serve my own selfish ends.

Many in positions of authority seem to specialize, as I did, in using words to oppress and intimidate. They are accomplished at putting people down, weakening their egos and contributing to shame and guilt. This use of words is especially damaging when used on the young by authority figures like parents, teachers or employers. Even pastors and others in Christian ministry can be guilty of verbal oppression. Since all authority comes from God (Romans 13:1–7), it is ultimately spiritual. Such misuse is likely to result, therefore, in spiritual damage.

Words can also be used (as we pointed out in chapter 2) to curse (James 3:8–10). This is a particularly heinous misuse of authority. It is an easy trap to fall into, however, when we are angry or hurt. Words such as "Damn So-and-so" or "I wish So-and-so were dead" or even "I hate So-and-so" need to be taken very seriously here on earth. The number of times we in ministry are called on to break such curses to bring freedom to people indicates that they are taken seriously in the spirit world. We need to heed James' warnings concerning how we use our tongues. More on this in chapter 8.

3. When Scripture Is Mishandled

Authority is misused when pastors or exhorters quote Scripture in such a way that people feel unnecessarily condemned. There are actions and attitudes we need to condemn, of course, if we are to be biblical. But when a verse such as Philippians 3:13—"Forgetting those things which are behind. . ." (KJV)—is used to give the impression that God commands us to simply forget past hurts, great damage can be done.

In context, that verse has nothing to do with past hurts. Paul is advising us to put behind us past *victories* so that we can win the race we are now running. But when those badly hurt from past abuse hear such a verse thus misused, they go away further abused, wondering why they cannot "just forget," as the preacher advised. How are those people to know God does not want such hurts simply swept under the rug? Far from it! God wants people to face such wounds openly and to forgive, in order to enter His freedom.

Preachers misuse their authority when they thus misrepresent God and hurt their hearers. I am afraid we will be judged harshly by God for such misuse.

4. When People Are Led from God

Authority is misused when it is wielded by religious or political leaders to lead people away from God. The leaders of Israel abandoned the true God over and over to follow false gods. In 1 Kings 16–22 we read of wicked King Ahab and his wife, Jezebel, who with hundreds of priests led the people of Israel in worshiping the Baal gods. The true prophet Elijah was given authority by God to confront those prophets and destroy 850 of them (as we saw in 1 Kings 18). Later God led His prophet Jeremiah to speak harshly against the false prophets he encountered for prophesying lies. He also spoke against the wicked priests who ruled "by their own authority" (Jeremiah 5:31, NIV).

These prophets attempted to represent God and work in His authority without ever hearing from Him. God said:

> "I did not send them, nor did I give them any orders or speak one word to them. The visions they talk about have not come from me; their predictions are worthless things that they have imagined."
>
> Jeremiah 14:14 (see 23:18)

We have such leaders today as well. Many who claim to be hearing from and speaking for God are counterfeits of the real thing. Leaders of several of the major U.S. denominations fit into this category. For they "obey lying spirits and follow the teachings of demons" (1 Timothy 4:1), and often stand for untenable positions with regard to foundational truths of biblical Christian faith, using the authority of their offices to mislead people. We need discernment to discover and warn the Body about such false leaders.

5. When God's Work Is Opposed

Authority is misused when it stands against God's authentic working. Scripture often recounts the persecution of those exercising God's authority and power. As Jesus said in His lament over Jerusalem, those in authority misuse it to "kill the prophets, [and] stone the messengers God has sent" (Luke 13:34). The authority Pontius Pilate claimed, even though ultimately from God (John 19:10–11), was being used for Satan's purposes rather than the purpose for which it was intended. And Jesus Himself received persecution and death at the hands of those using their human authority to serve the enemy.

I just heard about a publisher who has broken the contract of a friend of mine because he feels the author is serving the wrong master. As closely as I can tell, my friend is listening carefully to God and following Him closely. The publisher holds a different position on certain issues, however, and is using his authority, I believe, to block the authentic working of God.

I am afraid there is much of this kind of misuse of authority going on in contemporary Christian circles.

6. When Authority Is Counterfeited

One misuse is a bit more difficult to explain: the counterfeiting of authority in animism and magic. *Animism* is the term used by missiologists to label the majority religion of the world. Most of the tribal peoples, plus most of those who claim to follow a world religion, are really animists. A common form of animism involves belief in a high God who is good and benevolent toward humans, and can therefore safely be ignored most of the time. But between this God and us are a multitude of dangerous spirits or gods who must be kept happy if life is to go smoothly. Animists spend lots of time, energy and money attempting to manipulate these spirits. By doing or saying certain things, they think they can control supernatural beings, so much of their effort is put into doing or saying those things to magically bring about the desired end.

Animistic thinking is prominent among Old Testament peoples, who are condemned, and even among the Israelites. All the idolatry God reproached was animistic. Among the many examples is the likelihood that, when God commanded Moses to speak rather than strike the rock to get water (Numbers 20:7–12), He was trying to break an animistic reverence for Moses' rod. Whenever

101

Israel accepted the belief that the true God was a god of the mountains, while the Baal gods were in control on the plains (1 Kings 20:23–25), they were submitting to an animistic system and lowering the true God to the level of the territorial spirits. By doing so, they could subject Him to the same kind of manipulation that non-Jews practiced on their animistic gods. In Jesus' day we see animistic and magical attitudes toward the Temple (Matthew 23:16–21) and the keeping of the Sabbath.

But it is counterfeit authority when animistic and magical ideas lie behind it, rather than commitment and obedience to the true God. They are practicing animism today who expect automatic results that coerce God into doing their will when they use "sacred" phrases or "sacred" objects. Among the phrases used: *the blood of Christ,* words concerning binding and loosing, certain Scriptures and special words used repetitively in prayer (including the word *just* preceding a request), with the often unconscious expectation that these words or phrases will work to bring about the desired result. When name-it-and-claim-it Christians choose something they want, even healing, and assume that when they claim it, God is obligated to do it for them, they are practicing animism, not Christianity.

Among the objects used magically are crosses, anointing oil and the Bible. Such items can be effective in conveying a blessing. (More on this in the next chapter.) But when believers regard words or objects as *containing* the power of God, rather than *conveying* it, we are manifesting a magical attitude toward them. Or when we speak of "the power of the Word," the Bible, rather than recognize that God's power is flowing *through* His Word, we are unconsciously betraying an animistic attitude.

To use the authority God gives us responsibly means not to misuse it. Further, if we are to be responsible in our use of the authority God has given us, we do well to become aware of any misuse on the part of others. The Scriptures show that, because Christians have a multitude of responsibilities to God, others and ourselves, we are to use our spiritual authority responsibly in carrying out all obligations and the privileges that come with them. The fact that there are frequent misuses makes it important for us to seek the advice of those with gifts of spiritual discernment when evaluating ministries that purport to come from God.

What Jesus' Disciples Did Not Learn

Jesus was patient with the Twelve as He taught them what life in the Kingdom is all about. He took them everywhere He went, so they got to watch and listen as He carried out His Father's will. As He walked, talked and carried out His ministry, they learned how to be like Him. He taught them by both word and deed. *Jesus' primary teaching method was demonstration.* He not only spoke as He expected them to learn to speak, but He showed them what their ministries were to be like. Since He expected them to heal and cast out demons, He showed them how to do that. And in His healing ministry as well as in His teaching, He demonstrated how to use the authority the Father had given Him and that He had passed on to them. The next step was for the Twelve to launch out and use that authority.

But they did not learn easily. As usual, they were sometimes up and sometimes down. After they had watched Jesus for quite a while, they found themselves in the teeth of a storm on Lake Galilee. They woke the Master to rescue them and He did. But He rebuked them for their lack of faith (Luke 8:25). Could it be that Jesus expected the disciples to use the authority He had already given them to calm the storm? If so, they failed the test.

The next time, though, in Luke 9:1–6 and again in 10:1–12, Jesus gave His followers power and authority "to drive out all demons and to cure diseases" (9:1) and sent them out to minister on their own. Apparently they did well and got a taste of what this God-given authority was all about. They marveled that "even the demons obeyed us when we gave them a command in your name!" (Luke 10:17).

In the very next event after the disciples were sent out in Luke 9, we see a hungry crowd of five thousand or more and only a small boy's lunch to work with. The apostles were wringing their hands in concern for the people's physical needs, so Jesus told them to "give them something to eat" (Luke 9:13). That is, "Be creative. Use your authority to produce the food to feed them." It must have puzzled Jesus' friends to hear that He expected them to take care of the situation, for they were just learning what this authority business was all about. So they hesitated, and Jesus did the job.

The same chapter records that Jesus and His followers headed for Jerusalem via Samaria, where some Samaritans refused to give them lodging (Luke 9:51–55). James and John, angered over this affront, asked Jesus for permission to "call fire down from heaven to destroy them" (verse 54). Finally they had gotten the idea that they had been given great authority, but now they wanted to use it in a wrong way—to hurt rather than to help! Jesus refused to allow this and rebuked them for their desire to use their authority irresponsibly.

The same temptation exists today. And many in positions of authority in Christian institutions, and many others who function in the spiritual authority God has given them, misuse that authority. When this is the case, God does not always take the authority away from them.

The status of the Pharisees, for example, gave them power and authority both in the human social context and spiritually. Note what Jesus said concerning the need to grant them the honor due their position (Matthew 23:3), though He was quick to caution against imitating their behavior.

The demons were not fooled by the sons of Sceva when they tried to assert an authority that was not theirs, but humans *do* often get fooled. But even so, Jesus forbids us to "pull up the weeds," lest in doing so we pull up some of the wheat also (Matthew 13:28–30).

Jesus Doesn't Like It When We Wake Him

If I have a secretary and ask her to go to, say, an office supply store to purchase some supplies, I expect her to do it. Suppose she has been working for me for some time and knows what we need to make our office work. Suppose, too, that I have taken her with me on previous trips to buy supplies, so I am sure she knows the ropes. Furthermore, I trust her and give her the money (or my credit card) so the materials can be paid for.

Suppose, then, that after I have asked her to run this errand and have given her the money to do it, I find out the next day that she has not carried out my request. Nor does she do it the next day, or the next. I might reprimand her. I might even fire her. But if she continues to ignore what I have requested, I will do it myself.

This is what happened in the boat that day when the disciples and Jesus encountered the storm. I have suggested that I believe Jesus expected His followers to calm the storm themselves. He did not appreciate it when they woke Him up. And later He expected them to feed the five thousand. How disappointed He must have been to have to do it Himself!

An important part of responsibility, then, is not to ne-glect it. I wonder how often we have neglected the authority Jesus has given us by not applying His power to illness, weather, poverty or other life situations that He expects us to deal with as His agents. How many people does Jesus heal directly because we do not participate? Or, worse yet, how many go unhealed because we who have been commissioned to operate in Jesus' authority and power have neglected our responsibility?

The Apostle Paul on Authority

In the passage beginning with 2 Corinthians 10:8 and concluding with 2 Corinthians 13:10, the apostle Paul, while defending his own authority, demonstrates how leaders should exercise their authority. In those two verses he speaks of "the authority that the Lord has given us [me]—authority to build you up, not to tear you down." In short, Paul seeks to exercise considerable authority with a large amount of gentleness and love.

Missionary D. Michael Crow, currently a doctoral student at the Fuller Seminary School of World Mission, has found fifteen characteristics of spiritual authority articulated by Paul in the passage enclosed between the above verses. I find these so helpful that, with Crow's permission, I list them here, worded as I understand them. Before listing them, though, let's note two things about the way Paul goes about his argument.

First, at the beginning and end of his statement (10:1–2; 13:10), Paul implies his right to be harsh with the Corinthians but his desire to be gentle, kind and loving. Though the issue at hand involves a serious challenge to his apostolic authority, Paul chooses to exercise that authority in love and gentleness.

Second, Paul grounds his discussion in a context of spiritual warfare. I believe he is affirming what I suggest in the next chapter—that every human event, even a disciplinary problem, has an important spiritual dimension. For Paul says in 2 Corinthians 10:3–5 that, although "we live in the world, . . . we do not fight from worldly motives." Nor are our weapons worldly ones. They are "God's powerful weapons, which we use to destroy strongholds . . . false arguments . . . [and] every proud obstacle that is raised against the knowledge of God." So "we take every thought captive and make it obey Christ."

Thus Paul shows us the basis for spiritual authority (Spirit-led motives) and some of the goals we are to aim at in our assertion of that authority. Crow's list:

1. Spiritual authority has a territorial dimension. Paul asserts his authority in 10:12–18 over an area he believes God has assigned him—an area that includes Corinth.
2. Spiritual authority flows from a burden to see a love relationship between those served and Christ (11:1–6).
3. Spiritual authority is grounded in a substantial knowledge of God and His activities in the human sphere (11:6).
4. Spiritual authority must operate without being tied to payment. Paul exercises his spiritual authority as a servant without charging the Corinthians (11:7–12) or anyone else.
5. Spiritual authority involves an uncompromising opposition to charlatans—those who masquerade as true Christian leaders but who teach lies (11:13–15).
6. Spiritual authority serves even to the extent of readily sacrificing and suffering (11:16–33). Paul, in exercising the authority God gave him, has endured incredible hardship on behalf of those he has ministered to, mostly at the hands of those who oppose him.
7. Spiritual authority involves direct revelation from God (12:1–6). Paul was taken up to "the highest heaven" and heard things there "which cannot be put into words, things that human lips may not speak."
8. Spiritual authority is exercised in weakness and ordinariness, even with God-allowed satanic reminders to keep us humble. In 12:6–10 Paul speaks

of his weaknesses and of the "painful physical ailment" (verse 7), or "thorn in the flesh" (kjv), that God has allowed "as Satan's messenger to beat me and keep me from being proud."

9. Spiritual authority is authenticated through the operation of spiritual gifts (12:12). Paul points to signs and wonders as proving his apostolic authority.

10. Spiritual authority is ready and able to rebuke and discipline those who persist in disobedience (13:1–2).

11. Spiritual authority can be tested by checking the presence and activity of Christ in those who have responded to the message presented by the one who claims that authority (13:5–6).

12. Implied in the passage is the fact that spiritual authority is not contingent on a given personality type.

13. Neither is spiritual authority contingent on one's ability to preach or communicate in other ways. Spiritual authority precedes these abilities, acting as a life-giver to these means but not restricted by whether or not one is a gifted communicator.

14. True spiritual authority affirms rather than puts down others, encouraging them to operate in all the gifting and authority God has given them.

15. Spiritual authority can be exercised in a multitude of unique ways. Rather than being a mere "doing" thing, it is to be grounded in and exercised out of a person's very being.

We see in Paul's teaching, then, several characteristics of the one who would use spiritual authority responsibly. And we note that these all apply to the way Jesus exercised His authority.

One way to test whether or not the way we exercise our authority is on track is checking to see how well we measure up to these characteristics.

The Place of Experimentation

We have imprecise guidelines for much of this territory. That is, we do not always know how to go about using our authority responsibly in situations that occur in our lives but that are not addressed in Scripture. Even when situations are addressed in Scripture, we often experience twists and turns that we do not see dealt with there. (Many such twists and turns occur when dealing with demonization.)

In such cases I recommend experimentation. My rule of thumb is, *If in doubt, experiment.* This is the only way I know to discover what works and what does not. It is responsible, I think, to experiment. Otherwise, how are we to discover what Jesus promised the Holy Spirit would teach us (John 16:13)?

It is as an experiment that I first began saying, "If this is the enemy, stop it!" when something seemed to be going wrong, either in general circumstances or in relationships. I mentioned that this command is often effective when interpersonal conflict seems imminent. It has also worked sometimes (not always) when a baby starts to cry in church or when the students in class seem distracted. It seldom works, however, when I am caught in traffic on the Los Angeles freeway system! But once I spoke this command after a flight my wife and I were scheduled to fly on was canceled, at which point we saw a major improvement in a difficult situation. Did that change come about by chance? Perhaps. But maybe it was another of many experiences I have had in which the enemy's attempts to disrupt my life were thwarted when I claimed the authority Jesus has given me.

It was likewise as an experiment that I began to suggest to the head of a family that he (or she, in the case of a single parent) assert his protective authority over the family by saying to the satanic powers, "I am the head of this family, so if you want my wife or children, you will have to go through me." For many this action has brought release from attacks on family members.

One man reported that after he asserted this authority, his fearful three-year-old daughter changed immediately and has been a happy little girl ever since.

109

A couple whose ten-year-old boy was being picked on unmercifully by his schoolmates did the same thing. That very day the youngster came home from school to report happily that the children who had been taunting him had all changed now and become his friends.

I have experimented a lot in dealing with demons, and found that most of the experiments work. I have learned, for example, that during a session it helps, in keeping track of the demons, to lock each group in a spiritual "box" until all are collected and it is time to send them to Jesus.

This practice started as an experiment several years ago when we were in the middle of a deliverance session at the end of class one day. The members of the class had to go home, and I wanted to pick up at the same place the next morning when class reconvened. So without knowing how (or if) it would work, I commanded the demons into a box overnight. As we started working on them the next day, I asked them where they were. They said angrily, "Right in the box where you put us!" From this I learned of our authority to lock them up—an authority I have been able to use to good advantage over the years. Similarly I learned by experimenting that we can cut off the demonic communication system (see chapter 6).

More Prerequisites to Authority

If we are to work effectively in Jesus' authority, there are certain prerequisites. We have already considered several of these, including the need for intimacy with our Master, the obedience requirement, the recognition that we are at war and the importance of knowing who we are in Christ. In addition:

1. Ask for the Release of the Holy Spirit

It is necessary to start where Jesus started—with the baptism or filling of the Holy Spirit (Luke 3:22). We have noted that Jesus did no signs and wonders before that point in His life. Then, when He ascended to heaven, He told His disciples to wait until the same Holy Spirit who had empowered Him would come upon them and empower them before they went out to minister for Him (Luke 24:49; Acts 1:4). They, like Jesus, were to do no signs and wonders, or witness to God's loving concern for humans, until they were under the complete control of the Holy Spirit.

Some distinguish between the baptism of the Holy Spirit and the filling of the Holy Spirit. The only distinction I make is to regard the baptism as the first infilling. We receive the Holy Spirit when we accept Jesus as Savior and Lord (Romans 8:2, 4, 9, 16). At that time we have the potential for being filled with Him. We can, however, hinder the Spirit's full release within us. So most people need at some later time to ask Him to take over in His fullness, as the disciples did on the Day of Pentecost (Acts 2:1–4).

From my perspective, *such a filling is more like the release of the Spirit, who already resides in us, than like the pouring into us of something from outside.* Such release can and should take place many times as we live and minister with and for our Lord. Thus, I can agree with those who say there is one baptism but many fillings or releases. And I believe it is appropriate to ask God for a new infilling or release of the Holy Spirit daily.

The need to be filled with the Holy Spirit (though the concept is often abused) is scriptural. Jesus needed it; so do we. What the fullness of the Holy Spirit brings is power (Acts 1:8) and gifting—the power and gifting we need to go with our authority as Jesus' disciples. And it

111

is our privilege to receive the fullness of the Holy Spirit simply by asking for it (Luke 11:13). There is no required ritual, place, time or level of emotion in order for the fullness of the Holy Spirit to be released.

We should dissociate ourselves, therefore, from all unbalanced, unscriptural forms of belief and practice. Becoming Spirit-filled does not require us to become more emotional or fall under the power of the Spirit, though many find that they grow in their ability to feel and express emotion, especially in worship. Nor should such release result in arrogant, unloving behavior toward those who do not seem to be Spirit-filled. Such behavior is not what Jesus intends. Being Spirit-filled does not make us any better than we were before, nor does it assure us that what we sense as prophetic utterances or words of knowledge will always be right. And it certainly does not give us any right to boast or act haughtily. Indeed, it should make us more humble, loving and in every other way more Christlike. As for tongues, although those in Scripture who were filled with the Spirit often began to speak in tongues (Acts 19:6), Paul says not everyone has this gift (1 Corinthians 12:29–30), and he suggests in 1 Corinthians 14 that the gift of tongues, as valuable as it is, is the least of all the gifts.

For some, the release of the Spirit comes with the laying on of hands. It is good to seek it this way, but this is not the only option. For to others the gift is given directly by God in private, as God's quiet response to our request for His filling. However received, this gift, like all others that come from God, is given as an expression of His mercy and grace apart from our merit. We do not qualify for it by our righteousness, goodness or achievements, but by our openness and yieldedness to God.

In addition to the empowerment and gifting that the release of the Holy Spirit brings, another major purpose is for us to overflow with the fruits of the Spirit: "love, joy, peace, patience, kindness, goodness, faithfulness, humility, and self-control" (Galatians 5:22–23). Overflowing, not containing, is what we are to do. I like the story I heard once of a little fellow who commented on the filling of the Holy Spirit, "I'm not big enough to hold much, but I can overflow a lot!" Let's receive the Holy Spirit till we overflow, and then continue to overflow a lot.

2. *Tend to Your Spiritual Condition*

A second important requirement is that a person working in Jesus' authority tend to his or her spiritual condition. God is usually generous to those He has gifted, even if they do not keep close to Him, but the enemy keeps track and may challenge a person's authority during a ministry session. Though this has never happened to me (yet), some have told me that demons they were trying to evict started listing their sins for all to hear, hoping to embarrass them enough to get them to quit! Then there are those whom the enemy has been able to keep from even engaging in ministry through accusations concerning their spiritual condition or through fear that their sins would be made public.

Many, on the other hand, who have not been in good shape spiritually but have been faithful in ministry anyway have been so humbled by God's graciousness to them that they have cleaned up their acts. This was true of a man I will call Chet who was in an adulterous relationship when he started to minister deliverance. He was so blown away by the fact that God would use even him in such authority and power that he confessed his sin and got right with God, his wife and everyone else concerned.

113

Likewise with a woman I will call Donna. She went with us on a ministry trip in spite of the fact that she believed firmly God could not use her in a healing ministry because she was not right spiritually. She came to me to confess her problem only after God had used her powerfully. Puzzled, she could not reconcile her spiritual condition—and the constant, accusing voice of the enemy—with what God was doing through her. She discovered an important principle: that the authority and power of the Holy Spirit, received when one is filled with Him, remains even when one's intimacy with God is impeded by sin. In response to the grace and mercy of God flowing to and through Donna, she repented and got right with Him.

Just as we do not kick toddlers when they fall down while learning to walk, so God is patient with us, reaching down a hand to help us up, knowing that eventually we will learn (Isaiah 42:3; Matthew 12:20). He reads our hearts and makes a clear distinction between the mistakes we make, even sometimes willfully, and whether what we do is the result of confirmed rebellion. God knows what to do with those who have confirmed their wills in rebellion. But He is merciful to those of His children who fall frequently while learning to walk.

3. *Know That Authority Is Ours*

A further prerequisite to authority is to accept the fact that it is ours. Jesus gives us the authority to imitate Him, to be as close to God the Father as He was, to do what He did and even more (John 14:12). These are our rights as Jesus' followers and friends.

Many Christians think, as I have said, that they have no right to make this kind of assertion. They fail to recognize the extent of Jesus' self-imposed limitations and what that means for us. If we ignore the fact that Jesus never used His deity while on earth, choosing to work entirely under the power of God's Spirit, we will have no confidence in our ability to function in the authority He has given us. Many without such confidence hold back, fearing they might overstep their bounds as Christians. What a tragedy, and what a victory for Satan!

Scripture allows a much greater possibility of imitating Jesus than evangelicalism has ordinarily allowed. As we obey Jesus' command to imitate Him by being filled with the Holy Spirit (Luke 24:49; Acts 1:4–5, 8), we receive Jesus' authority to move into a ministry like His and actually do what He did.

4. Garner Prayer Support

It is important for anyone engaging in spiritual warfare to be supported by as much prayer as possible, especially intercession by those who know how to pray with authority. We are not expected to fight all by ourselves. We are to enlist others, especially those with the gift of intercession, to keep our ministry constantly before the Lord and the enemy. We are parts of a Body, and those of us who assert our gifting in ministry need the support of those whose gifting gives them special authority in praying.

The equation is simple: The more prayer support, the more authority; the less prayer support, the less authority. The kingdom of darkness knows and believes in the power of prayer, and it fears most those who have the most solid prayer backing. The message, then, is clear: Get as much prayer support as possible, with as many as possible who have the gift of intercession.

A good place to start to understand the importance of prayer for those who operate in Jesus' authority, and the way to go about building prayer support, is with C. Peter Wagner's book *Prayer Shield* (Regal, 1992). In this book he discusses three kinds of intercessors needed by those in ministry. He calls them:

I–1 Intercessors. These are one or more persons with whom we have a close relationship, who possess the gift of intercession and who commit to praying continuously for us, agreeing to be available to us and to the Lord for whatever the Lord wants to say or do in relation to prayer (and often prophetic) support. Wagner suggests we need at least one but no more than three of such persons.

I–2 Intercessors. These have a casual relationship with us but covenant to pray daily for us. Some will have gifts of intercession; some will simply be faithful pray-ers. For those in public ministry, it is good to have one hundred or more at this level. For others the number may be smaller. But it is good in any case for us to know who they are and to keep them informed concerning what is going on in our lives.

I–3 Intercessors. These have a more remote relationship with us, and we will not necessarily even know who they are. They may pray for us sporadically or regularly. Those in public ministry should have a large number at this level. For others the emphasis should be on building up the I–2 level, even if there are few I–3s.

How much prayer support do we need? I have no idea, but I try to get on as many prayer lists as possible. The way God frequently works, especially on ministry trips, makes it obvious that the people back home are supporting us in our part of the battle.

5. Find a Spiritual Mentor

It is good, especially when we are first starting to work in Jesus' authority, to have a spiritual mentor to assist and encourage us in our learning. Even after we have been at it for a while, it is important for us to be accountable to someone else. As we begin to learn about our authority and to assert it, we often assume naïvely that we can go it alone. On the contrary, it is especially important for those of us who assert Jesus' authority over the enemy to have one or more mentors, since we are the ones most likely to be attacked by Satan. Many of the Christian leaders who have fallen from high positions might still be effective for Christ if they had been accountable to another human being.

In addition to mentoring and holding us accountable, such persons should minister to us. Even though we are in active ministry ourselves, we often carry wounds that need to be attended to. At best we are "wounded healers," and it is good for us to work constantly toward greater health for ourselves. We also need the kind of encouragement and blessing from such mentors that we seek to give others.

The Responsible Thing to Do

Actually getting out and doing some of the things we are suggesting may seem scary. We may assume that the rest Jesus promised us in Matthew 11:29—"You will find rest"—involves freedom from having to be concerned with Satan and his kingdom. Some actually believe Jesus got rid of all the demons while He was on earth, or that He has worked things so that they cannot affect Christians. Sorry! Neither of these things is true. Some try to pretend the enemy kingdom does not affect us, or that spiritual authority is a gift others may possess, but not us. Some will try rationalizing, ignoring, theologizing or explaining away the warfare terminology in the

Scriptures. They will do almost anything to avoid having to recognize that we are at war.

Unfortunately, none of these approaches changes the facts. Satan is still on the loose (though I do not pretend to understand why God allows it) and we are at war, whether we like it or not.

This being true, we had better prepare to fight! We have been given the authority and power to fight. Why don't we accept the responsibility God has given us? Here are three agenda items that will, I hope, open us more to work in and with the authority we have been given.

1. The first priority on our agenda needs to be to *shed our ignorance.* My own ignorance was profound! So I began to take steps to learn what spiritual warfare is all about. I read everything I could get my hands on and looked for those who would disciple me, or at least let me watch while they worked in God's authority to do His works. Since I am a teacher, I sought opportunities to teach on physical healing, inner healing and deliverance, and, as part of each of these areas, the authority God gives us to do His works. I felt the responsible thing to do was, on the one hand, get prepared, and on the other, to start taking steps in ministry. These steps led me through what I consider my *paradigm shift* and my *practice shift.*

2. Second on our agenda: to *shed our fear.* Once people begin to move into spiritual warfare, they often begin to experience fear. The enemy does all he can to impress us with his power in order to chase us off. We hear stories of battles that have been fought with demonized persons and we get scared. Television and movies, when they deal with demonization and deliverance, focus on the sensational aspects of the subject. Satan loves to have these stories repeated; they make him look so good! But as Paul said to Timothy, "The Spirit that God has given us does not make us timid [or fearful]; instead,

his Spirit fills us with power, love, and self-control" (2 Timothy 1:7).

In this power, love and self-control, we need to accept the responsibility given by our Master and engage ourselves in the war He has called us to. As we are commanded in Ephesians 6, we are to put on the whole armor of God, to stand when our Master asks us to stand, to attack when He asks us to attack. We need to ask for and accept the filling of the Holy Spirit (Luke 11:13) and move out in the authority our Leader has given us, first to protect ourselves, our families and our ministries, and then to communicate God's love through words, through healing, through deliverance and in whatever other ways our Master shows us. Once again, as Jesus did when He was on earth, we are to do what we see the Father doing (John 5:19), speak what the Father shows us (John 8:38) and do what the Father wants us to do (John 5:30).

3. A third agenda item is to *work toward spiritual maturity.* Just as physical, intellectual and emotional maturity enable us to handle the everyday problems of life, spiritual maturity enables us to handle problems that are spiritual in nature. It is sad that many Christians would rather not even think about spiritual warfare. I asked one pastor, "If there are demons, would you rather know or not know?" He replied, "I'd rather not know!" Would we take the same position if someone asked us if we would like to know of the danger of fire or poison? Would we contend that young people do not need to know of the potential problems that can arise if they are careless in driving? Or with sexual intercourse?

A choice for spiritual ignorance is a sign of spiritual immaturity. We need to grow out of an immature approach to understanding and dealing with the enemy forces all around us, forces to which the Bible refers frequently. Often when those of us engaged regularly in

119

spiritual warfare mention demons and their activities, we are accused of looking for a demon under every rock and behind every bush. Our attempts to bring scriptural balance to our lives and ministries—in spite of the prominence of spiritual conflict and demonic activity in the Bible—are greeted with accusations that we are off-balance.

Spiritual maturity involves a Scripture-based recognition of the forces that fight against us, plus the scriptural good news of our authority over those forces. It also includes nurturing what the Church has traditionally recognized—love and the other fruits of the Spirit, much prayer, worship, witness and other spiritually edifying activities. But we cannot speak of spiritual maturity without including the subject of spiritual warfare and our authority under our Master in that conflict.

With this discussion of our responsibility behind us, let's consider some of the rules that govern the relationships between the human world and the spirit world.

5

Rules for Authority in the Spirit Realm

You can't get this family free. You don't have the authority."

It was difficult for Josh, one of my ministry team
members, to hear these words from a man with
prophetic gifts. If it was a word from the Lord, it means
he will not succeed in his ultimate goal—to bring that
family into freedom from demonic oppression.

We still do not know the full implications of this
prophecy since, as I write, the situation is unresolved.
In fact, we are not sure we know exactly how to interpret the prophecy. Nor are we sure if we need to rectify

the lack of authority by turning the ministry opportunity over to someone with greater authority, or whether others need to be present to add their authority to Josh's.

What this prophecy points up, however, is that there are rules in the universe that must be obeyed concerning the exercise of authority. If they are not obeyed, the results we seek will not happen.

I receive telephone calls regularly from a woman I will call Virginia. She lives at some distance from me and is engaged in spiritual warfare constantly. Though Virginia is in her forties, she has adopted me as her father, giving me legal rights in the spirit realm to protect and free her from demonic harassment. It surprises me that when her husband uses his authority to attempt to free her, it often does not work. The demons respond quickly, however, when I assert the authority Jesus has given me.

In another case, I was working one day to free a young woman I will call Cathy (who has also adopted me as her father) from a demon. The demon had an especially strong grip on Cathy since her mother, who was into witchcraft, had dedicated Cathy to this spirit before or soon after she was born. We were unable to break the demon's power until I said something to the demon like, "She calls me Daddy. So I assert my authority as her father to take away all your rights given by her mother." This broke the demon's power, and we were soon able to banish him.

My relationship with Cathy has changed, however, so that recently, in struggling to rid her of another demon, I claimed the same authority and it did not work. We were eventually able to get rid of the demon, but the fact that the father-daughter relationship we once had has now been "reduced" a bit had authority implications in dealing with the demon.

In another kind of case, we struggled for two and a half hours to release a man I will call Joe from a demon. Although we had the authority to cast out demons and knew it, nothing seemed to work. Then Joe confessed a sin he had committed (adultery). As soon as he confessed his sin and received God's forgiveness, the power of the demon was broken and we had no trouble getting rid of him. It was Joe's confession that, according to a rule of the spiritual universe, allowed our (and his) authority to be effective in dealing with the demon.

I do not claim to understand all that is going on in cases like these. But I know there are rules concerning authority that must be obeyed—rules as firmly fixed in the universe as the law of gravity. And as we learn what these rules are, we can be more effective in dealing with spiritual reality.

Our God is a God of order. He has created an orderly universe. Whether we are looking at the way the material universe is put together or the intricacy of the human mind, everything works according to rules. The same is true of the spiritual world. There are rules and principles by which the spirit world operates. Among the most important of these: the rules that govern authority relationships.

It is clear from Scripture that the beings in the universe are arranged hierarchically. God is at the top, of course, with humans made in His image (according to Psalm 8:5) immediately under Him. The separation between God and humans is distinct. But since the resurrection of Jesus, a Man, the God-Man, has assumed the highest position in the universe (Philippians 2:9–11).

In the human world, each status carries its own authority. (More on human status and authority in a minute.) Below humans there are angels (including demons) and animals. Angels, too, seem to have various rankings (see below). Perhaps animals do, too.

123

As far as the cases I just described: It seems clear that no one has the authority to banish a demon so long as a person hangs onto sin or unforgiveness. The rules allow the enemy specific rights in such situations. With respect to cases in which I claim my authority as a father (even a father by adoption), the rules appear to give me great authority in a "daughter's" life—an authority I no longer have if our relationship lessens. With respect to Josh's situation, there sometimes appear to be rules requiring the authority of several people, or rules permitting certain people, but not others, the necessary authority.

As we minister, we often discover techniques that work. Often (as I have said) this is the result of experimenting. When ministry colleagues and I experiment, we try to share any successes, as well as any failures we pick up along the way, with one another. Then we can try new approaches in our own ministries and report on them at our meetings. In this way we are building up a body of insight to add to what we learn from Scripture, Christian books, lectures and sources from outside our group.

What follows is an attempt to codify some of what we think we have learned so far about the way spiritual authority operates in the universe.

The Spirit World and the Human World

Scripture is clear that there is a close connection between the spirit world and the human world. In spite of our habit of regarding spirit things and human things as separate, in Scripture these realms are not compartmentalized from each other. They are tightly interrelated, with events that go on in the spirit realm having repercussions in the human realm, and vice-versa. Furthermore, the same rules seem to govern the interaction between humans and God and humans and Satan. The authority of God to do what He wants, for example, seems enhanced when His devotees obey, acknowledge the authority of, pray to or worship Him. Likewise, the authority of Satan to do what he wants is enhanced when his devotees respond in such ways to him.

It looks as though a major principle is this: *The way authority is exercised in the human sphere affects what goes on in the spiritual realm, and vice-versa.* We spoke in chapter 2 of the fact that binding or loosing on earth has effects in heaven. And when human beings commit themselves to God, we are told that there is a reaction in heaven: rejoicing (Luke 15:7). I suspect there is a similar reaction on the part of the satanic kingdom when someone commits himself or herself to their side.

The close relationship between the realms is seen in the conversation in which Satan challenges God to allow him to attack Job (Job 1). The resulting agreement has tremendous repercussions on the lives of Job and his family. In Daniel 10:13 we see a spirit being called the prince of Persia able to prevent the answer to Daniel's prayer from being implemented. Apparently such activities in the spirit realm can have great impact among humans without our knowing it.

All such interactions and repercussions stem from the ways in which authority relationships are used. There is, first of all, *inherent authority.* This is the authority that is automatically part of the position and power of the various beings in the universe, whether spirit beings or human beings. Much of this book is about inherent authority and the rules that pertain to that authority.

In addition to the authority inherent in a being's position is what we may call *specially granted authority.* This is the authority granted at specific times to given beings, whether spirit or human, for particular purposes. In addition to the authority inherent in his position in the universe, Satan was granted special authority over Job and his family. He was also given special authority to afflict the apostle Paul with what Paul called his "thorn in the flesh" (KJV) and "Satan's messenger" (2 Corinthians 12:7). There have probably been numerous times in history when Satan has appealed to God for similar special authority and been granted it.

Many human positions carry with them inherent authority. Among these we think of various statuses and giftings. We will deal with these throughout these pages. But humans, like angelic beings, may be granted special authority at particular times as well. A frequent instance of this is when God chooses to use us to minister in ways for which we have not been gifted. When He uses a person to heal who does not have a gift of healing, for example, it is by means of specially granted authority. Likewise when one who does not have gifts of hospitality or administration is called on to serve these functions, and is temporarily given by God the authority and gifting to do a good job of it.

The Importance of Obedience

One rule we may miss in Job's story (and in many other biblical stories) is that God had great opportunity to work in Job's life because of his allegiance and obedience to Him. In fact, it was Job's obedience that lay beneath his righteousness and that engendered Satan's animosity toward him.

When people are obedient to their masters, the ability of their masters to work in and through them is increased. Both God and Satan gain new rights and authority when humans choose to obey them. Furthermore, when people, especially people of status, obey one or the other, the one obeyed seems to gain more au-

thority to work in the human context than was otherwise true, leading to this principle: *Through human allegiance and obedience to one or the other, God or Satan
gains greater authority than otherwise to work in human
affairs.*

A corollary of this principle is that there seem to be
limitations to what God and Satan can do in the human
realm, based on the cooperation received from humans.
That is, if certain people, especially those with status,
stand for God and against Satan, Satan will have a difficult time carrying out his will in the sphere of influence of those people. Likewise, if certain people stand
for Satan and against God, God will have difficulty doing
what He wants to do within their sphere.

Let's put it another way. On God's side, obedience to
His rules—including such principles as committing ourselves to Christ, praying, worshiping, doing righteousness, loving others, confessing sin and (in Old Testament times) sacrificing—enables God to do what He
seeks to do both in and through us. On the enemy side,
disobedience to God's rules—by sinning, not forgiving,
hating, committing oneself to Satan, seeking help from
him, worshiping him and doing unrighteousness—gives
Satan authority to work in and through us.

So long as Adam was obedient, God could work His
will in Adam's life without hindrance. When Adam disobeyed God by obeying Satan, however, the enemy
gained the right to infect Adam and all that he had authority over, including his descendants and the physical world. The obedience of Noah gave God the authority
to reach down into the human world and rescue a rem-
nant at the time of the Flood. The obedience of Abraham enabled the Lord to raise up a people who would,
He hoped, be faithful to Him. When Abraham's descendants obeyed, God was able to do mighty things
through them. When they disobeyed (meaning they

127

obeyed Satan), God's plans were thwarted, at least at the time.

The Need for Human Cooperation

The ramifications of obedience affect the strategies of both God and Satan. The exercise of their authority in any given situation can be thwarted by a lack of human cooperation. God's plan for His people to enter the Promised Land had to be revised when they refused at Kadesh to obey Him (Numbers 13–14). On the enemy's side, it took some time for Satan to get a pharaoh who would obey him by harassing Israel. Finally, however, a pharaoh came to the throne who did not honor the agreement made with Joseph (Exodus 1:8), and Satan was able to get that king to carry out his plan. Then, on God's side, through a family that was faithful to Him—plus an Egyptian princess who disobeyed both Pharaoh and the gods of Egypt and unconsciously obeyed God—God was able to appoint and train Moses to rescue His people.

A similar circumstance occurred shortly after Jesus' birth, when Satan was able to get Herod to work with him to kill the boy babies in hopes of killing Jesus (Matthew 2:16). Joseph and Mary, however, in submission to the authority of God, were able to save Jesus (Matthew 2:13–15).

When a person is tempted but refuses to go along with Satan, what the enemy tried to accomplish does not happen. If, for example, a person is tempted by a demon to commit suicide but does not carry out the act, the death cannot happen. A spirit cannot bring about suicide without the person's agreement. Likewise, when God seeks to enter a person's life, it will not happen unless the person gives Him the authority to enter. When believers do not obey God by praying and witnessing, people are lost, in spite of the fact that it is not God's will for "anyone to be destroyed" (2 Peter 3:9). When God's people obey by praying, repenting and turning away from evil, however, God has promised to forgive and bring revival (2 Chronicles 7:14).

When a person disobeys his or her master, whether God or Satan, the relationship is weakened though not broken, unless the person pledges a new allegiance. If a Christian sins but continues to be committed to Christ, the relationship is damaged but not forfeited. And if he or she repents quickly in obedience, the relationship with God is restored to what it was before.

When those committed to Satan in occult organizations such as New Age or Freemasonry assert their wills to change their allegiance and begin following Christ, a new relationship is begun that replaces the old. And although demons left over from the previous commitment to Satan remain in the person, they can function only as hindrances to that person owned now by a different Master, not as representatives of the one (Satan) who owned the person before. (Unfortunately, those who come into a relationship with Christ carrying demons do not attain complete freedom in Christ until the demons are ejected.)

On the positive side, the more the followers of either master, God or Satan, practice obedience to that master, the closer their relationship to their master grows. As Jesus said, "If you love me, you will obey my commandments" (John 14:15), and, "If you obey my commands, you will remain in my love" (John 15:10). Obedience brings and maintains closeness (John 8:31).

Satan's working is frequently frustrated by God's. But even God does not get His way all the time. He does not, for example, want anyone to go to hell (2 Peter 3:9), but apparently many will. God wants great things to be done in the areas of evangelism, healing, deliverance and church-planting, but much of it does not happen because God's people do not cooperate adequately. Jesus prayed that we, His people, would be one, as He and the Father are one (John 17:21). But this has not happened yet either. Apparently Satan, through the obedience of humans to his designs, has been able to frustrate many of God's plans.

But God frequently frustrates the enemy's plans as well. Down through the ages He has been able to gain the allegiance and obedience of millions of people who have converted to Christ and served Him faithfully in ministry. I have encountered many frustrated demons whose major problem was that they could not get the persons in whom they lived to do their will, because these persons were busy obeying God. "I can't get him to look," said a frustrated demon of lust to me once. "Every time I bring a pretty girl across his path, he turns his head." Although this man's obedience to God did not succeed in getting rid of the demons, it did hinder them greatly in carrying out their plans.

The Power of Rituals

Rituals such as sacrifice (in the Old Testament), worship and prayer seem to especially enable God or Satan. When God is honored through such rituals, enemy forces have to stand back and cannot carry out their purposes. When Satan is honored in these same ways, the forces of God are pushed back. Again, obedience seems to be the key. When we obey God by praying, worshiping, fasting and living faithfully by His commands, we grant Him authority to do what He wants in and through us. The same seems to be true on the other side.

A hierarchy of rituals, with accompanying increases of authority, seems to make things happen by spiritual

130

power. Blood sacrifices are the most powerful kinds of sacrifices. Among pagan peoples, as well as with the Old Testament sacrificial system, we see this spiritual rule exemplified. The sacrifice of animals was at the low end of the scale of blood sacrifices. Much higher on the scale was human sacrifice; and near the top, the sacrifice of the heir to a king's throne. The clearest scriptural example of the enemy's use of this principle is recorded in 2 Kings 3:21–27, in which the king of Moab sacrificed his oldest son to the Moabite god Chemosh on the city wall.

The sacrifice of Jesus, another Heir to a throne, was the most powerful sacrifice in all of history. It unleashed an incredible amount of God's power and has had cosmic consequences. But there were also immediate, lesser consequences stemming from the power unleashed at the sacrifice of Jesus. Among these: an earthquake, the rending of the Temple curtain and the emergence of many dead people from their tombs (Matthew 27:51–53). Another result, I believe, was the spiritual cleansing of Jerusalem so that such spectacular events as the coming of the Holy Spirit and the conversion of many could take place (Acts 2).

Below blood sacrifices, several other kinds of sacrifice involving food and drink can be used to enable either God or Satan. There are also various kinds of non-sacrifice rituals, including prayer, worship, fasting, Bible reading, meditating on Jesus, practicing intimacy with other Christians, giving, witnessing, sharing with those in need and many more. All these enable God to do more of what He wants to do, because they are done in obedience to His will.

Obedience in areas such as these is crucial to authority. The reason such obedience is so effective and important is that there is a rule in the spiritual realm that empowers it. When we pray, worship or fast, we tap into

131

God's rules for the interaction between the spirit world and the human world to bring about the ends our Master seeks. Unfortunately, the same rule applies on the satanic side. Those who pray, worship, fast, meditate or share on the basis of an allegiance to Satan enhance his authority and help accomplish his ends.

An Angelic Authority Structure

Under God there seems to be a hierarchical structure of spirits that we call angels, archangels, cherubim and seraphim. The function of these beings is to serve God, and they play important parts in the operation of the universe. From various statements made in Scripture, we can infer that angels at different levels have differing levels of authority.

The discussion in Daniel 10, for example, leads us to infer that the angel assigned to take God's answer to Daniel was outranked by the demon called "the angel prince of the kingdom of Persia" (verse 13). The original angel, however, was able to get help from the archangel Michael, who outranked the prince of Persia. At the highest level under God that we know of, then, we have the archangels. Two beings at this level are mentioned by name: Michael, who is called "one of the chief angels" (an archangel) in Daniel 10:13 and "the chief angel" in Jude 9; and Gabriel, who introduced himself to Zechariah as one who "stand[s] in the presence of God" (Luke 1:19). It was Gabriel's assignment to announce the conceptions of John the Baptist and Jesus. An archangel is also mentioned in 1 Thessalonians 4:16.

It is likely that Satan was one of the highest, perhaps *the* highest, archangel before his rebellion (Isaiah 14:12–15). Thus would God have delegated to him a large amount of power and authority. It is clear that

Satan still possesses great power and authority—perhaps the same amount he had before he rebelled. But he, like any other angel, has no power or authority apart from God's permission.

We have no names for the remaining ranks of God's angels. Under Satan, however, we are told in Ephesians 6:12 that there are demonic angels with names (depending on the translation) like *rulers* or *principalities, authorities* or *powers,* and *cosmic powers of this dark age* or *mighty powers of darkness.* Though there is some debate over whether these names represent a hierarchy, it seems probable to me that those terms represent a hierarchy, with at least three levels in it, before we get down to the ground-level demons—the footsoldiers of the satanic kingdom. These footsoldiers may be divided into occult demons and "ordinary" demons, with the former wielding more power. If there is such a hierarchy, we can assume that the demons higher on the ladder have more authority than those lower down.

We know that at least some angels have specific responsibilities that apparently involve greater or lesser authority. The cherubim and seraphim seem to have important assignments relating to the presence of God (seraphim, Isaiah 6:2, 6; cherubim, Ezekiel 10:5) and protection, lest humans come near the Tree of Life (Genesis 3:24). Then there are the nameless angels, sometimes referred to as *the angel of the Lord,* that appeared to Abraham (Genesis 18:1–15), to Gideon (Judges 6:11–21) and in the fiery furnace with the three Hebrew men (Daniel 3:25). These were given authority to carry out specific important assignments, and were, therefore, probably of high rank.

Some angels have assignments, and consequent authority, relating to children (Matthew 18:10). There are, I suspect, several levels of authority among God's angels, and many angels down through the ages have been assigned by God to such specific tasks with accompanying authority.

In addition to these assignments, we find when we are dealing with demons that God apparently assigns certain of His angels to assist us, giving them whatever authority they need to handle the situation. As I work to free people of demons, I sometimes hear the demons comment on the activities of angels. They report such things as that we are protected by angels as we minister, that they, the demons, are surrounded by angels and that the angels punish them when they lie or disobey us.

A picture of the two angelic hierarchies, based on the names we have in Scripture, might look like this:

God	
Humans	
Archangels (Michael, Gabriel)	Archangel (Satan)
Cherubim, seraphim?	?
Angels	Rulers/principalities
Angels	Authorities/powers
Angels	Cosmic powers/mighty powers of darkness
Angels	Occult spirits/demons
Angels	Ordinary demons

Our enemy is allowed by God (as I pointed out in chapter 1) a certain degree of self-determination, as well as the authority and power that go along with the position granted him, even though he uses these to oppose God. He has, then, set up his own kingdom within which he dispenses authority and power. There are certain restrictions, however, under which he works. These are important for us to know in relation to our understanding of both Satan's authority and our own.

Some of the restrictions and principles on which they are based are as follows:

1. *In spite of the amount and extent of Satan's power and authority, they are much less than God's.* Though we talk of two kingdoms headed by two kings, and may be impressed with Satan's power, the kingdom of Satan is *infinitely* smaller and weaker than the Kingdom of God.

2. *Although the two kingdoms are at war with each other, there is absolutely no chance that the satanic kingdom will emerge victorious.* Satan was defeated miserably at Jesus' cross and empty tomb. Beyond that, Satan and his followers have been "made a public spectacle" and led "as captives in [Jesus'] victory procession" (Colossians 2:15). Thus, Satan's authority is restricted by both his limitations and his defeat.

3. *Satan's power and authority continue only at the level God allows and only as long as God allows it to continue.* God, working in terms of the rules He has built into the universe, limits Satan's activities, and will sooner or later call a halt to Satan's ability to function (see the book of Revelation).

4. *Satan gained authority over creation from Adam.* As in that event, whatever authority Satan presently holds or gains is that permitted by humans.

5. *The satanic kingdom is literalistic in the way its members follow the rules that have been laid down for them.* When working to get rid of demons, we find that they obey the letter of the law with regard to authority structures and every other area. So must we.

Humans: A Certain Degree of Autonomy and Authority

Though there is a bit of repetition in what follows, I believe it is important to review the human authority situation.

Flowing from the fact that humans have been created second in the universe (Psalm 8:5) with a good bit of freedom and authority, are facts and principles like the following:

1. Since we are created in the image and likeness of God (Genesis 1:26–27), *we are higher by creation in both position and authority than even Satan and his angels.* We are God's masterpiece, created high above every other creature, including the angels.

2. *At creation God gave Adam authority over the created world* (Genesis 1:26, 28). It was apparently God's intent that humans live in obedience to Him as stewards over His creation.

3. *God also built into the universe certain authority rules for humans.* Among these are the authority of:

- Husbands over wives (Ephesians 5:23; 1 Timothy 2:11–14);
- Parents over children (Ephesians 6:1–3; Colossians 3:20);
- Pastors and other leaders over the people in their churches (Ephesians 4:11–12; 1 Timothy 3);
- Rulers over their people (1 Timothy 2:2; Romans 13:1–2);
- Masters over slaves (Ephesians 6:5);
- Leaders over followers (1 Peter 2:13–14);
- Jesus over the Church (Ephesians 5:23);
- And, I believe, older people over younger.

Although the authority in each case (including that of Jesus Christ over the Church) is exercised by humans in the human world, it is a spiritual authority. Clearly, however, *the one with greater authority does not have greater value than the one with lesser authority.* Indeed, I would argue that what we call authority in this regard is more a matter of those with so-called "higher" authority being assigned the task of protecting those who are more vulnerable than of possessing the power to take advantage of those under their authority. Indeed, the principle by which those with greater authority are to be governed is the principle of service (Mark 10:42–45). These authority rules, then, are a matter of organization, not value. And there seems to be at least one counter rule: that of the believing wife (1 Corinthians 7:14), who has authority both in relation to her unbelieving husband and to her children.

In dealing with demons, we have found that they take all these authority relationships, including this counter rule, very seriously. They regard the authority of husband over wife, parents over children, leaders over followers as well-nigh absolute. We must, therefore, take such rules seriously in dealing with demons, regardless of whether, as contemporary Westerners with our own views of authority, we like such rules. We will discuss these matters again later.

4. *Adam squandered the authority he was given through his disobedience* (Genesis 3). This gave Satan the authority he bragged about in Luke 4:6.

5. *Through the work of Christ appropriated by faith, however, humans can regain their lost relationship with God.* Those who receive Jesus through faith in Him are given "the right [authority] to become God's children" (John 1:12). On this basis, then, we who are committed to Jesus in faith have the authority to do what Jesus did and "even greater things" (John 14:12).

6. *The proper relationship with God means the restoration of the authority we were intended to have over the creation and even over evil spirits.* As we learn from the sons of Sceva (Acts 19:13–16), those without a relationship with God do not have the authority to cast out demons. Jesus and His followers, on the other hand, demonstrated that such authority is available to those with this relationship.

Spirit World–Human World Interaction

Satan is, as I said, a literalist—or, rather, he is required by God to strictly obey the rules of the universe. Both God's Kingdom and Satan's are bound by whatever authority relationships God has set down. Among the principles governing these relationships:

1. *There are conditions under which humans can give authority in their lives to either God or Satan.* Human obedience, as we have seen, whether to God or to Satan, gives whichever master specific rights in a person's life. God's purpose for Adam was that he live a life of obedience to Him. But not until Jesus, the second Adam, do we see what human life was intended to be. Disobedience to God (sin), which is automatically obedience to Satan, gives the satanic kingdom rights over the person. And when a person wallows in sin, Satan has the right to send a demon to live in him or her.

2. *Dedicating a person to God or Satan, whether self-dedication or dedication by someone in authority over that person, gives whichever master authority over him or her.* When people commit themselves or their children to God, a kind of spiritual label is put on that person that says, *This one belongs to God.* Likewise with any dedication to a satanic being. Many people in non-Christian religions or occult organizations dedicate themselves to false gods or spirits, thus putting themselves under the authority of a demon, cult leader or false religion. Others who belong to organizations such as Freemasonry or Scientology commit themselves *unconsciously* to the enemy. When a parent dedicates a child to Satan, the parent gives the enemy authority to work in and through that child's life.

3. As I have indicated, *the spirit world honors human authority patterns, both natural and delegated.* We have spoken of the "natural" patterns—those relating to the

authority of husband over wife, parents over children and the like. But delegated authority is also honored by the spirit world. I have frequently been authorized by people to take authority over demons in themselves or in their houses. When I do so, I work with their permission and under their authority. Once I ministered to a man in his thirties who had carried a demon since he was five, authorized to be there by a babysitter! When his parents had turned him as a child over to the babysitter, they had given her their authority, which she used to invite one or more demons in.

As husbands, we can delegate to our wives our total authority over home and children when we go on a trip. Likewise, the leader of an organization can delegate his or her authority for certain purposes. When we do so, the spirit world has to listen to the one to whom authority is delegated, as if that person were the top authority figure.

4. *What leaders do with their authority affects those under them.* Those in authority over others need to be careful not to take their authority lightly. We see in Scripture that disobedience on the part of those in spiritual or civic authority over others (for example, Israel's kings) affects the whole group over which they have authority. In the case of Achan (Joshua 7), the sin of one, apparently not even a leader, affected the relationship of the whole nation to the Lord. Many evangelical churches in our day are hindered spiritually by the fact that some of their leaders are under satanic authority through immorality or occult involvement with such practices as horoscopes, fortune-telling, Eastern mysticism, New Age or Freemasonry.

5. *Any commitment, dedication, curse or blessing entered into by a person in one generation may give authority to either master—God or Satan—over that person's descendants.* Commitment to God in one generation

blesses its descendants, especially if they do not turn their backs on God. But satanic power may enter the family line through conscious or unconscious commitments, such as those mentioned above or through cursing. If such commitments are not canceled, the interference gets passed on to the following generation. Because of this rule, many children come into the world already demonized because of agreements their ancestors made with the enemy.

Exodus 20:5, part of the second of the Ten Commandments, may mean that such satanic interference is limited to four generations. I sincerely hope so. I have frequently found demons, however, that claim to have been in a family for many generations, stemming from such commitments or curses. One way or the other, we observe from Scripture a mystical relationship between members of the same family, which means that children participate in commitments made by their parents.

God kept His commitments to Abraham for many generations, even after Israel ceased to be faithful to Him. We also see the blessing of God on David extending to Solomon and to one after another of his descendants (1 Kings 11:34–36), in spite of the fact that first Solomon and then many of his descendants were unfaithful to the Lord. In 2 Kings 8:19 we learn that "the Lord was not willing to destroy Judah, because he had promised his servant David that his descendants would always continue to rule." This they did until the fall of Jerusalem (2 Kings 25). When God curses, as He did in the Garden of Eden, those effects, too, go on from generation to generation.

6. *On the basis of relationship and obedience to either master—God or Satan—these spirit powers delegate authority to humans.* Spiritual empowerment in the human world can be granted by either God or Satan. On God's side, we note again that Jesus gave His disciples au-

thority and power over all demons and diseases (Luke 9:1) while He was on earth. After His ascension, He sent the Holy Spirit to empower His followers (Acts 1:4–8) to do the works He did, and even more. With the Holy Spirit within us, Christians carry the authority and power of God Himself.

Satan, too, can give people authority to work in his power to do miraculous things. The amount of authority and power available to individuals on Satan's side depends on the rank of the inhabiting demons. Higher-ranking demons can give a person power to do signs and wonders, as with Elymas (Acts 13:8–11) or the demonized girl in Philippi (Acts 16:16), even to move around out of body as in astral projection.

Authority over and through Cultural Forms

Cultural forms such as words, material objects, places and buildings can be instruments of authority and power. Blessings and curses, talismans and shrines, rituals and music all fit under this principle. The empowerment of words is basic to most of the ways in which spiritual authority is wielded. Words usually serve as the vehicles through which other items are empowered.

1. *Words used on the authority of God or Satan are empowered.* Blessings and curses spoken on the authority of the one to whom the speaker is committed are ordinarily empowered, with one exception (noted below). As Christians we have the authority to bless individuals with specific endowments like peace and joy. We can also use our authority to bless objects or places such as cars, homes or offices with protection from enemy interference.

Although blessing in the name of God or Jesus gives rights to our side, there is also a satanic "blessing" that

141

can be engaged in consciously or unconsciously by his devotees. And there is cursing, by which enemy authority can be introduced into a person's life. I am not sure I know all the conditions under which a curse can be effective, but we are told in Proverbs 26:2 that a curse cannot land without a reason. By implication, then, a curse *can* land when there is a reason, such as sin in a person's life.

The exception to the source of empowerment I mentioned above is when a servant of God speaks words that serve Satan's purposes rather than God's. Negative words spoken against God's people, even on the part of Christians, can be empowered by Satan since they are in obedience to his temptations and are invested, therefore, with his authority. This means we have to be careful how we use our words.

I find that many people have cursed themselves or those close to them through negative statements. Self-cursing, often when a person simply says nasty things to himself or herself, gives the satanic kingdom rights to affect, influence, even live inside that person. Vows and oaths not made in God's will, or else vows made and broken, also give the satanic kingdom rights. Satan is quick to empower and take advantage of vows and oaths designed to harm people or to win power or prestige in the human or spirit worlds.

Words blessed on the authority of God or Satan and used for such purposes as dedication, sermonizing or witnessing are also empowered.

2. *Blessings and curses are the property of those who utter them.* We have seen that when Jesus gave His disciples authority and sent them out to witness, He commanded them to bless a home as they entered it, then to retract the blessing if they were not welcomed there (Luke 9:4–5; 10:5–6). The very fact that the disciples had given the blessings meant they could also retract them.

142

The power of their words lay under their own authority. If we have cursed ourselves, then, we retain authority over those words and can renounce them and be freed from the power we have unleashed. We can usually break such curses fairly easily by saying something like, "In the name of Jesus, I renounce all curses I have put on myself/my body/my. . . ."

3. *The dedication of objects to spirit beings enables spiritual power to flow through those objects.* Substances like anointing oil, water, salt and food, when dedicated to God, convey God's blessing to the user. In Scripture the Ark of the Covenant (1 Samuel 4–7; 2 Samuel 6:11), Jesus' cloak (Matthew 9:20; 14:36) and Paul's handkerchiefs and aprons (Acts 19:11–12) are examples of objects that conveyed blessing. Jesus' and Paul's items, moreover, conveyed God's power for healing and deliverance.

In ministry we often (but not always) find blessed oil to be effective in healing (James 5:14) or lessening the power of demons. Some people find it effective in ministering healing to bless and use such objects as water, salt, a cross, a Bible or the Communion elements. Lest we take a magical attitude toward such items, though, we must recognize that the power is not *contained* in the object itself, as animism would contend. Rather, the power comes from God and is merely *conveyed* through the blessed item.

The power of Satan is invested through dedication in such things as idols, cups and tables of demons (1 Corinthians 10:21), even doctrines (1 Timothy 4:1). In many societies it is customary for those who make implements used for worship, work, decoration or other functions to use their authority to dedicate those items to their gods or spirits. Many groups of Christians use the authority we have from Jesus to dedicate articles used in worship, including sanctuary furnishings, anointing oil, the Communion elements and holy water.

143

Once dedicated, objects are enabled to convey the power of the God or god to whom they are dedicated.

4. As with the Ark (1 Samuel 5) and cursed items retained by the Israelites in Joshua's day (Joshua 7), *empowered items in the hands of the other side can cause great disruption.* Apparently dedication and cursing are able to carry the authority of the being behind them into the territory of the other being. Often when missionaries or Christian travelers bring back objects from other societies and keep them in their homes, there is disruption by demons until the objects are either cleansed spiritually or gotten rid of. My colleague C. Peter Wagner had such a disruption in his home several years ago until he got rid of a group of items he and his wife had brought back with them from Bolivia. Unknown to them, these items had been dedicated to evil spirits.

5. *We can use our authority to empower non-material cultural forms as well.* Music is frequently empowered through dedication to either God or Satan. So are rituals, dances and other worship activities. The blessing we feel in Christian worship is likely due to a combination of the pleasantness felt at the human level and the blessing of God flowing from the spiritual level.

Certain musical groups active in America and Europe serve Satan openly and use their authority to dedicate their music to him. There are probably other groups that do so unconsciously. Such music conveys satanic power to its devotees. Dr. Ed Murphy has recounted how his committed Christian teenage daughter unknowingly became demonized through association with certain rock music groups and their followers. (See Murphy's article listed in the Bibliography.)

As Christians we have the authority to empower worship music to convey God's power to those who sing and listen to it. Blessed music played in our homes and cars

144

is effective in suppressing enemy activity and protecting against satanic attacks in those places.

Authority over Places and Organizations

Authority rules govern the relationship between God or Satan, on the one hand, and places or organizations, on the other.

1. *Spiritual authority can be used to invest buildings, land or other places with spiritual power.* Christians and non-Christians alike dedicate buildings to their divinities. Such dedications or blessings in the name of God or Satan give that spirit being specific rights over the building. The Old Testament Tabernacle, the Temple and contemporary churches are dedicated places where God manifests His presence in special ways. The homes, land and other possessions (for example, cars, furniture, clothing, computers) of Christians can be dedicated as well, giving God specific authority over them.

Places like churches, buildings, shrines, homes and land can be made spiritually clean by being dedicated to God. They can also be dedicated to Satan, giving him authority over them. Or they can become empowered satanically through regular use for evil purposes like prostitution, gambling, pornography, homosexual activity, financial swindling, abortions and occult meetings. I have found that places like Masonic lodges, pagan shrines, temples, occult bookstores, abortion clinics, offices of occult and sin-enhancing organizations, and some establishments doing commerce in health food, environmental concerns or martial arts can be dangerous for Christians to enter without claiming God's protection.

When Adam sinned, he gave away his right to the land and its productivity (Genesis 3:17–19). So it was that

145

Satan could claim ownership of the whole world (Luke 4:6). The enemy gains more specific rights, however, when people consciously dedicate property to him. Pagan temples, the meeting places of false religions and cults, shrines, occult bookstores and even the homes of those committed to Satan often show tangible evidence of his property rights. Those sensitive to spiritual things can feel the enemy's presence in such places.

On occasion I have been asked to clean out homes and rooms, spiritually speaking, that have been dedicated to Satan or that have come under his power due to people's sin and rebellion against God. A demon I once found in a woman claimed the right to inhabit her because she lived in a house in which a previous occupant had committed adultery. Only when we claimed the woman's authority as the new owner of the property, in order to break the power granted the demon by the previous owner, were we able to cast him out. I have dealt with other demons who seemed to have rights to homes through occult activity or a death that occurred in the home and, on one occasion, a claim to a church through adultery that had been committed in the building.

I was once consulted by a mission leader concerning one of his colleagues who became disruptive during mission meetings. I asked the leader if he cleansed the meeting place spiritually before each meeting. He did not, but started to do so after our conversation. The disruptive person's behavior changed dramatically when he was in that meeting place. Several teachers have told me they have found their students' behavior changed for the better after they started blessing their classrooms.

2. *Cosmic- or higher-level spirits wield authority over territory.* In Daniel 10:13, 20 and 21, we are introduced to this concept overtly by the angel who has to deal with the ruling spirits called "princes" (NIV) of Persia and Greece. Territoriality of high-level spirits is implicit in

much of the Old Testament, however, especially in the historical books, in which we see that the Canaanite people (and probably many in Israel) assumed Yahweh was a mountain God, while the Baal gods ruled the plains. In 1 Kings 20:23 this belief is stated explicitly, and Yahweh, whose authority over the plains is questioned, demonstrates that He is more powerful than the pagan gods even in "their" territory.

3. *The territory over which spirit beings wield their authority seems to be defined by humans.* It is humans who work out the boundaries over which they will have authority. These human boundaries seem to be honored in the spirit world. The fact that the territories of Persia (Daniel 10:13, 20) and Greece (Daniel 10:21), over which satanic principalities held sway, are labeled by human territorial names points in that direction. So does the impression gained by those who study and deal with territorial spirits that there are national spirits, regional spirits, spirits over cities and spirits over sections of cities.

C. Peter Wagner's book *Engaging the Enemy* (Regal, 1991) recounts the story of a missionary distributing tracts in a small border town along a street that divided Brazil from Uruguay. He found that people accepted the tracts on the Brazil side but refused them on the Uruguay side. Furthermore, some who had refused them on the Uruguay side received them gladly after they had crossed over into Brazil. The missionary's interpretation: that the prayer of Christians in Brazil was what made the difference. There were gradations in the enemy's ability to control the responses of the people on either side of the human political border, calibrated to the authority exercised by the Christians to break through the enemy's defenses.

4. *There seem to be cosmic-level spirits with authority over organizations, institutions and activities.* Probably

there are cosmic-level spirits whose job it is to promote pornography, abortion, homosexuality, prostitution and occult organizations. These spirits probably aid, empower and encourage organizations devoted to such sins. In Evanston, Illinois (according to Wagner in *Engaging the Enemy*), Pastor Steve Nicholson was fasting and praying in an attempt to discover why his church was not growing. As he did, he was approached by a high-level demon who identified himself as a spirit of witchcraft and claimed to own the area in which the church was located. Steve felt led to claim a certain amount of territory for his church and was able to break the spirit's power over it. From that point on, his church began to grow, largely through a steady flow of converts from witchcraft.

In the Kingdom of God we know of angels assigned to children (Matthew 18:10) and to churches (Revelation 1–3). Why not also to Christian activities like missionary and other parachurch organizations? Institutions such as churches, seminaries and Bible schools probably all have high-level angelic spirits and also high-level enemy spirits assigned to them. Possibly social institutions like marriages, governments and educational institutions do, too.

5. *In order for spirit beings to have authority over territories and organizations, they must have legal rights.* Such rights are given them through the allegiances, dedications and behavior of the humans who now use and have used the territories and organizations in the past. Land and organizations can be dedicated consciously to the Kingdom of God or the kingdom of Satan. They also seem to be consecrated by the purposes for which they are used, whether to God or Satan. Such dedications appear to continue from generation to generation until broken by the current authority figures. The ded-

ication of a place or organization can be weakened, sometimes broken, by subsequent opposite usage.

In Papua New Guinea, I learned that a whole mission compound was built on territory formerly used for tribal warfare. In an American community I was told that a church and high school were built on an ancient Indian burial ground. In neither case does it appear that the power has been broken simply by opposite usage. Until the power given to the enemy over those territories by evil activities is broken by those with authority to operate in the power of God, Satan will continue to have great ability to interfere with God's activities in those places.

Authority to Counteract Authority

When one with authority confronts another with authority, the one with the greater backing has the better possibility of winning.

Through bluff, however, mice are able to defeat elephants. The same is true with satanic spirits, if those of us working in God's power do not know what we are doing. One reason for this book is to help us know we have greater authority than that of the enemy's servants, and know how to exercise that authority to defeat them.

1. *By working in the authority and power of God, we can free people who are in satanic bondage.* Under God we have the authority to cast out demons, and minister in other ways that cancel enemy rights at ground level. We will deal with this more specifically in chapter 8, "Authority in Ministering to Others."

2. *The rules for breaking the authority given by people through the dedication of territories, buildings and organizations are parallel to those for breaking such authority over individuals.* The dedication to God or Satan of

149

such places or institutions can be weakened, sometimes broken, through either the opposite dedication or through usage for the opposite purpose. This parallels how the authority given through dedications or commitments of individuals can be broken.

With individuals committed to Satan, we need to look for and clean out the garbage that gives satanic spirits rights in the individual. For territories, buildings and organizations, it is crucial to find and break the power of commitments, dedications, curses and sins that have been made on the land, as well as agreements forged consciously or unconsciously by those in authority over the land that gave legal rights to the enemy.

Examples would be cities, buildings or organizations dedicated to or by occult groups such as Freemasons (for example, Masonic lodges, plus cities such as Washington, D.C., and several Argentine cities dedicated by and to Freemasons); places where blood has been shed unjustly (for example, Wounded Knee, South Dakota, and buildings where murder took place); and buildings, sections of cities and organizations given to violence, prostitution and homosexuality. It is an important step in breaking the enemy's power for the people of an infested place (just as with individuals) to confess sin, repent and turn from their wicked ways (2 Chronicles 7:14).

The power of the enemy over areas infected by sinful usage can be weakened, perhaps broken, through repentance on the part of those now in authority over them. We call this *identificational repentance*. It consists of contemporary representatives of groups that sinned against other groups taking responsibility for the sins of their ancestors and repenting (preferably in public) to contemporary representatives of the groups wronged. Both Nehemiah (Nehemiah 1:5–11) and Daniel (Daniel 9:4–19) model identificational repentance. Such ground-level human activity prepares the way for more aggressive offensives against evil powers.

3. *There are rules for exercising authority in attacking the spirit, good or evil, assigned to territories and organizations.* For servants of God attacking evil spiritual beings, and servants of Satan attacking God's Kingdom, the most important weapon of attack is prayer, especially intercession. Servants of God and Satan, as individuals and groups, attack regularly through prayer, worship and fasting. God's servants need to add repentance, both individual and corporate. Those praying need to rid themselves of as much internal garbage as possible, so that the enemy can find nothing in them on which to get a grip (John 14:30).

In prayer we need to give attention to breaking all historical and contemporary commitments, curses and dedications holding a territory or organization in Satan's grip. We must repent of any sins committed in that territory. Next, in authoritative praying, we speak the power of God over "the spiritual powers in space" (Ephesians 2:2), laying claim to the territory or organization in the name of Jesus.

Learning the Rules

I have tried in this chapter to articulate the rules I have become aware of that relate to spiritual authority. As in all of God's creation, the spirit world is organized according to the principles and rules God has laid down. These rules are, I believe, as firm as any of the laws of physics or mathematics; and they will, when discovered and recorded, constitute a science in the spiritual area.

But little attention has been focused on the study of the rules governing the spirit realm (unlike the study of the rules governing the physical universe), especially those governing the relationship between the spirit world and the human world. So we understand little. But in dealing with spiritual authority, and the relationships between that authority and what goes on in the world above and the one below, we do well to find out what these rules are and how to operate by them.

Now it is time to begin discussing specific areas of application of these principles.

6

Authority in Our Personal Lives

Just who are you?" the demon said with a strong, arrogant voice.

"That doesn't matter," I replied. "I don't come in my own name. I come in Jesus' name. Do you recognize that name?"

"Oh yes," he replied, his voice much weaker. "I know Jesus."

"And do you recognize that I have the authority of that name?"

"Oh yes," he answered again, his voice weaker still.

"What does this mean?" I asked.

"It means I have to obey you."

"In that name, then, I command you to obey," I said. And he obeyed.

I have had this kind of interaction with many demons. (Although some question whether we should let demons speak, I have found that a short conversation like this can be very helpful to the client as a clear demonstration of who is in charge. For further discussion of talking to demons, see the section on this topic in chapter 8.) In such confrontations with the enemy, I never cease to be thrilled over the privilege Jesus has given us to use His name, His authority, to free others. Unfortunately, most Christians do not seem to know the authority they have in Christ, so demons harass us at will, interfering with all aspects of our lives and crippling many.

The apostle Paul said that we know the enemy's schemes (2 Corinthians 2:11). But we who live today are much less likely to know them. The people of Paul's day understood the spirit world. We, due to the blinding effects of our worldview, do not. And because we do not know our enemy in a time of war, we fight (or hide or run) at a severe disadvantage.

I believe (as I have said) that Satan attacks us primarily in the area of self-image. He is desperately afraid we will discover who we are and make life difficult for him. Like a mouse bluffing an elephant into fearing a creature with much less power, the devil bluffs us and often wins because we do not know who we are. As Dean Sherman points out in *Spiritual Warfare for Every Christian,* Satan does his best to keep us from "confidently believing in the authority God gives us." He wants us "out of the race, sidelined by our doubts, fears, and weaknesses." It is up to us to accept the truth of who we are and to operate on it. God's Spirit does live within us, no matter how we feel.

It is absolutely true that "the Spirit who is in [us] is more powerful than the spirit in those who belong to the world" (1 John 4:4). "But if we don't embrace that truth," writes Sherman, "then it might as well not be true. We will agree with Satan's lie" and submit to our feelings and circumstances as they are manipulated by the enemy. But God's truth is God's truth. We need to believe it in the depths of our being. We need to speak it out to let the enemy know that we know who we are, and then we need to act on it.

To again quote from Sherman's helpful treatment:

> The basis of our spiritual authority is a legal one. It is a legal reality that does not waver because of our unbelief, and is as real as any transaction. In fact, it's a legal arrangement much like marriage. When I ask people if they are married, I never hear, "Well, I'm not sure. Sometimes I feel married, and sometimes I just don't know." They always say, "Yes" or "No." If we are married, we are totally convinced of it at all times, and have a legal document to prove it. Feelings, thoughts, and personalities do not change the reality of that legal arrangement.
>
> Our spiritual authority is just as real and legal as marriage. It is not just a concept; it's an actual thing.
>
> p. 110

This legal authority God gave us at creation was so important to Satan that he stole it from our ancestor Adam. And it is still at the top of his agenda to steal it from us.

We Are to Fill Jesus' Shoes

The position and authority we have been given is to "fill Jesus' shoes." He said, "As the Father sent me, so I send you" (John 20:21), and He meant just that. As mem-

155

bers of God's family, then, we are commissioned by Jesus to continue in the world what He started. When He sent His followers to do His works throughout Palestine, He assigned them to do two things (Luke 9:2; 10:9): to communicate that the Kingdom had arrived, and to heal (including to cast out demons). Furthermore He said to them, "I have given you authority, so that you can walk on snakes and scorpions and overcome all the power of the Enemy, and nothing will hurt you" (Luke 10:19).

There are four ways we do this.

1. We must start, once again, where Jesus started: *with the filling of the Holy Spirit* (Luke 3:21–22). That is, to fill Jesus' shoes, we must first be filled with His Spirit (Acts 1:4–5).

2. Once empowered by the Spirit, we need, like Jesus, *to be present and engaged.* We are not filling Jesus' shoes by receiving His empowerment and then simply sitting still. Jesus was representing the Father in the world with a mandate to establish His Kingdom here in enemy territory. He did not shun His responsibility, even though He knew He would not be treated gently in a world ruled by the enemy. He did not run away or hide from engagement. He was a man with a mission, which required that He be present and engaged. Being present, He provided a major threat to the enemy's reign on earth.

We, too, are to be present and engaged with the hostile world. As Jesus' representatives, we are to be a threat to the enemy kingdom. Too many Christians accept Christ, then lead basically secular lives, as if all Jesus expects us to do is wait for Him to come again. But that is not the picture of the Christian life that the New Testament paints for us. There we are told to put our uniforms on and go to war "against the wicked spiritual forces in the heavenly world, the rulers, authorities, and cosmic powers of this dark age" (Ephesians 6:12).

3. Third, we need to consider *the matter of protection.* In order to do what Jesus was commissioned to do, He needed a certain level of protection. The enemy came around frequently, whether as himself (Luke 4:1–13) or through Pharisees, government officials or other humans. In Nazareth the people tried to push Jesus over a cliff, but the Father protected Him (Luke 4:28–30). In the boat on Lake Galilee, likewise, the Father protected Him (Luke 8:22–25). And doubtless there were other situations in which the Father ordered angels to protect the Lord Jesus because "his hour had not yet come" (John 7:30; see 2:4; 7:6; 8:20).

God grants us, just as He did Jesus, an incredible amount of protection as we battle the enemy. As God granted His protection to Job, David and scores of others mentioned in Scripture, I believe all of us are protected by God in ways beyond number. I wonder how many accidents would have happened to us that did not, because God kept them from happening.

But there is another level of protection we need to be concerned about: anytime we challenge the enemy and enter territory specifically dedicated to satanic use. At this level we cannot be passive, but must claim greater protection than normal. I have mentioned the need to claim such protection in health food stores, occult bookshops, pagan temples and when driving or staying in motels.

Jesus claimed such protection for Himself regularly, I believe, as He fought the enemy. He also claimed it for His followers. During the days before His crucifixion, as the intensity of opposition grew, Jesus said to Peter, "Satan has received permission to test all of you. . . . But I have prayed for you, Simon, that your faith will not fail" (Luke 22:31–32). Even so, as we know, Peter failed. But later he came back.

Living and carrying out warfare in Jesus' shoes, then, means that we need protection at both levels, normal and beyond. And although we need not fear the enemy because the normal level of protection is great, we do need to be conscious of our need to claim extra protection. Often God Himself tips us off to the need to claim more.

Dick Margeson, a ministry colleague of mine, was used in a special way recently to minister to students in a class I was teaching. After he left to return home, one of the members of the class felt nudged by the Holy Spirit to ask if we could take a moment to claim God's special protection for Dick. We did, and found out later that as he was driving along the freeway, a large sign slid off a truck in front of him. It was headed for the windshield of his car, sure to smash it and hit him in the face, when it lifted and went over his car, merely scratching the roof as it flew by. We know God protected Dick, although we do not know whether this was God's normal protection or a special protection granted because of our prayer.

4. A fourth indication that we are filling Jesus' shoes is that *all we do in His authority is done in love.* As I pointed out in chapter 3, only if God's power is wrapped in love is it truly used in God's way.

With God's love, then, and with the infilling of His Holy Spirit, our own presence and engagement and God's protection, we are prepared to use the authority credit card in ways Jesus demonstrated for us—doing the things He did in the ways He did them. He passed on to us the authority to heal, cast out demons, bless and forgive. We will discuss these one by one. But first let's return to the important issue of authority asserted in love and power.

The Relationship of Our Gifting to Our Authority

We are told that when Jesus ascended into heaven, He "gave gifts to mankind" (Ephesians 4:8, 11) and that "each one of us has received a special gift in proportion to what Christ has given" (Ephesians 4:7). Some of these gifts are listed in Romans 12:6–8; 1 Corinthians 12:1–11, 28–31; and Ephesians 4:11. I believe these gifts are given at conception. This is why the enemy works so hard to gain control of those with the most spectacular gifting.

On occasion, as I have engaged in inner healing and deliverance, I have asked demons why they work so hard to keep a particular person in bondage. The demonic response is something like, "We don't want him [or her] free to live for Jesus," or "We're afraid of what she [or he] might do for Jesus." Demons seem to understand that *certain individuals have greater potential than others to serve Jesus Christ and, therefore, to hurt their kingdom.* Over and over I have found people with gifts such as words of knowledge, discernment, prophecy or healing who have been tormented by the enemy from childhood. People with the greatest gifting seem to be more often attacked by the enemy.

One dimension of gifting is the fact that God has given different gifts to different people. And different giftings designate a different range over which one has the right to exercise authority. (One does not have authority over someone else's bank account or credit card.)

There are at least three kinds of gifting. I will call them *role, ministry* and *office.*

The most obvious kind of gifting is what I call *ministry gifting.* When a person has a gift of healing or intercession or teaching, and exercises it regularly, we can say he or she has a ministry of whatever that gift is. Per-

159

sonally I have been gifted by God to help people get free in emotional and spiritual areas. By exercising this gift, I have a ministry of inner healing and deliverance. I also have a gift of teaching. If I exercised this gift as a layperson, it would classify as a ministry gift. But because I am employed as a teacher, I am in the office of teacher and am using this gift as an *office gift*.

The distinction between ministry gifting and office gifting is, thus, simply a matter of whether or not one is appointed (and usually paid) by an organization to function in one's gifting. I know people who are appointed as official intercessors, and one who is ordained to a deliverance ministry (office), though without pay.

What I am calling *role gifting* is when a person is put on the spot, needing to function in an area in which he or she is not normally gifted, but God supplies the gift needed for the occasion. As nearly as I can tell, I have little or no gifting in the hospitality area. But when my wife is not at home and I need to fill in, the Lord is gracious and gifts me for the occasion. Nor do I think I have the gift of physical healing, since many of the people I pray for do not get healed. But God often uses me to bring physical healing as part of inner healing (within my gifting), and not infrequently to bring purely physical healing (as role gifting).

Given what we think we know about gifting, then, it looks as though we have greater authority in areas of our gifting than in other areas. Even when the gifting is a matter of role, the authority can be great, if only for that single occasion. There may be times in role situations, however, when God does not give a person enough authority to do the job.

I once foolishly visited a Buddhist temple in Taiwan during a "holy" month when the temple was specially empowered. I came away with a bothersome pain under my sternum. Several people prayed over me during the next three weeks without success, before the one whom God used to relieve me of the problem. As I was being prayed for unsuccessfully by those people, some of whom may have had the gift of healing at a ministry level, I believe I was just as receptive to God's working as I was later. So I do not think (though I could be wrong) that the difference was in me. I conclude, rather, that God did not give the others the authority to deal effectively with my problem.

The level of authority in ministry or office gifting (unlike role gifting) is constantly high. Not that the success rate is one hundred percent; but those who know their gifts and practice them regularly develop a high degree of confidence about what the results will be. They are, therefore, ready to tackle any problem within the area of their gifting, knowing they carry authority into every situation commensurate with the problem. They know who they are—both in general, and in terms of their specific gifts and calling.

Those who do not take seriously their responsibility to use and develop their gifts, however, may find after a while that these have been removed. Or such persons may retain the gifts in much diminished measure, at least until such time as they begin to use them again regularly.

What Authority Comes with Our Status?

The human and spirit worlds are, as we have noted, tightly connected. One of the implications of this fact is that the level of one's status in the world affects one's spiritual authority. Leaders in human affairs, for example, carry great authority in the spiritual realm. As we can see from the history of the kings of Israel, the spiritual fortunes of God's people were tied to the faithfulness or unfaithfulness of their leaders.

God does not take lightly the responsibility over precious people given to those who lead politically, corporately, educationally or in any other context, large or small. For "no authority exists without God's permission, and the existing authorities have been put there by God" (Romans 13:1). Those in authority, therefore, are directly accountable to God for what they do with that authority. I tremble to think of the punishment awaiting leaders who stand for the murder of pre-born infants and who cater to the unreasonable demands of certain homosexual groups. And by the same token, as with ancient Israel, God is a rewarder of leaders who stand for righteousness.

Since spiritual authority and status are thus linked, we need to be especially careful how we exercise whatever human authority comes with our status. Those of us who are parents need to recognize that the decisions we make regarding our children have spiritual implications as well as human ones. We husbands need to recognize the same with regard to the way we treat our wives. Teachers are accountable for the way we treat students and co-workers. We who are older should use the status of age carefully and responsibly. Heads of organizations need to take seriously their responsibility before God for the ways in which they treat His people. When we use our authority to oppress, we are offending God as well as those we encumber. When we bless people and treat them lovingly, we are using our status the way God intended it.

I have already recounted stories of problems that stopped when teachers took the authority of their status over their classrooms. One fourth-grade teacher I will call Martha was having an awful year. Her kids were unruly, apparently undisciplined and not learning much.

162

Then a couple on my ministry team suggested that Martha begin first to pray for specific children, then start getting to class a little early each morning and going around to each desk, anointing it with oil and blessing it. They further urged Martha to take authority over her classroom and kick out any demonic intruders, and to take the same authority silently whenever the children showed signs of becoming unruly, as if a demon were causing it. Martha followed these instructions, and God transformed her year as well as several of her students.

A friend who served as an interim pastor told me a similar story about a badly divided church he was asked to serve. Discouraged and desperate, he went into the sanctuary several Saturdays in a row, exercising his authority as pastor over each seat and its occupant as he visualized the person who regularly sat there, in order to break any bondage that person might be under. My friend also consecrated pulpit, choir loft, musical instruments, Communion table and everything else, and prayed fervently for unity. Unity soon came, as the exercise of his authority as pastor banished the enemy spirits that were disrupting the congregation.

Claiming Authority over the Past

One of the areas covered by our authority is not obvious to many: our right to cancel any claims the enemy may be able to make on us due to events and agreements of the past. Our aim, as with regard to claims Satan may have on us stemming from things we do in the present, is to be as "clean" as Jesus was. In John 14:30 Jesus referred to Satan as "the ruler of this world," but He stated that he "has no power over me"; or, as other versions translate it, "He has no hold on me" (NIV), or "He has nothing in me" (NKJV), or "He has no rights over me" (NEB).

Some of the rights the enemy has over people come through inheritance. Believers have the authority, however, to cancel those rights. The place to start is with the recognition that God has planned and chosen each of us from before the creation of the world (Ephesians 1:4). We can then assume that He has superintended the coupling of each pair of our ancestors and the transmission of both genetic and spiritual influences down through the generations. Then, according to Psalm 139:13, He formed and framed us in our mothers' wombs so we would come out just right.

Nevertheless, the enemy has had ample opportunity through this process to influence—and often to intrude on—our ancestry by way of demonization. Through choices our ancestors have made, doors have often been opened into our bloodlines, permitting the enemy to produce damage and insert his agents that will be inherited from generation to generation.

To help free people from any such bondages, I find it important to take authority over five major areas to cancel all rights the enemy may have gained through *vows, curses, dedications, sin* or *trauma*. It is important for us, whether by ourselves or with the help of another, to take authority over these issues in our ancestry in such a way as to cancel any rights the enemy may have gained in our lives deriving from the past.

Vows

The first area is *vows. Merriam Webster's Collegiate Dictionary* (Tenth Edition, 1993) defines a vow as "a solemn promise or assertion . . . by which a person is bound to an act, service, or condition." People vow regularly to do things or not do things. Vows that fall in line with Satan's purposes in our lives get empowered by him. One such vow that is commonly made and looks fairly innocent is, "I will not be like my mother [or father]." Somehow the enemy is able to use such a vow to establish a stronghold in a person. Some other damaging vows that come up fairly often are these: "I never want children" (from someone who had a difficult upbringing or who gets disturbed by children's behavior); "I will never allow myself to enjoy sex" (from abuse victims); "I will never let another man [or woman] get close to me again" (after a broken relationship); "I refuse to grow old"; "I'll never amount to anything"; and "I'll never be able to get it right."

I ministered to a man once who had vowed at age five never to cry again. Many men and a few women have made similar vows. A colleague of mine dealt with the descendant of a woman who had made a more openly evil vow. She had actually written a letter to Satan, vowing to give him her firstborn son, and every firstborn son thereafter of her descendants, if he would make her rich and famous. She became rich and famous, but her descendant, a firstborn son, was in deep trouble.

Two kinds of negative vows need to be broken: ancestral and those made by the person himself or herself.

To break the power Satan is able to wield in our lives through ancestral vows, we simply claim authority in the name of Jesus to break their power. Doing this in a general way usually takes care of things. But sometimes the power of Satan through a given vow is so great that we must discover what the vow was and break it quite specifically. God can reveal what we have to know in order to break the vow, either through a word of knowledge or by forcing a demon to tell us. Usually I deal with ancestral vows—as well as curses, dedications and sins—in each ancestral line, father's and mother's, separately. I usually say something like this: "In the name of Jesus, I take authority over all vows in the father's [or mother's] line to cancel any power given to the enemy, and to break his power through vows that may have been made by anyone of [name of person]'s ancestors in his [or her] father's [or mother's] line."

In addition to ancestral vows, any vows made by the person also need to be broken. This can be done in the same way. It is good to be as specific as possible.

Cursing

The second kind of past event that needs to be canceled is *cursing*. It is likely that both we and our ancestors have been the target of curses, whether leveled at us formally (for example, through a set ritual) or informally. This is especially likely if we or our ancestors have served in non-Western societies where curses are commonplace. Missionaries and others attempting to witness for Christ are frequent targets of such cursing.

Unfortunately, many of the curses that need to be broken have come from parents or other close relatives. An unwanted baby may be cursed while in the womb by mother or father or both. Many whose parents did not want them, especially those who have been adopted, can usually count on having been cursed. (More on this in the next chapter.)

A common form of cursing is *self-cursing*. I have ministered to many who grew up with strong negative feelings toward themselves or some part of themselves. Many people curse their bodies during their teenage years. Victims of abuse often curse their sex organs. Many women tell me they have cursed such things about themselves as their hair, faces, breasts, hips, minds and personalities. A man often curses such things as his emo-

tions, his sex drive (for example, in relation to mastur-
bation), his sex organ and his ability to perform tasks
such as job or athletics.

Another kind of curse that needs to be broken is the
one recorded in the New Testament when at Jesus' crucifixion the Jewish leaders said, "Let the responsibility
for his death fall on us and on our children" (Matthew
27:25). A friend of mine of Jewish ancestry experienced
a radical change in his life when the one ministering to
him broke the effects of this curse on him. As we have
spoken against this curse in others of Jewish ancestry,
we have often seen major changes. The testimony of
demons (for whatever it is worth) is that all Jews are affected by this curse and that the demons' power is significantly lessened when the curse is broken. In one of
my recent ministry sessions, a Jewish believer experienced major physical as well as emotional and spiritual
changes when this curse was broken and the demons
attached to it were expelled.

Cursing, whether from others or from oneself, often
gives Satan a right to a person. But we have the authority
to take away all rights the enemy has obtained over ancestors or over the person himself or herself.

My practice is first to claim God's power to cancel any
rights over ancestors through cursing that affect the person I am working with, then have that person renounce
any self-curses and finally to break the power of any
curses leveled at the person from conception up to the
present.

Dedications

The third category of past events that need to be canceled is *dedications.* Individuals who come from (or
whose ancestors came from) Asia, Africa or Latin Amer-

167

ica, or those with American Indian ancestry, can count on the fact that they or their ancestors have been dedicated to false gods and spirits that are really demons. People who have belonged to false religions such as Buddhism, Hinduism, Islam, Shintoism (Japan) or shamanism (Korea), or to cults such as Freemasonry, Mormonism, Scientology, New Age, Christian Science and the like, or if their ancestors have belonged to such false religions, need to have the effects of dedications broken.

My practice is to cancel any power the enemy is able to wield—especially over non-Westerners, but over Westerners, too, just in case—through ancestral dedications, whether I suspect they are there or not. Better to be safe than sorry. I treat any specific dedications that I know about, whether ancestral or in the person's life. To do this, I simply assert the authority of Jesus Christ to cancel any enemy rights and to break all power gained through dedications (to the specific god or spirit, if known). Then I speak the covering of any rituals used in these dedications with the blood of Jesus Christ.

Sin

The fourth aspect of past influence that needs to be dealt with is *sin*. Often Satan has gained rights in our lives through sinful behavior on the parts of various ancestors. Many of us know of alcoholism, aberrant sexual behavior or even criminal activity in our family tree. Such behavior allows the enemy rights, on the basis of which he can often make claims on us. Any wallowing in sin on our part can, of course, give the same rights.

With the authority we have in Christ, we can claim freedom from satanic interference in our lives coming through this channel as well. We simply assert the power of God to break any power Satan has gained in our father's or mother's line through sinful behavior. It is a good idea to precede such taking of authority with identificational repentance (mentioned in the last chapter), claiming the authority that is ours as the current representative of our family line and *repenting for the sins of our ancestors.* Like Nehemiah (Nehemiah 1:6–7) and Daniel (Daniel 9:5–11), we identify with our ancestors in their sinfulness, taking responsibility for their sins as if they are ours, and confessing our participation with them. We then assert our authority to repent on their behalf to remove family guilt from ourselves.

We do not have the right to grant our ancestors forgiveness, but we can free ourselves from any guilt that attaches itself to us, and any rights their sin gives the enemy over us. To do this, we may say something like, "As the current representative of my father's [or mother's] family, I assume responsibility for the sins of my ancestors, and humbly repent for their disobedience in the name of Jesus Christ, who paid for their sins as well as mine." This act of identificational repentance breaks this dimension of the enemy's power over us.

Trauma

The fifth area to cover when breaking enemy rights through inheritance is *trauma.* We often find, in dealing with demonization in the present, that the enemy is able to enter when a person experiences trauma or abuse. Given the fact that such experiences may have happened to various of our ancestors, it is good to cancel any rights the enemy may have gained through trauma in our family line. This is done in the same way as recommended above for any of the other four areas.

Our authority over the past extends to land, buildings, cars, curios and other items that come into our possession. We need to assert our authority to break any agreements that have given the devil any rights over such property before we acquired it. See chapter 7 for more on taking authority over homes and land.

And we can mention again that objects we bring back from foreign places may have been dedicated to enemy gods and spirits. Usually these can be prayed over and the power in them broken quite easily. I pray routinely over whatever I buy overseas or from Native American sources or places that may have New Age connections. I am told (though I have not experienced it) that some objects contain so much enemy power that it is better to destroy them than to fight continually with the spirits in them. Perhaps as a rule of thumb we can say, if the object has no purpose other than a religious one, it ought to be destroyed. But I do not believe in simply destroying everything that looks suspicious. We should be capturing things from the enemy rather than giving in to him.

Another dimension of the authority God gives us over the past is highlighted in chapter 8 in the section on deep-level healing. Most of us have experienced emotional wounds in the past that have the power to affect our present life negatively. In prayer most people are able to take themselves back to those events, and first to feel the pain again, and then to picture the truth that Jesus was there when the event happened. Jesus does not change what actually happened, but He enables us to experience the fact that He was there, keeping His promise never to abandon us (Hebrews 13:5). This usually brings tremendous healing, whether for ourselves or for those we minister to.

The authority that enables people to see and experience Jesus in a past event is the key to great freedom from the crippling effects of bad memories.

Claiming Authority in the Present

As we have mentioned, we can assert God-given authority in the present over a home, classroom, office or church building. In addition, it is important that we assert the authority of Jesus over our workplace(s). Those of us who work in offices should cleanse them by claiming the presence and power of Christ to banish any enemy spirits. We may or may not use anointing oil in the process. As I cleanse an office, I like to make the sign of the cross with blessed oil over the doors and windows. Then I speak a blessing of Jesus' presence on the office and all that goes on in it.

What is the "shelf life" of such prayers for cleansing? The cleansing lasts until demons are given another right to enter. When a room is utilized by others between the times we are using it, it is a good idea to cleanse it whenever we are again in charge of it. As far as workplaces like classrooms, workstations and offices that others (including cleaning personnel and night watchmen) enter after hours, I suggest we take authority over them daily to reclean them as often as they are likely to get reinfected.

We do not need to discuss protection again, except to note that this is a present authority we have been given. God's promise "to put his angels in charge of you to protect you wherever you go" (Psalm 91:11) is important to claim. We should also claim special protection for our children (Matthew 18:10). (I will discuss authority within the family in chapter 8, including the authority that goes with our responsibility as parents to protect them.)

It appears that, at least on certain occasions, we can use our authority to disable or disrupt the enemy's communication system to keep demons from hearing what we are saying. I do not know whether there are restrictions as to when we can do this, but I have been experimenting. When leaving on a trip, for example, I take authority over the enemy's communication system, forbidding it to be used to inform burglars or others who might do mischief or damage.

One Wednesday a woman called me to ask for prayer from a city about twenty miles away. As we talked it became obvious to me that she was probably demonized, and I decided to go to her home to minister to her. But before I made the appointment, I spoke to the spirit world, saying something like this: "In the name of Jesus Christ, I forbid any spirits to hear what I'm about to say." Then we made an appointment for that coming Saturday. In dealing with one of her demons three days later, I asked if he had known I was coming. He replied, "No. She knew but wouldn't tell us." Then I asked if he had consulted the demons in the Pasadena area, where I live, to find out about my coming. "I couldn't," he answered. "You built a hedge around me so I couldn't get to them."

In dealing with demonized persons, I have frequently found it helpful to explain to them what my strategy is and why I am doing something. But before doing so, I forbid the demons to hear what I will say. It seems to work, for when I have tested to see if they know what I talked about during the "blackout" period, they do not seem to.

We need to remember when we do this, however, to release demons from their inability to hear when we are finished dealing with the confidential matters. Otherwise they will not respond to our direct commands, since they cannot hear us.

Guidance is another of our present needs that we have authority to claim. When Jesus said He did only what He saw the Father doing (John 5:19), and said only what He heard the Father saying (John 8:28), He was speaking of guidance. He lived by that guidance—a blessing

He could claim on the basis of His relationship with the Father, not something He had to ask for. In claiming His right to guidance, though, He had to keep His eyes and ears open to the Father so as not to miss Him. This was Jesus' right. It is ours also.

The Nature of Personal Attack

I already mentioned that I am often asked, "If I get into spiritual warfare, am I or my family in danger?" My answer is usually something like: "Yes, but you're already on Satan's hit list by virtue of the fact that you're a Christian. And if you're not fighting, you're losing every time. Wouldn't you like to learn how to win when you're attacked?"

Personally I can reflect with a good bit of regret on nearly four decades of such failure after my conversion. My ignorance of the authority God has given us enabled the enemy to keep me from either offensive or defensive interference with his activity. I have sometimes complained to God about the fact that He allowed me to be so ignorant for so long. He never answers such complaints, of course, but He did bring home to me an important truth while I was on a plane returning from an overseas trip.

The night before, I had fought for more than five hours unsuccessfully to free a woman from a demon. In any war there are battles lost as well as battles won, and we had lost this one. Now, as I sat on the plane, I began to complain to the Lord about the fact that He had not enabled us to win this battle. Sometime during the discussion came the inaudible but distinct reply, *Well, at least this time when you lost a battle, you were fighting!* It was true. This time I had not been avoiding the battle out of ignorance, nor had I run or hid. And the Lord, without explaining why we had lost, was expressing His pride in me that for once I had done the right thing.

There must have been many battles the Lord wanted me to wage during the first 38 years of my Christian life. But I lost them because I did not even know I was in a war. My commitment now is never to go down knowingly without a fight. And most of the time we get to win.

The enemy does not like it that we are here and connected with God. Frequently he attacks spiritually. Sometimes the attack is in the emotional area. It may even be physical. During one of my seminars a woman told me she had been accosted by a man with a gun. Having learned the authority she has in Christ, and assuming an evil spirit was motivating the man, she spoke to the spirit and forbade it to attack her. Looking straight at the man, she said something like, "I belong to Jesus Christ and forbid you, foul spirit, to harm me." At that, the man's hand with the gun in it fell to his side, he turned around sheepishly and walked away!

Another woman told me of an incident with a dog. As she was out for her daily walk, she noticed a large, fierce-looking Doberman coming at her. Suspecting there might be a demon, she spoke to it authoritatively, much as the woman had addressed the spirit in the man accosting her, and the dog turned and slunk away without touching her.

The enemy likes to attack us when our resistance is down. When we sleep, we relinquish conscious control over our senses. This makes it easier for either God or Satan to get through to us. If the enemy has rights either to us as persons or to the building we are occupying, we can be attacked. Such attacks usually seem to happen, for some reason, between twelve midnight and three A.M. To prevent them, it is a good idea to claim the Lord's protection before going to sleep.

Often when a spirit attacks at night, people feel pressure on their body or on some part of it. They may even experience a kind of paralysis. A friend of one of my colleagues was asleep one night when she was attacked. She could not move and woke up in a panic, thinking she was dead. Although she was unable to talk, she could pray in her mind, and pretty soon she could say the name of Jesus. As her tongue was loosened, she began to rebuke the demon and it left her. Shaken, she called a friend, and they spent the rest of the night praying together. Later, in a deliverance and inner healing session, the woman was delivered from a spirit of death that was generational. It seemed to be trying to scare her in her sleep.

On several occasions, another friend woke up during the night with the impression that claws were digging into his face. The pain in his eyes and mouth was so great that it prevented him from speaking. Each time he began calling on the name of Jesus in his mind, and before long he could speak Jesus' name aloud. Once he could do this, he could rebuke the demon and go back to sleep. It turned out that the owners of the house in which he lived kept a large collection of Indian and tribal art objects, many of which were infested with demonic power.

Not infrequently the enemy attacks in dreams. Some people have reported to me that when they were attacked this way, they were able to stay in the dream long enough to invite Jesus into it. Then Jesus took over and, in some cases, cast demons out of them during the dream.

Whether by night or day, attacks can often be stopped by using the authority we have to pray in tongues. One friend tells me that whenever he begins to move into a mode of stress and fear in his work situation, he spends a few minutes at his desk quietly speaking in tongues.

Invariably the tension lifts and God's perspective for his work returns. Whether through prayer or tongues, though, the result is merely to suppress the demonic activity, not to stop it permanently. To make the demons quit permanently, their rights have to be taken away. This entails discovering what gives them their rights and then taking those away from them forever by the power of the Holy Spirit (see chapter 8).

What to Do When Attacked

When we are attacked or suspect we are in danger, we need to assert our authority to protect ourselves. With it we can tell the enemy to back off because we belong to Jesus Christ.

There are several ways to assert our authority. My favorite way is to say, "If this is the enemy, stop it!" Sometimes simply calling out the name of Jesus is effective. At other times reminding the enemy that we are members of God's family and under the blood of Jesus is appropriate; or speaking in tongues or referring to or quoting Scripture. In any case, it is important to address the enemy directly in the authority of Jesus Christ.

Spiritual and Natural Weapons

When we are attacked, we must resist with both spiritual and natural weapons. If we are too tired and worn out to resist, we must sleep. If we have not eaten, a good meal may give us the strength to resist. We may need to exercise. We may need to cut some things out of our schedule so we have more time for God. He will not protect us much in disobedience.

A weapon that is both natural and spiritual is the support of the Body of Christ. Incredible strength can be imparted to us by those with like faith when we are under attack. We can join their authority to ours and be helped and uplifted by their gifting. When members of the Body of Christ find themselves under the weight of spiritual attack, therefore, calling on other believers for such things as prayer, advice and encouragement can enable them to overcome and defeat the enemy. The ones successful in spiritual warfare are those who have learned to surround themselves with other believers who share the struggles with them.

A man we will call Jared discovered the importance of the Body one Sunday when he came forward in church for ministry. Through tears he explained that the day before, he had been driving on the freeway when an intense fear overtook him in the driver's seat. He got pictures in his mind from every angle of people around him trying to kill him by ramming their vehicles into his. The enemy was whispering in his ear, *I'm going to kill you. All these people want to ram you. You're going to die right here in traffic.* His drive turned into a nightmare of fear that almost paralyzed him in his seat. He was barely able to make it home, and he remained gripped by fear even after he got there. All that night the enemy came to him with threats, until by the time he came forward for prayer, he was a jumbled mess of frantic nerves.

As the team members prayed with Jared, they asked the Holy Spirit to enable them to break the power of this irrational fear. They asked God to show him that the threats he was hearing were lies, and they commanded the enemy to "stop it in the name of Jesus!" They claimed protection for Jared by the power of the Holy Spirit, and felt impressed to speak strongly and decisively against fear, and to proclaim the truth to him that God's protection rested on him as a believer and as one who walks with Jesus. They asserted the truth that, as a Christian, Jared was under the authority of Jesus, whose power is far greater than the power of the enemy. He was to respect the enemy's power and be wise to his schemes, but to reject any fear of him, especially irrational fear.

As the ministry team spoke to and prayed with Jared, his countenance began to change. The truth, more powerful than the lies, permeated his heart and mind. He began to breathe more easily and comfortably, resting in God's peace and rejecting the lies of the evil one. His tears dried up, while hope and courage were visibly restored to him. Jesus had broken into the jumbled mess of his emotions, reorienting them in the truth of His sovereign protection.

Using Scripture

One of the great privileges of the Christian life is the authority we are given to use Scripture when we are attacked. This is an especially good defense when the attack is sustained over a period of time.

One of the greatest arguments for using Scripture to counter enemy attack is the example of Jesus Himself. As Jesus submitted His life to God, moving into the wilderness for forty days of fasting and prayer, the devil tempted Him powerfully (Luke 4:1–13). Because Jesus was getting ready to begin His public ministry, the devil sought to divert Him from the Father's plan, getting Jesus (like Adam earlier) to give up His authority. But Jesus countered each temptation from the enemy with Scripture.

Satan's suggestion that Jesus use His authority to turn stones into bread was met with Deuteronomy 8:3, which says that "man must not depend on bread alone to sustain him, but on everything that the Lord says." The temptation for Jesus to use His authority by throwing Himself down from the Temple, in order to stage a rescue and be caught by angels, was met with a quotation of Deuteronomy 6:16: "Do not put the LORD your God to the test." Finally Jesus countered Satan's offer of a quick way to authority over the world by quoting Deuteronomy 6:13: "Honor the LORD your God, worship only him."

In dealing with the enemy's temptations, Jesus was modeling the way for us to use Scripture when we are attacked by the enemy. We can and should hide God's Word in our hearts, as we are advised to in Psalm 119:11: "I have hidden your word in my heart that I might not sin against you" (NIV). And we should speak it forth with our mouths to defeat the enemy in spiritual conflict—either quoting Scripture or reading it aloud.

The enemy does not like to hear Scripture! It is there that we learn we have the authority to "resist the Devil" and see him run away from us (James 4:7). The verse the enemy hates the most is the reminder in Colossians 2:15 of his defeat and humiliation. I have had demons cry out for me to stop reading that verse to them:

> On that cross Christ freed himself from the power of the spiritual rulers and authorities; he made a public spectacle of them by leading them as captives in his victory procession.

An especially rich source of scriptural ammunition to bring encouragement to those under attack is the Psalms. Many of these, called laments, were written by a person actually under enemy attack. Knowing that roughly forty percent of the Psalms are of this nature helps me to know I am not alone in experiencing enemy attack. Some of the most useful passages I have found: Psalms 3:4; 6:8–10; 72:12–14; and 82:1–7.

David and many other Bible figures really went through it! Reading about their experiences can be a source of great strength when I am under attack, because God can take me from a place of confusion to a place of clarity with Him.

Summary Suggestions

We can help people feel more comfortable with the pain and suffering they will undergo when they move into spiritual warfare. Although we want to help free them from any internal garbage the enemy is using to attack them, we also need to remember Jesus' prediction that since the world hated Him, it will hate us also, and will persecute us as it persecuted Him (John 15:18–20). Thus, when people come to me who are obviously under enemy attack, my first words to them are usually words of congratulation. They must be doing something right to attract the enemy's attention!

My friend and ministry colleague Mark White has developed the following list of ten suggestions to enable us to combat satanic activity:

1. *Always be alert.* Without becoming paranoid or mentioning spiritual warfare to any but those who understand, keep your spiritual eyes open to enemy activity. He likes to focus our attention on lies about ourselves and others and to disrupt relationships with others and with ourselves. Talk a lot to God about these things, claim His protection regularly and use your authority to plunder the enemy kingdom.
2. *Respond in love if Satan uses someone to attack you.* The enemy is the enemy, not the people he sucks into his operations.
3. *Respond in prayer.* Don't panic. Invite the Holy Spirit immediately into every volatile or potentially volatile situation. Use tongues if you have that gift.
4. *Do not fear.* Remember, there is nothing that can separate you from His love. You can trust this. Respond to the situation remembering this as a foundation.

5. *Be submissive to God.* The power for fighting lies in the place of reverent obedience to the Father.
6. *Rebuke the enemy with confidence and boldness.* Remember, the infinite power of God is on our side, and Satan's primary weapon is not power but bluff. Call his bluff and bring the love and power of Christ to bear on the situation.
7. *Ask the Holy Spirit to reveal any spiritual strongholds in you that need to be broken, and any activity or attitude in your life that may be inviting the spiritual attack.* Repent of any known sin and respond in forgiveness toward any person the Holy Spirit brings to your mind. When you find anything within yourself that you cannot take care of alone, seek others who know how to minister in God's power, and work with them to get free.
8. *Read Scripture aloud.*
9. *Worship.* Play worship music. The enemy does not like to hear Jesus glorified.
10. *If physical and emotional stress is involved, as it often is, do the natural things to reduce the problem.* Take a nap. Rest. Eat a good meal. Take a hot bath. Bless yourself. Bless your head, your mind, your heart, whatever part of your body is tired or in pain.

Since we are to assert our authority not only as individuals but in the context of our families, we now turn to family matters.

7

Authority in Families

I will call him Robert. He is a committed Christian who, like many fathers, has had great difficulty getting his children interested in family devotions. For years Robert tried everything he could think of, from enticement to coercion, to motivate his children to spend a bit of time each day with him and his wife reading the Bible and praying. But their cooperation was always grudging at best.

Then, in one of my seminar sessions at a church, Robert heard me suggest that fathers let the evil spirit world know they are in charge of their families by making a statement such as, "If you want my wife or any of my children, you have to go through me. And I'm not going to allow that."

Robert went home and spoke those words. Apparently the enemy kingdom heard them, for something changed.

A couple of days later, in a follow-up meeting to the seminar, I asked if any of the participants would like to share anything. Robert stood and, with tears in his eyes, said, "Many of you know how fervently I've been praying that my children would willingly participate in family devotions, and how resistant they've been. So the other day, when Dr. Kraft taught us to take authority over our families by forbidding the enemy to go around, over or under us to get to our children, I tried it. And this morning my oldest son came to me asking if we couldn't get together for family devotions. It's a miracle!"

The Authority of the Husband/Father

There is an ordering in the human world (as we have pointed out) that has spiritual significance. God is a God of order. And just as He has structured the universe in an orderly manner, He has structured the family so that each member has his or her place with its own privileges and responsibilities. As with the way gifting is intended to function in the Church (1 Corinthians 12:12–30), the purpose of differences within the family is that the members will work complementarily for the good of the unit. And, as with the body called the *Church*, so with the body called the *family*, different members have different authority (1 Corinthians 12:28).

We have to be careful, though, not to attach more value to greater authority or visibility. Difference of function or status in no way makes one person worth more than another. In God's sight all humans are of equal value, whatever their position on the human scene. To God the poorest, least significant person (humanly speaking) is just as valuable as the president of a country or head of a bank. Likewise, in a family, the youngest

183

child with the least authority is just as valuable to God as the father (to whom, according to Ephesians 5:23, God has given authority over the whole family).

Differences in authority have important implications, however, for what God expects of a person. Those with great authority carry great responsibility, as well as risk of harsh judgment, if they misuse their authority. In God's eyes, one in authority is a steward of that over which he or she has responsibility, and "the one thing required of such a servant is that he be faithful to his master" (1 Corinthians 4:2). Jesus underlined this point with parables like the Parable of the Talents (Luke 19:11–27), the faithful and unfaithful servants (Luke 12:42–48) and several others.

Faithfulness in heading a family is an awesome responsibility and challenge, especially since husbands are expected to use the authority we have been assigned as Jesus did—to love, serve and give ourselves to and for our families, even to death (Ephesians 5:25). "How did your family turn out?" is a question we husbands and fathers can expect God to ask us at judgment time.

Differences of authority are important not only to God; they are respected in the evil spirit world as well. It makes a difference, when we work to release a wife from demons, whether or not her husband is in favor. Often a husband's negativity toward our efforts makes it necessary for us to override his authority, as well as to break the demon's power, in order to get the wife freed.

One of my abiding memories from a recent seminar is the look of desperation on the face of a young wife who, though tormented by demons, could not get her husband's permission to receive ministry. With his agreement we could easily have freed her. Without his permission we could probably have freed her with difficulty. But he, probably following the orders of his own demons, watched her like a hawk and would not allow us to help her.

The apostle Paul was pointing to a rule of the universe when he stated that the husband has authority over the wife (Ephesians 5:23), extending even to authority over her body (1 Corinthians 7:4), just as the wife has authority over her husband's body. But although this rule confers privilege on husbands, there are corresponding rules for how this authority is to be exercised. Whatever privilege is thus allowed to husbands is to be tempered by their responsibility to exercise it according to God's guidelines.

Even though we are told that "a husband has authority over his wife just as Christ has authority over the church" (Ephesians 5:23), the rule is that such authority is to be exercised lovingly and with a giving, serving attitude, with Jesus Himself as our model (Ephesians 5:25; Colossians 3:19; 1 Peter 3:7). The command to love their wives was a shocker for first-century Greeks, since the ideal for a wife in Greek society was never to be noticed, either for bad or for good. By such a command, then, Paul was not only articulating God's rule but challenging Greek custom.

As husbands we are given authority under God over our wives. This is a law of the universe that, if broken, interferes with our prayer life (1 Peter 3:7). Let's dissect what this authority involves.

It is authority first to love, then to care for, to respect, to sacrifice for and to protect our wives as more vulnerable (even "weaker," according to 1 Peter 3:7) than we are. Ours is an authority to relate to our wives as Christ relates to His Church. Indeed, we are commanded to treat them as Christ treats the Church, giving our lives for them as Jesus gave His life for His Church. This is an incredible mandate. It is authority involving far more responsibility than privilege—an authority that challenges our tendency to see authority as more a matter of rights than of duties.

One important responsibility of a husband is to protect his wife and family. Gary Runkle-Edens, one of my ministry team members, writes about how he learned to take this responsibility:

> One day in a course I was taking from Dr. Kraft, I heard him mention that he believed we husbands have the responsibility to declare to all spiritual forces that they are forbidden to bother our wives. He advised us to speak out to the enemy powers in the universe, saying, "If you want my wife and family, you must go through me."
>
> Honestly, I didn't take this advice very seriously, feeling it was a novel idea but impractical. I figured demons would bother whomever they were going to bother. But a few weeks later I noticed that Betsy seemed not to be sleeping well. In talking with her, I noticed how stressed and bothered she was from all she had experienced recently—leaving her church, moving across the country, looking for a new church, etc.
>
> So one night I decided to do what I had been challenged to do. I declared to all cosmic powers, principalities and demons that I was God's appointed head to Betsy and our home. I ordered them to quit harassing Betsy, and told them they had to go through me from now on if they wanted to get to her.
>
> To my surprise Betsy's personal joy and zest for life seemed to return that week. She started sleeping better and being more carefree about life. I also noticed, however, that I seemed to be more spiritually attacked on all sides. A few days later it dawned on me that some sort of *enemy attack had been transferred to me!* So I started dealing with the enemy that was now harassing me.

This area is so important that I will give another testimony, this one from Natalie Stangl, a woman who attended our 1996 seminar in Zurich, Switzerland:

> I was used to fighting by myself against the attacks of the enemy. My husband would pray for me every day. But he did not know the authority and responsibility he had as the head of our family.
>
> I suffered for more than two years from one throat infection after another. There was not a month when I did not have throat pain and get hoarse to the point that I could not even speak. Since I am on the worship team at our church, this was a real problem. I began to get very discouraged.
>
> Many people prayed for me, but the problem continued. I went twice to a throat specialist because I feared there might be some kind of growth on my vocal cords. But after looking at my throat and vocal cords, the doctor couldn't find anything wrong except an infection. He simply advised me to use my voice very carefully and to wait it out. I took some treatments from a vocal therapist. These helped. But as soon as the therapy was over, the problem came back.
>
> Then, at a seminar led by Dr. Kraft, I learned that husbands can use their authority to protect their wives. So I went home and asked my husband, Andy, if he would start taking authority in the way Dr. Kraft suggested. He agreed, saying something like, "I, Andy, as Natalie's husband, take authority in Jesus' name to forbid that any evil spirits attack my wife. I take all such attacks on myself." He spoke this way every day.
>
> The results: From that day six months ago, I have been free from any attacks. Though recently I caught a cold, it had no effect on my throat. Andy, however, began to have the same kind of terrible throat pain and hoarseness that I had had! This went on for two weeks, then stopped.

(I suspect that since Andy had the authority to protect his wife, he could probably have spared himself the throat pain, too, by refusing to allow the enemy to attack him. See Dick Margeson's account on pp. 219–220.)

With regard to the spirit world, our authority is great when we obey the rules, but is interfered with if we do not use what is granted us as God intends us to use it. As Nee observes in *Spiritual Authority*, "If husbands wish to represent God's authority, they must love their own wives." Disobedience to God automatically means obedience to the enemy. If we men use wrongly the authority we have been assigned with respect to our wives and children, we cannot expect to be as resistant to satanic activity in our lives as we are meant to be. We will not be able to say, as Jesus could, that the ruler of this world "has nothing in Me" (John 14:30, NKJV).

Since parents have authority over children (as we will discuss in a moment), the husband/father's authority extends to the children as well. But again, there are rules. We need to treat our children well if we are to use in the spirit world the authority God has granted us (Ephesians 6:4; Colossians 3:21).

The Authority of the Wife/Mother

Wives are to submit to the loving authority of their husbands as the Church submits to the authority of Christ (Ephesians 5:24; Colossians 3:18; 1 Peter 3:1). They are to submit gladly, lovingly, respectfully (Ephesians 5:33) and sacrificially. Such submission makes wives beautiful, according to 1 Peter 3:5.

These commands and the ways they are to be worked out are the ideals we are to strive for. Other passages deal with less-than-ideal situations, such as when the husband is an unbeliever. But even then, Peter advises wives to submit so that if their husbands "do not believe God's word, [their] conduct will win them over to believe" without their speaking a word (1 Peter 3:1). And in 1 Corinthians 7:14 we are taught that an unbelieving spouse and his or her children are "made acceptable to God" through union with the believer.

We do not get as much help as we could wish from the Scriptures to deal with cases in which husbands abuse their authority. When love and patience do not win over the husband, but only allow abuse to continue, steps need to be taken to protect the wife and even get her out of the abusive situation. Here, I believe, our concern should be more for the need to protect a person God loves from the attacks of the enemy than for seeing to it that she fulfills the ideal of wifely submission.

The wife's authority in the family is second to that of her husband, but by no means small. I was experimenting with the use of 1 Corinthians 7:14 once in dealing with a "family demon" (one who resides in more than one member of a family) who lived in a woman I will call Grace. This verse says,

> For the unbelieving husband is made acceptable to God by being united to his wife, and the unbelieving wife is made acceptable to God by being united to her Christian husband. If this were not so, their children would be like pagan children; but as it is, they are acceptable to God.

> 1 Corinthians 7:14

Grace's husband, Jim, was not present but would be willing to be freed, we believed, if we could use his wife's authority to bring it about. Both Grace and Jim are deeply committed Christians. So I said something like, "On the basis of 1 Corinthians 7:14, and on the authority of this believing wife, Grace, I command all demons

189

who are under this demon's authority and living in her husband, Jim, to come here and be joined to this demon." At that, the demon exclaimed to Grace, "How did he know about that authority? Nobody knows about that!"

On the basis of the authority of the believing wife, then, we were able to banish her demons and at least some of his—those under the authority of the demon in her with whom I was dealing.

On another occasion I was working to get a demon out of a woman whose husband was a Hindu. As I was getting information from the demon concerning what gave him his right to be there, I asked him if he had any authority over demons in her husband. He said, "Of course." So, using the authority of the believing wife, I commanded all the demons in her husband over which this demon had authority (we had no rights over the others) to join him and to leave with him. The demon said they had to do this, and I believe they left the husband when the wife's demons left her. If so, it was a combination of the power of Jesus and the wife's authority over her husband that canceled the demons' assignments and enabled me to send them away.

A wife joins her husband in parental authority over their children. And since she is more likely than he to have primary responsibility for raising them, she may have more opportunity than he to exercise authority. She also has authority over her husband's body (1 Corinthians 7:4). And, in the case of a believing wife with an unbelieving husband, she may have even greater authority than he in the spirit world, according to 1 Corinthians 7:14 (quoted above).

The verse applies specifically to children but has broader application, I believe, to the spiritual authority of believing wives. Many women whose husbands are unbelievers have used this authority, though perhaps unconsciously, to protect their children from the vulnerability to satanic attack that would ordinarily be their lot. That is, since the head of the house belongs to Satan, the enemy would ordinarily have permission to do whatever he could get away with in that household. The presence of a believing wife and mother, however, automatically puts severe restrictions on what he can do in that family. If this woman becomes aware of her right to exercise even more authority, both over her children and over her husband, the enemy is restricted further and defeated at many points in his attempts to influence the family.

Probably we all can point to families that have been led spiritually by a believing mother because the father is either an unbeliever or merely nominal in his faith. Often the children in such families are well protected from spiritual attack as they grow up and become strong in the Lord, in spite of their father's lack of relationship with God.

It is common to hear of a mother's prayers and realize she has been making requests of God for her children from before they were born. This is a right and important kind of activity. But a mother should also recognize and employ her authority in relation to the spirit world, challenging the enemy's right to do what he wants with her children. Just as a mother, whether human or animal, is known for her ferocity in protecting her offspring physically, so she should be known for her refusal to allow satanic interference in her children's lives. She should exercise her authority regularly to restrict enemy activity in her children's lives, to protect them from the enemy and, if necessary, to attack the enemy if he bothers or threatens them.

In addition to a wife's authority over family members, she can claim at least delegated authority over such things as parts of a house (for example, kitchen or workroom), car or other personal possessions. She can and should spiritually cleanse the objects and spaces that are hers, either by ownership or because she is the primary user. The section "Single-Parent Families" later in this chapter discusses a woman's authority in less-than-ideal situations (1 Peter 3:1–6).

Male/Female Authority Relationships

In Numbers 30 we learn some important principles concerning how God regards male and female authority relationships, if we believe (as I do) that the whole Bible is inspired and to be taken seriously. Some dispute passages like this one on the basis of current sensitivities concerning male-female status. But since there is no New Testament contradiction of the teaching in this passage, and since the demonic world takes such father-daughter and husband-wife authority relationships seriously, I think we need to listen, whether we like the way God has set things up or not.

The principles come out in a discussion of God's rules concerning vows, especially those made by women. At the beginning of Numbers 30, the author shows the direct authority relationship between God and males:

> When a man makes a vow to give something to the LORD or takes an oath to abstain from something, he must not break his promise, but must do everything that he said he would.
>
> verse 2

The rule for a widow or divorced woman is similar; it is directly between her and God with no intervening authority. She "must keep every vow she makes and every promise to abstain from something" (verse 9).

For an engaged or married woman, however, the rule is that any vow she makes can be broken by the man in authority over her, so long as it is canceled by the day after he hears about it. A young woman still living at home must keep any vow she makes unless her father uses his authority to cancel it (verses 3–5). But if she gets married and her husband does not agree to her vow, he can use his authority to cancel it (verses 6–8). The vow of a woman already married, then, can be annulled by her husband if he does not like it, as long as it is within the one-day time period (verses 10–14).

This passage gives us insight into several ways the authority of males operates in the spiritual realm. First we see the authority of a father over his unmarried daughter. Then we see the change that takes place when that daughter gets married and begins to function under her husband's authority. In both cases, although the women who made the vows are accountable directly to God for them, the men in authority over them are responsible to God to either approve or annul the vows. (Males, widows and divorced women are responsible directly to God without the possibility of someone in authority over them annulling their vows.)

Horizontal and Vertical Authority

A mystical, spiritual unity exists between members of the same family. It has both horizontal and vertical dimensions. Horizontally we are connected tightly to siblings. Vertically we are connected tightly to parents and ancestors on the one hand, and to descendants on the other. We may diagram these relationships as follows:

Such relationships involve authority. Since spiritual authority seems to be calibrated to human status arrangements, the normal horizontal authority hierarchy for most societies would be older siblings over younger ones (although in some societies the youngest son has a special position). In all patriarchal societies and most matrilineal societies, brothers exercise authority over sisters. In Jewish and Greek societies, like most patriarchal societies, the first son has priority over the rest of the children in the family, and a status about equal to that of the father. Again, brothers are over sisters.

Given these differences in status (not value), those with greater authority should exercise it to protect and bless those with less. On several occasions I have recommended to older sisters or brothers that they make use of their authority to break the enemy's power in what looks like an attack on a younger sibling. In some cases it seems to have worked. In other cases, either there was no report or else things did not seem to change.

A woman came to me recently as the youngest sibling in her family, and the only Christian, to express great concern for the salvation of her parents and other siblings, especially an older sister. My suggestion was for her to assert the authority of a believing younger sister (whatever that might be) and claim the breaking of the blinding spoken of in 2 Corinthians 4:4 in the lives of her loved ones. I have not heard yet whether there are any results.

I would recommend, however, that my readers experiment with taking such authority in similar situations.

Generational Ramifications

As for our vertical relationships, we have already pointed out that what we do with our authority has ramifications for our descendants. We see several examples of inherited blessing in the Old Testament. God was generous to Israel, in spite of their disobedience, for several generations because of the faithfulness of Joseph (Exodus 1:7), Moses, Joshua (Joshua 24:31) and, of course, David (1 Kings 11:34–36; 2 Kings 8:19), among others. The faithfulness of these men of God resulted in blessing and protection for a certain number of their descendants.

But God's patience is not without limits. He says in the Ten Commandments, "I bring punishment on those who hate me and on their descendants" (Exodus 20:5). We find references throughout Scripture to the accountability of succeeding generations for the sins of their ancestors. As Lamentations 5:7 states: "Our ancestors sinned, but now they are gone, and we are suffering for their sins." People like Daniel, Shadrach, Meshach and Abednego, who found themselves in captivity in Babylon (Daniel 1, 3), were not being punished for their own sins but for those of their predecessors. And Jeremiah 15:4 states that "all the people of the world" would be "horrified" at Israel's plight several generations later as a result of God's judgment on King Manasseh.

Among the most vivid examples of God's visiting judgment on later generations is what He did to the descendants of Eli. God wiped out Eli's house because he did not rein in his sons, Hophni and Phinehas (1 Samuel 2:27–34; 4:11). The punishment was not simply because of his sons' disobedience but because of Eli's negligence (1 Samuel 2:29). God expected Eli to assert his authority to keep his sons on track even after they were grown. But Eli's sons had become "scoundrels" (verse 12), and although he attempted to bring them back into line, "they would not listen to their father" (verse 25). God held Eli responsible, therefore, and cursed his family because of the behavior of his sons, "so that no man in your family [except one who will become blind] will live to be old. . . . And all your other descendants will die a violent death" (verses 31, 33).

There is a single passage, however, that seems to counter the general teaching and illustrations from Scripture concerning the accountability of descendants for the sins of their ancestors:

> The LORD spoke to me and said, "What is this proverb people keep repeating in the land of Israel? 'The parents ate the sour grapes, but the children got the sour taste.' As surely as I am the living God," says the Sovereign LORD, "you will not repeat this proverb in Israel any more. The life of every person belongs to me, the life of the parent as well as that of the child. The person who sins is the one who will die. . . . It is the one who sins who will die. A son is not to suffer because of his father's sins, nor a father because of the sins of his son. A good man will be rewarded for doing good, and an evil man will suffer for the evil he does."
>
> Ezekiel 18:1–4, 20

Whether God has changed the rules, I cannot say. But we learn from this passage that each of us is responsible for our own behavior, regardless of whether our guilt gets passed down to following generations. An important part of the vertical oneness of families is our need to repent for the sins of our ancestors. In Leviticus 26:40

the Lord predicts that, while in exile, "your descendants will confess their sins and the sins of their ancestors," and that this will lead to His forgiveness and restoration. In Jeremiah 14:20 the people of Judah confess both their sins and those of their ancestors. Such accepting and repenting for the sins of ancestors were an important part of Nehemiah's reforms (Nehemiah 9:2). Daniel, too, was led to confess the sins of his people and ask forgiveness for his ancestors (Daniel 9:5–19).

The Father as Spiritual Gatekeeper

A major implication of the headship of the father/grandfather is the fact that he is the spiritual gatekeeper for the family. This means that whatever spiritual influences enter the family come as a result of the exercise of his authority to consciously or unconsciously give or withhold permission. The father is in the position either to allow negative or to invite positive spiritual influences into his family. He is thus responsible to protect his family from enemy intrusion. Unfortunately, many men (like Andy, whose wife kept getting throat infections) have no idea of their authority and responsibility in this regard, or how to exercise it. Consequently the enemy specializes in going around, over or under the heads of family who neglect their responsibility as spiritual protectors.

I have ministered to many people whose lives are scarred by the influence of evil spirits invited by fathers or grandfathers who gave themselves and their families over to spirits of Freemasonry. Most of these people have not belonged to a Masonic organization or taken any Masonic oaths themselves. All the rights the spirits of Freemasonry had over them came from the authority granted by their fathers or grandfathers.

These spiritual authority figures had not simply joined an organization. Through the oaths they had taken and the allegiance they had pledged to the god of that organization (Lucifer), they had committed themselves *and their families,* often quite unconsciously, to Satan.

A father is in a position, by the same token, to provide protection and even rescue for his family. I have given several examples of fathers who were able to free their children from problems by asserting their authority against the harassment of the enemy.

The husband/father's authority carries with it responsibility for whatever goes on in the home and family. He is to be the one who protects by providing the necessary prayer covering; who guides by listening to and following God's instructions; who rises up to defend when the family is attacked. "You can't have access to my wife or children" is his constant word to "the spiritual powers in space" (Ephesians 2:2). His shield of faith[fulness] is raised constantly on his and his family's behalf "to put out all the burning arrows shot by the Evil One" (Ephesians 6:16). His ears are to be open constantly to the voice of God.

Like the patriarchs of old, the husband/father is the family priest with responsibility and authority both under God and toward the family. This authority and responsibility relate to the spirit world, too, both to demons and to God's angels. And the authority of the husband/father over the family has a cosmic dimension, which seems to be the reason that Adam, not Eve, is blamed for the entrance of death (Genesis 3; 1 Corinthians 15:21–22). It was in Adam, not Eve, that we all sinned and forfeited our relationship with God and our sovereignty over the created world.

Authority of Parents

Ephesians 6:1–4 and Colossians 3:20 speak of the duty of children to obey and honor parents. This commandment, Paul says, is the first one with a promise attached: "So that all may go well with you, and you may live a long time in the land" (Ephesians 6:3). The authority of parents, although not stated explicitly, is assumed, and respect for that authority required.

But again, there are rules for the exercise of parental authority. As parents we are not to "treat [our] children in such a way as to make them angry. Instead, raise them with Christian discipline and instruction" (Ephesians 6:4). We are not to "irritate [our] children, or they will become discouraged" (Colossians 3:21).

I am not sure how long parental authority remains in effect over one's children, or how this relates to their own choices. Do I still have the authority to protect my grown children after they marry and establish their own families? I think I do. And I would point to the patriarchal structuring of Old Testament families, like those of Abraham, Isaac and Jacob, as possible bases for such exercise of authority. The way in which authority and honor were structured in those families may be more than simply cultural. It may be a transcultural pattern that points us to God's ideals for families of every society.

So I take what I believe to be my responsibility by exercising my authority as the head of my home, claiming protection regularly for my children (even though they are grown and on their own), their spouses and their children (my grandchildren). I let the spirit world know that access to any of my children, their spouses or my grandchildren has to come through me, and that is not going to happen because of the authority Jesus has granted me.

199

If my children or grandchildren choose to disobey God, however, I am not sure how much influence my claim of protection has in their lives. The tragic story of the prophet Eli and his wayward sons seems to relate to this topic as well. Eli probably claimed protection for Hophni and Phinehas, but because of their choices could not keep them from ruin. On the other hand, their bad choices probably stemmed from a lack of proper early training. Eli and his wife seem not to have done a good job at this.

As in our relationship with God, then, a father's desires can be thwarted by a child's choices. Even so, fathers carry a major responsibility for their children's choices and actions.

Dealing with Adoption

When children are adopted, there are special considerations. The first thing to remember, once again, is that the spirit world works according to human authority rules. When the adoption is official on earth, it is official in heaven. And from the time it is official, the new parents have the right to assert their authority over the child.

But the fact that the child is under new authority does not automatically cancel whatever rights the enemy may have had over the child. And the circumstances that led the biological parents to give up their rights to the child often mean there are enemy spirits present with rights over the youngster. A child conceived in rape, adultery or violence, for example, or carried in a situation of abuse, unwantedness, mixed emotions, contemplation of abortion or abandonment is likely to be demonized.

This means the adoptive parents need to take authority over both the ancestry and the circumstances of the child's conception, gestation and birth in order to break any enemy power the child may be carrying. (More on this in a minute.) It can be done while the child is asleep, if he or she is small, or with his or her participation.

The key thing to take care of is the cancellation of all rights the enemy may have gained through the birth parents' family line, and any rights he has gained due to the circumstances of the conception, pregnancy, birth and relinquishing of authority by the biological parent(s). Among these rights may be those that have come through cursing, through abandonment by the father, through contemplating or attempting to bring about an abortion or miscarriage, or through any of the other circumstances mentioned above. Much of this information may be hidden from the adoptive parents during the negotiations leading to the adoption. Even so, it is good to take authority over such things, even if one is not sure they happened. Why? Because it is better to clean a house that is not dirty than to leave it dirty simply because one is not certain that it needs cleaning.

In one seminar I was approached by an eighteen-year-old I will call Joe, accompanied by his adoptive parents. He could not understand why he hated them since, by his own admission, they had treated him wonderfully all his life. Joe was asking for prayer ministry to try to break through this problem. In addition, he hated himself and had wanted to die for as far back as he could remember.

To start with, I led him in a discussion of the probable circumstances of his biological mother's decision to give him up. My aim was to help Joe understand what it must have been like for an unmarried young woman who had made a mistake by getting pregnant and whose boyfriend had run off, taking no responsibility and perhaps even pushing for an abortion. Knowing nothing about the actual circumstances, we assumed all this, plus the dilemmas his biological mother must have faced over when and how to tell her parents, whether or not to abort the child and what to do with the child once she chose to carry it to full term—all the while hoping for a miscarriage. Joe could understand how his biological mother had probably concluded that adoption would be the most loving thing to do, rather than the irresponsible decision to abandon her child.

On the basis of these understandings, then, and with the help of the Holy Spirit, Joe was able to forgive his biological mother, and also his natural father. After this forgiveness step, we took authority over his ancestry (as outlined in chapter 6) and, in the name of Jesus Christ, canceled any enemy rights to him through sin, vows, curses or dedications in the family lines of his biological father and mother.

Having done this, I challenged any demons that might be there, and found four main spirits. (I think they were fear, anger, hatred and self-rejection.) These spirits were severely weakened because we had gone over Joe's ancestry and he had extended forgiveness. So all we had to do was cancel the rights they had been given by his natural parents during his gestation and birth, and any rights Joe had given them during his life to this point. They went quietly, leaving Joe incredibly free and, for the first time in his life, expressing genuine love and gratitude as he hugged his adoptive parents.

To break enemy authority over adopted youngsters, we may use words such as the following:

> In the name of Jesus Christ, we take authority over all the circumstances of this person's conception, gestation and birth. He forgives his biological parents for their mistakes and thanks God for allowing him to be adopted. On the basis of the authority given us by Jesus

202

Christ and by his adoptive parents, we cancel all rights
the enemy has been given, consciously or unconsciously,
by his biological parents, grandparents or any others.

At this point I usually challenge any demons that
might be there and seek to find out what, if any, addi-
tional ground they may have been given by those in authority over the person, or by the person himself or herself. Then I take that ground away and send the demons
to Jesus.

Just the other day I received a telephone call from a
distraught mother I will call Adele. She could not figure
out how to stop what was going on with her eleven-year-
old daughter, adopted at age three from a war-torn country in Southeast Asia. Apparently the daughter had spells
of rebellion characterized by temper tantrums that dis-
rupted the family greatly. Worse than this, she had, according to Adele, a very low self-image and spoke of suicide a lot. In fact, she had already made several small
attempts to end her life, and the family feared she would
accomplish her goal. Adele and her husband had taken
her to a series of counselors, but the problem persisted.

Since this call came from a distance, I needed to advise Adele how to work with the Holy Spirit to bring
freedom to her daughter. So I made several suggestions,
all with the aim of helping her "do it herself," since she
has the same Empowerer I have. Thankfully the family
is Christian, so I could assume the power of the Holy
Spirit at their end.

These suggestions can serve as a sort of outline of
what to do if you find yourself, as Adele did, far from an
expert in spiritual warfare.

1. *Assert authority over the family*. The first thing is for
the father to assert his authority over his family. As we
have seen from several illustrations, it is important for
him to do this before the evil spirit world, in order to

cancel whatever other authority there might be, and to break whatever power the enemy has been able to gain. Adele's husband needed to make obvious to the spirit world that he had legal authority over the child (since we have seen that the previous authority over the child continues until it is overtly canceled by the present legal authority).

I advised Adele to ask her husband to state to the spirit world something like this: "I am the head of this home, the protector of my wife and children. If anyone out there wants to get at them, they have to go through me. And I refuse to allow this."

2. *Take authority over the child's ancestry.* It is important to take authority over *any* child's ancestry, but especially important for adoptees, and crucial for those coming from societies in which it is routine to dedicate children to spirits. I advised Adele to join her husband in canceling all rights the enemy may have gained over their child through agreements made by her biological parents and ancestors, in both father's and mother's lines.

We have already noted that this involves the breaking of all vows, curses (both from outside and self-curses), dedications (in this case, generations of dedications to Buddhist and shamanistic spirits), rights given through sin and rights taken by the enemy at times of trauma and distress (such as probably happened in the warfare situation in which the child's parents lived).

3. *Cancel any direct dedications.* A third area to cover is the possibility that the child may have been dedicated to spirits or taken to spirits for healing or blessing. Given the girl's cultural background, it is likely that her parents dedicated her to their family spirits. It is also probable that she was taken to spirit healers at various times when she became ill in the three years before Adele and her husband adopted her. It is important, therefore, to

cancel all rights the enemy may have gained through dedication to or healing by evil spirits.

4. *Do housecleaning.* Next I advised Adele to do some housecleaning. I suggested that she and her husband take complete authority over their home and the land on which it sits. They needed to cancel any rights of the enemy to their property, gained through agreements or through sin that occurred under past owners or users, by asserting their rights as the present owners to break any power the enemy still had. Then I suggested they go through the house room by room, taking authority over every space—especially their daughter's room—for Jesus.

At that point Adele told me she had already had a disturbing demonic visitation one night in their bedroom. This suggested to me that the enemy probably has some rights in their home, stemming from either past agreements or rights related to their daughter.

5. *Assert your authority verbally.* A fifth suggestion I made is that Adele and her husband make use of the command "If this is the enemy, stop it!" It is likely that the assertion of such authority will help when the daughter acts up, when there is an argument or when there is indication that the daughter is struggling with thoughts of self-destruction or other problems.

6. *Get deep-level healing.* A sixth important area to deal with is the deep-level healing the daughter needed. For their little girl, working on self-image and early-life trauma is probably very important. She needs to experience the fact that Jesus was there protecting her during what may have been very traumatic experiences before she was born and during her first three years. She must also come to know deep inside herself that she was planned "before the foundation of the world" (Ephesians 1:4, NKJV) and that she is now a princess in the Kingdom of the most high God. When she assimilates

these truths, they will transform her self-image and set her on a new course of freedom in her life.

Authority of Children

What authority, if any, does a child have? All the previous rules apply. Children have rights over whatever they own or whatever they are granted authority over. In the former category fall toys, bicycles, athletic equipment and other possessions. In the latter, a youngster who is assigned a bedroom has authority over that room.

At a seminar where I had been teaching on authority in the home, I was approached by an Asian young woman concerned over the ability of the enemy spirits in her home to influence her. She asked, "What rights do I have in my parents' home where I live? I'm a Christian, but they are devout Buddhists with a very large and obvious ancestral shelf in the living room, and countless Buddhist artifacts everywhere except in my room."

I recommended that she focus on three goals: keeping herself clean spiritually, so the enemy would not have rights to her; claiming protection for herself when she was in any part of the house other than her own room; and asserting her God-given authority over her room and any other parts of the house she had rights over.

These three areas are important for anyone to tend to, especially if living in a place belonging to someone else.

Authority to Bless Unborn Children

Although there is some controversy over what pre-born children are aware of, my experience leads me to accept what Dr. Thomas Verny and John Kelly have written in *The Secret Life of the Unborn Child* (Dell, 1981). The following perspective assumes, with Verny, that life begins at conception and that a preborn child begins gaining consciousness of what is going on in the outside world after about six to eight weeks of gestation. Every attitude and event that goes on in the mother's life from at least that time, perhaps even earlier, gets recorded in the baby's brain and can affect him or her subconsciously. Thus, experiencing rejection at this early age can become a major problem later in life.

For this reason it is important that each child have a good experience in the womb. Verny's studies and others seem to show that preborn children know quite a bit about what is going on in the lives of their parents and siblings. If there is fighting, violence or abuse, the preborn child senses an uncongenial environment. And if the parents prefer a child of the opposite sex, or do not want a child at all, the preborn child knows it and may even make the birth difficult.

Prospective parents can use their authority, on the other hand, to bless and communicate love and acceptance to their preborn child. The best guide I know for expectant parents is Francis and Judith MacNutt's book *Praying for Your Unborn Child* (Doubleday, 1988). Taking the authority we are given to pray over unborn children, as they point out, makes a big difference in the children's lives.

One of the illustrations recorded in the book contrasts a pregnancy without prayer with one in which the parents and their three-year-old daughter, Jenny, daily "took time to talk and pray with our baby." They prayed:

"Dear Lord, we ask you to bless and protect our baby, to fill it with your love, your peace and your joy—to surround this little baby with the warmth of your love. We ask you to help it grow and develop into the beautiful child you want it to be. Thank you for this baby and for blessing us and entrusting us with this new life."

p. 16

Although the mother had been sick during most of her first pregnancy, before they had learned to pray over a preborn child, and labor and delivery had been "long and hard," things were different with this one. The second pregnancy was "much better physically—and much more peaceful." The birth took place in a "relaxed atmosphere" in a birthing room, and Jenny was allowed to join her parents soon after the birth. The baby, Albert, "just looked around and was very peaceful and content." The mother continues:

> He seemed to recognize each one of our voices, especially Jenny's. As the weeks went by, we noticed how happy and peaceful he was, and, to our surprise, others also commented on Albert's joyful personality. Finally, we realized that our praying for Albert in the womb accounted for his peaceful, pleasant personality. Now he is a year and a half old; his personality is still joyful and peaceful.

pp. 16–17

Former members of my ministry team, Gary and Kathleen Hixson, who now minister in Spain, had a similar experience with their firstborn daughter. Just as soon as they found out they were expecting, they began to systematically bless and communicate with their little one. Never has a preborn child been the recipient of more love, care and the impartation of the love and blessing of God than this one! Though we cannot be sure, I regard it as highly likely that this prebirth activity has a lot to do with the fact that little Sarah, now nearly two, may be the happiest, most content and best adjusted child I have ever seen (including my own grandchildren).

Authority over Our Homes

The authority of the head of a household extends to the territory in which the family lives. The head of the family, and the other family members as well, have legal rights in the spirit world over the family's residence. This right of ownership is respected in the spirit world. So are the legal rights granted through a rental arrangement, the loan of a residence or a less formal arrangement.

Sometimes a family buys or rents a home that has been dedicated to the enemy or over which Satan has gained authority through sin. Sins such as adultery, violence, occult activity or wrongful death that occur in a house may give the enemy enough authority to make life very difficult for the next owner or occupant. Again, the rules for such authority apply regardless of whether we know, understand or agree with them.

If a house or apartment has been used for evil purposes before we bought or rented it, the enemy may have rights to do things there without our permission. Our legal right to own or rent that house or apartment also gives us the authority, however, to cancel any claims the enemy can make because of previous agreements, whether those agreements were made verbally or through behavior. Likewise with land and other property.

A woman I will call Sue experienced strange fears and other disagreeable feelings when she got up in the night to feed her baby. The feelings always seemed strongest in the hallway just outside her bedroom door. Then we learned that a previous occupant of the house had been practicing New Age rituals in that hallway. Indeed, there were still traces of candle wax there. So with the encouragement of her husband, we claimed their authority as the present owners of the house, plus the power of Christ, to cancel all previous agreements, and we were able to get rid of whatever enemy spirits were operating there. There has been no such problem since then.

We said something like this:

> In the name of Jesus, we assert the authority of the present owner of this house to cancel all agreements with previous owners and all rights given to the enemy by them. We thus break all satanic power over this house and the land on which it stands, and we bless them with the power of Jesus Christ.

Then we anointed the doors and windows of the whole house with anointing oil that had been blessed, making the sign of the cross in oil on each place. (It is not necessary for the anointing to be in the sign of the cross; that is just the way I choose to do it. Some simply rub the oil on.)

With houses and land, it is good to pray back over their history, asserting the present owner's authority back to the beginning of time to cancel any enemy rights. Although I cannot claim to know all that is going on, I have been involved in many situations in which taking authority to break satanic power, obtained through events that have occurred in homes, has made a big difference. I have prayed for land that served as the regular place of warfare, land that was once Indian burial ground, houses in which violence and even murder took place, a college dormitory in which a New Age devotee had lived and other places in which strange things were happening, although we did not know the specific reason. To my knowledge, there were major changes in each place after we prayed.

In one case a demon claimed to have influence over a woman herself, not just over her house, because of adultery that had occurred there prior to her purchase of it. When we asserted the power of Jesus to cancel all authority given through the previous owner's sin, the demon's power was greatly weakened and we had no difficulty getting him out.

The way the enemy works and what to do about it is well described by Gary Runkle-Edens in recounting a personal experience:

> After Betsy and I got married, I moved into the beautiful house and half-acre she had purchased when she moved to Ohio. Despite the fact that we were very compatible, excited and happy together, I became troubled. I found that when I was home, I had a lot of critical thoughts about Betsy. I was thinking about all the ways she needed to change and grow. This began to affect our relationship.
>
> As I prayed about it, I felt God revealing to me that I was being attacked spiritually. So I proceeded to go through every single room in our house, anointing them with oil and taking authority over any demonic intruders. Within a few hours I noticed a tangible difference in the atmosphere (and my thought life) in the house. But I failed to notice that when I went outside to do yardwork, these thoughts continued to bother me. Because we had a huge yard, I was outside a lot, especially during the summer months. I worked really hard and fast, and tried to think about anything other than Betsy's faults.
>
> Finally one day I got down on my knees and said, "Lord, haven't I prayed over the house? Why is this still happening?" I heard the Lord reply, *You forgot the yard.* Though surprised that I would have to take authority over the yard, too, I went right to it. I grabbed my anointing oil and proceeded to walk the perimeter of our half-acre lot, taking authority over it.

211

After that I had some of the most peaceful and wonderful yardwork experiences ever! Not only did I not think critical thoughts about Betsy, but in the following months God used my outdoor work as a time to birth an incredible new vision for ministry. If I sensed enemy attack in the yard after that, I commanded it away, and away it would go!

But this was not the end of Gary and Betsy's problems. When they moved across the country to California about a year later, they found themselves at each other's throats in the new apartment. Thinking this was due to the stress of the move, Gary did nothing about it at first, even though the unease and temper flare-ups lasted a full six weeks. Then Gary records:

> As I struggled one evening in prayer, I heard the Lord say, *Go through the apartment and anoint it with oil and take authority over it.* Well, I was too worn out to do it that night. And the next day, in my busyness, I simply forgot about it. But by that next day, our sour moods became unbearable. It was then that the Lord reminded me again. So not only did I go through and take authority and anoint our apartment, but I even did this to the entire apartment complex! It was as if something broke immediately. Within a few hours we were back to being happy and compatible. God revealed to us that the enemy had lain in wait to ambush us on our arrival in California.

But that was still not the end of the story. Gary and Betsy were living in their apartment without a written contract, and when a notice came for them to appear at the housing office to sign their contract, they did not get around to it right away. Gary writes:

> Then we began to notice that our problem of short tempers and negative attitudes had returned. Despite

my taking authority over the apartment almost daily, these persisted. As I cried out to God over the matter, I sensed the Holy Spirit saying, *The enemy has found out you don't have a contract!*

It didn't take me long to get down to the housing office and sign our contract. That night it was as if the enemy was upset, and we had a difficult night. The next morning I declared to the enemy that we were now fully legal contractual renters and they must leave. We have been back to normal since that moment.

Delegating Authority

Authority can be delegated to someone else. This can be done anytime we leave home, even to go to work.

I mentioned in chapter 5 that husbands going on a trip can delegate total authority over home and children to their wives. And it is important for husbands to assert their authority to protect their families in their absence. My approach to this is simply to claim protection, regularly and pointedly, when I go away. If my wife stays home or if someone else is left in charge, I let the spirit world know that person has my full authority while I am gone.

Before we learned to do this, my wife, Meg, and I found that when I went away on a trip, things often broke down, or the children had accidents or got sick, and almost invariably she and I would have an argument before I left, and another when I returned. So I learned, first, to forbid the enemy to cause us to argue, and then to speak protection over our home and all the people and things that reside there. Finally I would state to the spirit world that my wife has my full authority while I am gone. Things have changed dramatically since I learned to do this. Now things rarely go wrong when I travel, and Meg and I rarely even have a difference of opinion.

This kind of protection is especially important when children are involved. One of my ministry team members, Dick Margeson, shares the following illustration from his life:

> I have been privileged to go on several ministry team trips. Somewhere along the way, it began to dawn on me that whenever I went away, my oldest son, Zachary, age five, would misbehave. He would often begin to misbehave as soon as I drove out of the driveway, and his behavior affected the other children. Out of concern for this problem, I consulted several I could trust, including a psychotherapist who had considerable experience with children. All felt, as I did, that Zach's behavior was in reaction to my leaving for these trips. Their suggestion was that I leave him with something of value that belonged to me.

> Before leaving for our next weekend trip, I let Zach keep my pocket watch. On the second day of the trip, I called home from Arizona to find out how things were. My wife reported that Zach was up to his usual misbehavior, but that at least he had slept well that first night. He continued to struggle that weekend until I returned.

> On my return, it finally dawned on me that the problem we were having had spiritual roots. I knew that the enemy spirit world takes the father's authority seriously, but that I hadn't taken the steps to assure the safety of my family while I was away. While the high priest of the family is away, evil spirits will search for any advantage they can get to attack those left behind, especially if the father/husband is in a ministry they don't like.

> So I decided to take the necessary steps to assure that there would be no more of this kind of spiritual problem, whether I am away or at home. The first thing I did was declare to all the spirits that I am the high priest in my family and that if I am away, at any time and for any

reason, my wife, Marcia, assumes my role. Second, I let the satanic world know that my children have been dedicated to the most high God and that evil spirits do not have my permission to disturb my family. Third, I declared that since I am the high priest of my family, any spirits who would like to destroy my children, and particularly Zach, must come through me first. And finally I told them that, in addition to refusing to allow evil spirits to attack my family, I as the husband and father in the position of authority in my home—a child of God, saved by the blood of the Lamb—absolutely forbade any of them to attack me either.

Marcia and I also embarked on a program to teach our children Scripture that they could speak out whenever they felt they were under attack. We instructed them that attacks might come in the form of dreams, temptations or anything that did not seem right. Teaching our children Scripture has given them authority of their own to deal with the enemy.

My next trip was to Toronto, Canada. This trip would be longer than the last, and busier. Before I left, I took authority over each member of my family, stating specifically that my wife was in charge both physically and spiritually. I also reminded Satan's army that I am a warrior in the army of the most high God, and that while I am away, my wife is the high priest in my absence.

Because we were busy in Toronto, I didn't get to check in at home until the second day. To my relief, Marcia was feeling great, the kids were doing very well and problems in general appeared to be minimal. The fact that I had passed on my authority to my wife seems to have done the trick.

And this approach has continued to work well. When I am home, I continually remind the enemy that the Spirit of the living God is in charge of our family. And when I go away, I let them know Marcia has my full authority.

If a husband goes to work and his wife stays home, especially if she has young children to take care of, it is a good idea to make explicit to the spirit world that she has her husband's full authority. A major reason for this: Demons are very active in attempting to disrupt family relationships. They like to goad children into behaving badly when Dad is away, even if he is just at work. Men have reported to me that after they started speaking to the spirit world in this way each day as they left for work, it made a big difference in the behavior of their children. And when they spoke protection over the home, they experienced fewer mechanical breakdowns in appliances or cars.

When parents go away and leave their children with someone else, they delegate their full authority—over the children and usually over the home as well—to those they leave in charge. It is good to recognize this when selecting babysitters, or even when leaving the children with relatives. When we turn our homes and children over to someone else, we are granting that person our rights for whatever period of time we are away. It is wise, therefore, to speak out into the spirit world that this person is operating under our authority, not simply on her or his own. This can keep pesky spirits from taking advantage of the situation.

Unfortunately, I have had to deal with several missionaries who left their children with the wrong caretakers, who either innocently or by design got their children demonized.

In chapter 5 I mentioned a man in his thirties who had carried a demon since he was five. When I asked the demon what right he had to be there, he told me the babysitter had given Arthur to him when he was about five years old and living with his parents in a Latin American country. It may be that, while Arthur was under the authority of the babysitter, he got sick and the babysitter did what she normally did, intending no harm, and called on some spirits to heal him. Or she may have been under demonic assignment and passed on a demon knowingly. In any event, the babysitter used the authority she was given over Arthur to invite demons into him. And Arthur, with no knowledge that the demons were there, had been struggling against them all his life.

Single-Parent Families

It is good for parents to take the authority God has given them. But what if either husband/father or wife/mother is missing? What about situations in which the mother or father is alone in raising the children because the spouse has abdicated responsibility or has died?

I believe the statements recorded in Numbers 30 concerning responsibility for vows point us to the right approach here. We noted in our earlier discussion that in verse 9, a widow or divorced woman has the same responsibility for her vows as does a man. I believe she has the same authority a man has as head of a home.

But some women are uncomfortable with this understanding of their authority. They prefer to find a man—sometimes a pastor, sometimes a relative—to be for them what is often called a "covering." This can be arranged simply by getting a man to agree to assume the spiritual authority that a husband or father would carry. This is an awesome responsibility, for it means (among other things) that any attempt to attack the woman might land on the man who has agreed to be her covering. If he is vulnerable in some way, he can encounter difficulty (as Andy did when he started getting the throat pain his wife had had). If the man is spiritually clean, however, so that the enemy can find nothing in him (John 14:30), any woman who puts herself under his protection gains great status in the spirit world.

To take such authority, the man must agree to be the covering for the woman. He may assume this role as a pastor, as a surrogate father or grandfather, as a leader of some group (for example, a Bible study) that the woman belongs to or just as a friend to whom the woman chooses to give this authority. In assuming this role, the man simply speaks to the spirit world, stating that he is claiming the spiritual authority over her that the woman has requested. Such arrangements speak loudly to the spirit world and provide great spiritual benefits to the women who make them.

I believe the same kind of covering can be effective with men as well as with women. Several men who work with me as members of a ministry organization find that my authority to protect or bring healing to them is greater than that of others who pray for them. I believe this is because they have granted me a kind of spiritual covering for them.

Relinquishing Authority

There are times and circumstances when we either relinquish or forfeit our authority. Less permanent forms of relinquishment occur when we give our authority to someone for a longer or shorter period of time. (We spoke about husbands giving their authority to their wives when they go on trips, and about parents turning over their authority to babysitters.)

At certain times we give over our authority gladly and voluntarily to someone else. I think of my daughter's wedding. At a point in the ceremony, the pastor asked, "Who gives this woman to be married to this man?" My response was, "Her mother and I do." At that time two things happened in the spirit world: My daughter came under the authority of her husband, and they both came under my authority (and my father's) as the patriarch(s) of the family. I retain some authority over my daughter, but the major transaction was one in which I relinquished to her husband my role as her primary authority figure.

A more permanent form of relinquishment can happen at death. A friend of mine has told me that his last words to his terminally ill wife were, "It's all right to leave." And as he left the room, she acted on his permission and died. In saying those words, my friend relinquished his authority over her, giving her permission to die. Another friend, who pastored Chinese congregations for a number of years, recalls several times when he gathered the families of terminally ill loved ones and asked them if they agreed that their loved one could die. In each case it was only a short time after they relinquished their right to keep the loved one alive that he or she died.

We can point to several times in Jesus' life when He relinquished His authority to the Father. The first was when He came to earth, giving up His rights as the second Person of the Trinity. Then, in John 5:19 and 8:28, Jesus stated that He had relinquished to the Father His authority to act and speak on His own behalf. It might even be said that He surrendered His authority to Pilate when He made it clear that the Roman governor had no authority over Him except that granted by God (John 19:11). In the agony of His final hours, then, having begged the Father to "take this cup of suffering away," Jesus relinquished His right to life itself, saying, "Not my will . . . but your will be done" (Luke 22:42).

Divorce is another kind of relinquishment. A divorced woman can, however, still be interfered with by her ex-husband unless she asserts her new position out from under his authority. My recommendation to such a woman is that when the divorce is legalized, she speak out to the spirit world asserting her freedom from the authority of her ex.

Using Authority Wisely

One of the most important areas in which we are to assert our authority is within the family. Those of us who are heads of families need especially to carry out our responsibility by making good use of this privilege. Those who are in positions in the family other than heads may have more spiritual authority than they realize. It is my prayer that this discussion will help us all to recognize the authority God has given us and enable us to use it wisely. It is sad that we have not learned more about this area in most of our churches. May this discussion contribute important insight to enable us all to make use of our authority to enhance God's work in our families.

Now let's turn to the authority Jesus gives us to minister to others. He came to set captives free (Luke 4:18), and He sends us to continue granting freedom to those harassed by the enemy.

8

Authority in Ministering to Others

A woman I will call Teri has written me about her discovery that she really does have spiritual authority. I was leading a seminar that she was attending at a California church. Teri and a friend had come along as apprentice ministry leaders and had just finished working with someone, when they became aware of another ministry group that seemed to be having difficulty. They had aroused a demon that was manifesting loudly and violently, and they were unsure what to do next. Although Teri was headed for her lunch break and had no experience dealing with demons, she felt led to help the group as she passed by. Then she remembered some of my teaching, and she rebuked the demon, forbidding it to be violent or to cause the person to throw up, thinking she would then go on to lunch.

The demon responded immediately, and the people in the group thought she was an expert! Teri suddenly realized she was now in charge of the ministry. Without a clue what to do next, she called on the Lord for help, and immediately felt led to ask the demon who had more authority, him or Jesus. The demon admitted that Jesus did. Teri writes:

> Then I told the demon that I came in Jesus' authority and that it had to obey me. What happened next really startled me! The demon agreed with me that I had authority over it, and it tried to convince me that I should let it stay in this man. It took me a few moments to get over the initial shock of discovering that the authority Jesus gave us is real. After a brief pause, I continued with deliverance, commanding the demon to leave the man and go to the feet of Jesus. It disagreed three or four times, then gave up and left the man.

Teri testifies that this experience brought about a major change, both in her thinking and in her practice. What we had been saying in the seminar about working in the authority of Jesus became more than mere theory. The discussions suddenly made practical sense as Teri became involved in doing something she knew she could not do alone. "My authority was no longer mere head knowledge and theology," she says. "It became reality! That was the start for me of learning to walk in His power and authority and to do the things Jesus did."

Authority to Invite the Holy Spirit

Jesus said that whoever believes in Him will do the works He did and "even greater things" (John 14:12).

Then He said He would "do whatever you ask for in my name, so that the Father's glory will be shown through the Son. If you ask me for anything in my name, I will do it" (John 14:13–14). What incredible authority these statements give us!

A few verses later, Jesus let us know what the first item on our "want list" should be: the Helper called the Holy Spirit (John 14:16). As we have mentioned several times, we are to start where Jesus started—with the empowerment of the Holy Spirit, whom (as Jesus said) God will give us if we ask for Him. As Luke 11:13 says, ". . . You know how to give good things to your children. How much more, then, will the Father in heaven give the Holy Spirit to those who ask him!" What an inestimable privilege—having the authority to invite the Holy Spirit to come and take charge of our lives and ministries, and being sure He will do just that.

We see the pattern in Jesus' life. He came into the world, committed to living in total dependence on the Father, as Adam's life was intended to be. We have noted Jesus' dependence in John 5:19: "I tell you the truth: the Son can do nothing on his own; he does only what he sees his Father doing. What the Father does, the Son also does." We have also seen that Jesus' dependence on the Father was worked out in such a way that He did no mighty works before the Holy Spirit came on Him at His baptism (Luke 3:21–22). And we have seen that whatever authority the Father granted Jesus before that time did not impress the people of His hometown, Nazareth, for they marveled at His authority and power once He began His public ministry (Matthew 13:53–58). They also rejected Him.

We are to follow the same pattern Jesus did: receive the Holy Spirit, then move out in authority and power. We start as the disciples did in Acts 2 by waiting (Acts 1:4–5) and, presumably, asking to receive the gift Jesus promised. We use our authority first to ask for the baptism in the Holy Spirit. But there is more. We are to live as Jesus lived—in the fullness of the Spirit.

But we note an ebb and flow of the Spirit's activity in Jesus' ministry. Although Jesus was filled with the Holy Spirit, we see that He did not have the authority to override the lack of faith of the people of Nazareth, and so "did not perform many miracles there" (Matthew 13:58). At other times the Holy Spirit came in a special way "to heal the sick" (Luke 5:17) and to fill Jesus with joy (Luke 10:21). I take it, then, that although the Holy Spirit is always with and in us, once we have invited Him in, He comes with special power and gifting at certain times, either by His choice or because we ask Him to come.

There are two times, then, when it is appropriate to use our authority to ask for the Holy Spirit. The first is when we ask to receive Him in His fullness. The second is when we want Him to come for some special purpose, such as ministry.

The purpose of this chapter is to discuss the various kinds of ministry for which the Holy Spirit empowers us. We will deal with these ministries under eight headings: blessing, breaking bondages, physical healing, deep-level healing, deliverance, forgiveness, death and higher-level spirits. As we look at Jesus' ministry, we see most of them in focus regularly. As He ministered in authority and power in these crucial areas, so should we.

Authority to Bless

First of all, we have been given the authority *to bless.* As usual, Jesus modeled this area of authority for us. In the Beatitudes He blessed people for specific behavior and attitudes (Matthew 5:3–12). When He sent His followers out to minister in Luke 9 and 10, He told them to bless those who cared for them (Luke 10:5). Blessing is especially noticeable after His resurrection (John 20:19, 21, 26). Then, when Jesus left the earth, He commanded His followers to teach their followers "to obey everything I have commanded you" (Matthew 28:20). And the command that His followers be taught to minister as Jesus did comes down to us. So, just as Jesus blessed, we are to bless.

The authority to bless (Matthew 5:44; Romans 12:14) is one of the most precious gifts God has given us. Genuine spiritual transactions take place when we speak blessing in Jesus' name.

The Bible is full of blessing. Not only did Jacob and other Old Testament fathers pronounce blessings on their sons (for example, Genesis 48–49), but Paul starts each of his letters with a blessing (for example, Romans 1:7; 1 Corinthians 1:3; 2 Corinthians 1:2; Galatians 1:3). Jesus was blessed before He was born (Luke 1:42) and afterward (Luke 2:34–35). Jesus blessed children (Mark 10:16), people who lived Kingdom values (Matthew 5:3–12), His disciples after His resurrection (John 20:19, 21, 26) and those present at His ascension (Luke 24:50–51). Further, He commands us to bless those who curse us (Luke 6:28).

We find about three hundred references to blessing in Scripture. There would undoubtedly have been more examples of blessing if it had not been so universally practiced by those with a Jewish worldview. The more familiar something is, the less it gets mentioned. Invoking God's blessing on those you favor was, for the Jews, almost as natural as breathing. The favorite Jewish blessing was peace. In each of Paul's letters, he spoke peace on his readers. And since he was working in the Greek world, he added a favorite Greek blessing, grace. Thus, his usual opening blessing was grace and peace. In his letters to Timothy, he added mercy, another favorite Jewish blessing (1 Timothy 1:2; 2 Timothy 1:2). In each case, these are not to be taken as mere words of favor but as the invoking of God's spiritual power for the benefit of those addressed.

The authority to bless is a wonderful gift from God. We are to use it often to minister to people. Blessing someone is a form of ministry in and of itself. I mentioned in chapter 2 that as I have blessed people with peace, many have experienced a noticeable peacefulness coming over them like a warm shower or mild electricity. I have blessed myself with peace many times when I have been upset, and found that it usually works wonders. People blessed with joy often find their minds filled quickly with God's praises. Once I blessed a woman with joy, and a demon manifested itself! The demon could not stand the praise for God that welled up in the woman's heart. On one occasion I blessed a woman with "a deeper experience of the love of God than you have ever had before," and the Holy Spirit started a major work in her life.

I make it a practice in my seminary teaching and seminars to bless the students as we close class. I have frequently blessed them with things like peace, patience, freedom from tiredness and good rest (after they go home from an evening class), and have had many remark on the changes these blessings seem to have initiated in their lives.

Blessing in Ministry

Blessing is also an effective vehicle for initiating more extensive prayer ministry. It is my practice to bless the person I am ministering to at the beginning of each session. Often he or she needs the peace of God to combat fear and discomfort. The blessing usually changes such fear to peaceful anticipation of what God is about to do.

Recently Gary Runkle-Edens began to take a new approach to working with a man who had been coming to him for several months. The man's male identity had been damaged in childhood through sexual abuse, homosexuality and much more. Gary began to bless his client with a rebuilt self-identity as a male. After a few sessions of such blessing, the client reported having "strange new thoughts" and urges about "working on cars and trucks, doing furniture refinishing and going fishing!" He did not know how to handle these urges. So Gary explained to him that he thought God might be rebuilding the male part of him. The client looked at Gary amazed by what it felt like to have male urges and surprised by God's power to do this!

While working with a man I will call Ed, I was finding no success in ridding him of a demon of defiance. So, more out of frustration than anything else, I began blessing Ed with an infilling of God's love. At this the demon started shouting, "No, no, no!" And soon the demon was willing to leave because he could not stand this influx of love through the blessing.

Partly as a result of reflection on the ministry session with Ed, I have begun to experiment with a new use of the authority to bless. At the end of our time together, I bless my client *with the opposite of whatever damage or demon we have dealt with.* If we have been doing inner healing for a damaged self-image, I bless the person with new self-love and self-appreciation. If we have just kicked out a demon of anger, rage or violence, I bless that person with gentleness and self-control. If the problem or demon is fear, I bless the person with confidence or faith. Sometimes I just use a general blessing, saying, "I bless you with the opposite of each of the problems [or demons] we have dealt with."

Kinds of Blessings

A blessing may be either general or specific. "I bless you in Jesus' name" is general. When we bless one another with peace, mercy, grace, patience or joy, we are being more specific. It may be that in the Beatitudes, Jesus intended His statements to confer specific blessings, not simply to describe the blessings available to those with the qualities He mentioned. Perhaps He was saying, "I bless you who are spiritually poor by giving you the Kingdom of heaven," and, "I bless you who mourn with the comfort of God" (Matthew 5:3–4).

Those who pronounce the blessings have authority over the blessings they speak and can take them back if they choose to. Jesus commanded His disciples to do just this (as we saw in chapter 2) if they were rejected when they went out to proclaim the Kingdom (Luke 10:5–6). They were to go to a home and ask for hospitality. If the homeowner invited them in, they were to accept the invitation. If not, they were to leave and take their blessing with them.

"Peace be with you" was Jesus' favorite blessing, especially after His resurrection (Matthew 28:9; Luke 24:36; John 20:19, 21, 26). This was probably the blessing He pronounced as He ascended (Luke 24:50–51).

I love to bless people! My favorite blessing (following the examples of Jesus and Paul) is peace. General blessings such as "I bless you in Jesus' name" are fun to use and minister God's blessing effectively to those who are receptive, although I prefer to use more specific blessings as often as possible. One formula I use often is, "In Jesus' name I bless you with [peace, forgiveness, confidence, release from worry/fear/guilt]."

Material objects such as food and the Communion elements may also be blessed. I believe it is the power of God conveyed through blessing that explains how

Jesus' garment (Matthew 9:20; 14:36), Paul's hand-kerchiefs and aprons (Acts 19:12) and Peter's shadow (Acts 5:15, if it worked) could bring healing. Jesus blessed food regularly. The disciples who walked to Emmaus with Him recognized Jesus as He blessed and broke the bread (Luke 24:30–31). Before distributing the food to the five thousand, He blessed it as He thanked God for it (Luke 9:16). With regard to the Communion elements, Paul spoke of blessing the cup used in the Lord's Supper (1 Corinthians 10:16, KJV). I have seen God minister healing to people during Communion as they ate and drank the elements that had been blessed.

I have gotten into the pleasant habit of starting and concluding both private and public ministry sessions with one or more blessings. This is one of the most wonderful privileges we have as representatives of the supreme Blesser. And He Himself has given us this authority.

Authority to Break Bondages

A second important area is the authority to break bondages. People can be in bondage to Satan due to such things as sin, soul ties, contemporary or genera-tional curses, self-curses and authority relationships. A relationship in which one person is dominated by another, for example, can be empowered by Satan. Likewise, participants in adultery become bonded by satanic power. Curses are obvious bondage-creators. And there seem to be generational bondages, often (perhaps always) reinforced by demons, in which par-ticular sins or compulsions occur generation after gen-eration. In each case we have the authority to renounce such bondages if they are in us, and to cancel them in others.

Cursing by Others

The topic of cursing has come up frequently in these pages. This is because we have to deal with cursing so often as we minister to people. Many societies have those who practice what may be termed "formal" cursing. With New Age and Satanist groups emerging in the U.S., formal cursing is becoming more prominent. In this kind of cursing, some ritual is performed, sometimes involving a sacrifice. During the ritual, words are said, and sometimes an image or statue of the person being cursed is used, in order to invoke satanic power against that person.

More common is "informal" cursing. This may happen through careless or angry words. Such negative statements as "I wish you [or I] were dead" or "I hate you [or myself]" or "You'll never amount to anything" or "You're worthless," especially if uttered by someone in authority over the person cursed, can convey enemy power into anyone who accepts the statement or prediction.

I was told by one of our ministry team members recently that he had to break a curse on a young woman put on her by her pastor! The pastor had happened to say something like, "Spiritually you're just a midget." Somehow this statement, made by one in authority, dug its way into her to such an extent that the enemy could use it significantly in her life. In ministry, my colleague treated those words as a curse and asked a fellow team member to stand in for the pastor, asking forgiveness on his behalf and renouncing the curse. At that time its power was broken and she became free.

Sometimes we have to break the power of a doctor's prediction based on a diagnosis concerning a serious disease or accident. The enemy's ability to use such predictions against us seems to relate directly to whether or not, under the guidance of the Holy Spirit, we accept the prognosis as valid. If we do, the enemy seems able to use that belief to empower the words as a curse. If we reject the prediction, its power as a curse seems to be broken.

Another form of informal cursing is embodied in curse words or swear words such as "You bastard" or "You son of a bitch," or perhaps even "God damn you" or "F___ you." Matthew 5:22 adds "You good-for-nothing" and "You fool" to the list. These and other negative words, especially when uttered by someone in authority over a person, especially if there is internal garbage the enemy can latch onto, probably invite enemy power into that person's life.

Or the curse may go back to prebirth, if the pregnancy was not wanted or if the parents wanted a child of the other sex. During pregnancy either parent may put a curse on the child by saying or thinking things like, "I wish I [we/you] weren't pregnant," or, "I hope there will be a miscarriage." It is amazing how much power the enemy is able to wield throughout a person's life when such words or wishes are uttered.

Can Christians Be Cursed?

Does the enemy have the authority to empower curses directed at believers? Unfortunately the answer seems to be yes. I have heard numerous accounts from missionaries who have experienced evil of various sorts after being the target of curses. Indeed, missionaries working in other societies, as well as Christian workers in the United States, seem to be special targets of such cursing. I have ministered to many of God's choicest people who have experienced significant freedom when we used our authority to break curses over them. In what follows, therefore (as throughout this book), I am speaking mainly to Christians.

A curse, according to Proverbs 26:2, must have someplace to land if it is to be effective. And internal garbage coming from various sources provides ample opportunity for the enemy to carry out at least part of his assignment in a person's life. Spiritual and emotional garbage can come by inheritance, by our own choices, by the choices of those in authority over us or by our reactions to difficulties and abuse. If any such conditions result in unresolved sins such as unforgiveness, bitterness, lust, anger, hate or self-rejection, even in Christians, these provide landing places for curses. The ideal, once again, is the condition Jesus could claim for Himself when He said, "The ruler of this world is coming, and he has nothing in Me" (John 14:30, NKJV).

A related question that comes to me from time to time: Does Satan have authority to afflict Christians who enter territory dedicated to him, such as temples, shrines, occult bookstores or Oriental martial arts studios? Again, I think he has that authority on the same basis as with curses: if there is something inside that he has a right to. I also believe, however, that demonic beings know if we are there as tourists or for warfare. I have toured many temples and, for the most part, suffered no ill effects.

But I have learned to be cautious, especially after my visit to the Buddhist temple in Taiwan when I got the pain under my sternum. Ceremonies were being conducted there in honor of the dead—ceremonies that I believe provided more power than normal for the spirits inhabiting the temple. So now I claim God's protection, and even ask for extra protecting angels when I visit such places.

Self-Cursing

Many curse themselves, usually without realizing it. I do not know when negative words uttered against ourselves constitute a curse. But I have ministered to numerous people whose problems were lessened when they took their authority in Christ to renounce any curses they had put on themselves. As with blessings, the person who makes the curse owns it. This means that he or she can break its power by renouncing it.

The most frequent target of such self-curses seems to be our bodies, often during adolescence. As our bodies develop, we may perceive ourselves to be the object of critical words or looks from peers, especially if the speed of our development differs from that of others. If so, we may say things to or about our bodies that constitute self-curses. I often minister to men who have cursed themselves, and whose struggle with shame is intense, due to the taunts of their peers in junior high locker rooms over the small size of their sex organs. Shame and insecurity over adolescent development is also a frequent problem in women. Either because of dissatisfaction with how they developed or because of abuse, I have found that many women have cursed themselves. Or they have cursed some part of themselves, such as their faces, breast size, hips, hair, mind, emotions or some other parts that they do not feel are adequate.

The impression that we should not have been born, or that we should have been male rather than female (or vice-versa), is often the source of self-cursing. I ministered to a woman once who was the fourth daughter in a Chinese family. She came to me because she had cancer in several parts of her body. I asked her if she had ever wished she were a boy. "Every second of my life!" she replied. Then she admitted to having cursed her body thousands of times. I helped her renounce those curses, and later received a letter from her that she was well.

Abuse can be another reason for self-cursing. A woman came to me whose doctor had discovered lumps on her breasts. As I asked God what to pray for, the word *abuse* came into my mind. It turned out that she had been abused sexually and that the abuser had focused on her breasts. So she had cursed the fact that she had breasts. After she renounced the self-curses, her next examination showed no lumps.

A general rule regarding curses is that the person who has put the curse on has the authority to cancel it. Those who have cursed themselves, therefore, usually need to simply renounce the curses in the name of Jesus to break their power.

Breaking Curses

Whatever the source of the curses, we have been given the authority to break them. Our gracious God wants to free people from any power of the enemy that has come through cursing. And we get to assist. Since the power in which we work is infinitely greater than that of the enemy, most curses are fairly easy to cancel once they are discovered or suspected. I usually say something like this:

> In the name of Jesus Christ, we take authority over this curse [or these curses] and speak the canceling of the curse, and all its effects, and the breaking of all enemy power that affects or has affected this person's life.

We have authority in Christ to break ancestral curses as well. Often I find demons that have rights in people through curses leveled at their ancestors. Routinely,

234

therefore, I speak the canceling in the name of Jesus of all curses that have given the enemy rights, either through the father's line or through the mother's, including curses coming from others and self-curses.

If we become aware that someone has cursed us, we are commanded to bless him or her (Matthew 5:44; Romans 12:14). I like to do what I learned from one of our ministry team members. If the source of the curse is a human being (as opposed to a demon), I say, "I return the curse to the sender as a blessing." Sometimes I make the blessing more specific: "I return the curse as a blessing aimed at bringing that person to salvation" or "I return the curse as a blessing of peace [or patience, or whatever]." If, as often happens in deliverance, the source of the curse is a demon, I return the curse to the demon as a curse. This usually stops him from cursing, since he is receiving what he is trying to send me.

Since we as Christians have the authority to speak empowered words, we need to be especially careful how we talk, especially when we are angry, lest we curse others or ourselves. But it is appropriate to curse germs, viruses and whole diseases when praying for healing. I have done this on several occasions, especially with "big ones" such as diabetes, arthritis and cancer.

Canceling Authority over Us

We spoke in chapter 6 about the need to break enemy power over our ancestors due to authority granted through vows, curses, dedications, sin and trauma. The authority to cancel such enemy rights may be referred to as the "authority to renounce authority" that has been given the satanic kingdom. This authority has been implied in several places throughout this book, but deserves a bit more focus.

We can renounce agreements (as we have seen) made by our ancestors. Since we are the contemporary representatives of our family line, we have authority over all such agreements. When anyone in our family line has made vows giving the enemy rights, it is our job to ferret these out and renounce them. Likewise with curses that our ancestors have put on themselves, dedications to occult involvement they have made and power they have granted Satan through sinful practices.

Often a general renunciation is sufficient to break the enemy's power through such ancestral involvement. The person seeking freedom can say, "I renounce all vows, dedications, curses and authority given through sin or reaction to trauma in the name of Jesus Christ." But sometimes the enemy's grip is so strong that we need to discover the specific occasion on which the ancestor gave the enemy authority over that person and his or her family. The Holy Spirit usually provides the information necessary to discover the event, either directly through a word of knowledge or indirectly through the confession of a demon. The rights can then be renounced very specifically.

Rights granted through vows, dedications, curses, sins and reactions to trauma should also be renounced if any has occurred in the life of the one being ministered to. A fair number of persons who come to me for prayer ministry have participated in occult activities such as palm-reading, Ouija boards, satanic computer games, organizations like Scientology, Mormonism, Freemasonry, Christian Science, Buddhism and even Satanism. The rights given the enemy through such involvement must be renounced. Usually it is best to have the person renounce them specifically, and to include the renunciation of all rights the enemy has thus gained over spouse, children and anyone else under that person's authority.

Canceling Soul Ties

Other authority-granting connections should be renounced as well. An important area to explore in ministry is the possible presence of soul ties. These bondings empowered by Satan come about in a variety of ways that usually involve sex, close friendship or dominating relationships. Sexual relationships bond people spiritually. This is why Paul put sexual sin in a special category—something that, unlike other sins, works within and against the body, which is God's temple (1 Corinthians 6:18–20). People bonded by sex to persons other than their marriage partners carry a major source of satanic interference in their lives. Likewise with those who are soul-tied (bonded) to people who dominate them, or with whom they have an unnatural or super-intense friendship or dependency relationship.

The bonding we call a soul tie often happens in situations in which a pastor is very dominating and produces a church that is cult-like in its demands on people. Often there are strict rules and regulations, and members are required to ask the leader's permission before they do anything major in their lives. A dominating relationship with a parent can also produce a soul tie. I have ministered to several women who were so dominated by their mothers, emotionally and sometimes even physically, that they could hardly turn around without consulting them. Often such women have to call their mothers every day, or even live at home to care for them, as if their mothers were children. An unhealthy codependent or dominating friendship with someone of either sex (even in marriage) can likewise produce a soul tie.

The way out of immoral sexual bonding or soul ties is to use our authority to renounce the relationship and claim the freedom Jesus gives when we break such enemy power. Usually it is enough for the person to state something like, "I renounce the sexual bonding [or soul tie] I have with [person] in Jesus' name, and break the power Satan has gained over me through this relationship." Breaking the power is often easier, however, than breaking the habits that have enabled the relationship. Once the power is broken, the person needs to work hard at establishing new habits. Although the habits are easier to break with the new freedom from enemy interference, they still may be a problem. Often the person needs others to assist.

Authority for Physical Healing

Physical healing is the third of our eight areas of authority in ministry. It is obvious that Jesus was active in this ministry. The Father gave Him incredible authority and power to heal the most difficult kinds of physical problems: leprosy, lameness, paralysis, hemorrhaging, blindness, deafness, dumbness. Contrary to the way we often speak, however, Jesus never prayed for healing; He commanded it. He took authority over whatever the condition was—for example, when He "ordered the fever to leave her" (Luke 4:39), or when He said to the leper, "Be clean!" (Luke 5:13), or when He cast out demons. When Jesus sent out His followers to speak about and demonstrate the Kingdom of God, then, He gave them authority to heal as He had demonstrated it—by commanding it (Matthew 10:1, 8; Luke 9:1; 10:9).

The ministry of physical healing that Jesus taught the Twelve while He was with them continued after He left. The book of Acts contains many references to healing through the apostles and others (Acts 2:43; 5:12–16; 14:3; 19:11–12; 28:8–9). General references to the healings of Stephen (6:8) and Philip (8:6–7), plus the specific reference to Ananias' healing of Saul's blindness (9:10–19), demonstrate that not just the apostles were involved. Peter and John healed a lame man (3:1–10), Peter healed Aeneas of paralysis (9:33–34), Peter raised Dorcas from the dead (9:36–41), Paul raised Eutychus from the dead (20:9–12) and healed Publius' father of fever and dysentery (28:8).

It is plain from history, and from the fact that many people today are being healed of physical maladies, that the authority to heal is still present. Marvelously gifted people like Benny Hinn, Pat Robertson and his associates on The 700 Club, my colleague C. Peter Wagner and many others are active in physical healing. Several years ago Paul Yonggi Cho, pastor of the world's largest church in Seoul, Korea, sent a woman suffering from degenerating hip bones to Peter Wagner for prayer. He took authority over the physical problem and brought healing to the woman. She announced it by giving us her crutches, which she had needed badly when she came, and walking out of our office without a limp.

Jesus did not distinguish between physical and deep-level healing (see the next section). When He extended forgiveness to the man let down through the roof (Luke 5:17–26), He healed him both physically and spiritually. Forgiveness is a major focus of inner healing and often results in physical healing as well.

Most of the purely physical healings I have been involved in have either been "small" or have been in conjunction with deep-level healing, since physical healing does not seem to be my gifting. But I have seen physical healing combined with inner healing in abundance. A woman has been free for several years now from what was diagnosed as terminal cancer, since I helped her deal with fear. At least two women were healed immediately from major back problems when colleagues and I helped them deal with certain emotional and spiritual issues, as was a pastor's wife when we helped her turn over to God the problems of others that she was in the habit of carrying herself. Many have been freed of stress- or unforgiveness-related stiff necks, headaches (some-times migraine) and stomach or back problems, as we dealt with their inner issues in the authority and power Jesus gives.

The point is, Jesus gives us the credit card to assert His authority over physical problems. Those gifted in physical healing see more such healing in their min-istries. Those of us with gifting in deep-level healing see many physical healings in the process of doing inner healing. Even those without these healing gifts may ex-pect to be used in the role of physical healer from time to time, if they will be faithful and use the authority they have been given in this area whenever possible.

Should we assume God always wants to heal a per-son with a physical problem? We do not know, except to say that Jesus never told anyone to simply grin and bear it. Whenever He saw someone with a problem, the Gospels show that He took authority and healed it. We also know, however, that He was getting His directions from the Father. And although the Scripture frequently shows Him healing everyone who came to Him, He must have walked past several hundred needy people to heal the one bedridden man in John 5. The key, I believe, is listening to God, on the one hand, and showing com-passion by ministering to any who come to us, on the other.

What about those who do not get healed? This is a tough one, especially when we feel deep compassion for someone who continues to live in both physical pain and the pain of knowing God has not chosen to heal him or her. Although I feel it keenly when I minister to some-one who does not get healed (and I have had many like this), I have determined not to allow my disappointment to lead me to stop ministering to people. It is a matter

240

of obedience to do as Jesus did by ministering to the hurting. And it is my responsibility to remain faithful to God by exercising my authority to help the hurting, no matter what the results may be. Those results are up to God.

Authority for Deep-Level Healing

Deep-level or inner healing is another area of ministry for which the Lord gives us authority. Most of the people who come to me are suffering from wounds in the emotional or spiritual areas of life, even if they come with a physical problem. So when they come describing a physical need, I have learned to ask when the problem started, and what else was going on in their life at the time. Again and again a physical problem becomes the occasion for claiming God's power to heal something much deeper. Indeed, I am often thankful for the physical need, since we can usually gauge the progress of the deep-level healing taking place by the way in which the physical problem lessens and goes away.

Often the person is unaware of the underlying problem when he or she first comes for ministry. For others the problem is obvious, but they have not been able to get rid of it—often in spite of much prayer, counseling and consultation. Problems like worry, fear, bitterness, unforgiveness, lust, shame, guilt, pride, inadequacy, unworthiness, rejection and depression come up again and again. And in each case God gives us the authority and power to minister His love and grace to His hurting children.

In dealing with deep-level hurts, the Holy Spirit gives us authority to go back deep into people's past to bring healing. Usually through picturing led by the Holy Spirit, we can help people revisit the hurtful event and

241

picture Jesus in it. It is true that Jesus was there at the time they were hurt, even though they were not aware of it. This experience of Jesus' presence in the event is usually very healing. As the person pictures the event, allowing himself or herself to feel the emotional pain, Jesus usually leads the person right through the pain, taking the problem and pain on Himself and bringing about a radical change of attitude.

Jesus died for our wounds as well as for our sins (Isaiah 53:4; 61:1). He thus releases the person from fear of the past and changes an emotional open wound into a painless and harmless scar. The memory of the event remains, since Jesus does not change history. But He does take away the fear of the past that Satan uses so effectively to cripple people, along with most, if not all, of the pain of the event. And the person goes free! The way Jesus treated Peter in John 21:15–19, as He reinstated him in ministry after his denials, is also classic inner healing.

Frequently God does not heal deep-level problems all at once. Ministry often requires several sessions, plus all the psychological skill and insight one can muster. Sometimes problems are reinforced by demonic beings that need to be banished. Such ministry provides great opportunity to demonstrate the caring and lovingkindness of Jesus. There is power in the authority we take and in the love we show.

Authority for Deliverance

Jesus' authority was most obvious in deliverance. Demons never questioned Jesus' authority over them; they responded immediately. He did not beg demons to leave, as we are told the Pharisees did. Nor did He pray to God the Father to release a person from them. He assumed they should not be there and He commanded them to go.

His is the example we are to follow. The authority Jesus gave His followers in Luke 9 and 10 included "authority to drive out all demons" (9:1). It is an authority that amazed the disciples (Luke 10:17) and one that He intended to be ours as well. As with Jesus, the authority we have is most obvious in deliverance. Demons recognize it right away, even before we challenge them. With it we have the privilege of confronting and defeating them regularly.

The satanic kingdom is active in this world, taking advantage of people as often as possible from inside. Apparently Satan has no access from the inside to those who are spiritually clean (John 14:30; Proverbs 26:2). But there are people (including many Christians) with enough garbage inside to make the enemy quite successful in his attempts to gain an inside position. I have found that many people, non-Christians and Christians alike, give demons opportunity to live within them by hanging onto emotions like bitterness, anger, unforgiveness, hate, fear, worry and lust. In addition, many inherit demons due to sins, vows, curses, dedications and trauma in their ancestral lines.

For demons are like rats, and rats go for garbage. With certain exceptions, then, it is the presence of the spiritual and emotional garbage that allows demons to enter if they have not come by inheritance, or to stay if they have. Furthermore, their strength is calibrated to the amount and kind of garbage present in the person. Those with lots of the kinds of problems listed above will have strong demons. Those with fewer of them will have weak demons. Though the presence of such problems does not in and of itself prove that there are demons present, if there *are* demons, it is because they have such problems to attach themselves to. Getting rid of garbage, then, weakens any demons that may be present.

One important implication of the rats-and-garbage situation is that demonic infestation always involves problems at two levels. There are, as it were, two causes of the malady, not just one. There is the human problem and the demon problem, for demons piggyback onto human problems. (This is why demons often go by function names such as *fear, anger, lust* and the like.) It is never *either* a demon or an emotional or spiritual problem; it is *both* a demon and an emotional or spiritual problem. If there are demons, there are automatically emotional or spiritual problems that must be dealt with, either before or after the demons are cast out. Because I do not like strong demons, and because I want my clients to be healed (not just delivered), my preference is to deal with garbage first, then demons. This approach weakens the demons so that we almost never have any violence.

When we think of the strength of demons, it is important to remember that the term *demon possession* (as I pointed out in chapter 1) is unscriptural. The Greek words translated *demon-possessed* in many of our English versions really only mean "have a demon." The translators have been irresponsible in using that phrase, and by so doing have given the impression that demons have more authority than they actually do. Demons have only the authority that a person (often ignorantly) allows them, and they never have complete control of a person all the time, as the term *possession* suggests. Even the Gerasene demoniac, who was more controlled by demons than any other scriptural example, came to meet Jesus of his own free will (Mark 5:6–8). It is inaccurate, then, to call even him "possessed" in the sense of being under demonic control at all times. The only possible validity for the term *possession* would be in cases in which a shaman calls on spirits to take over or possess him or her.

How to Proceed

To use our authority with demons, we usually have to challenge them. In most cases I try to do as much inner healing as possible before challenging demons (as I said), so that if some turn up, they will be weak. Although the demons recognize our authority and see their strength diminishing as we do inner healing, they usually hide until challenged (though sometimes, when they feel threatened, they will make their presence known to try to stop us). Once they surface, they try their best to bluff us into leaving them there. Most of what demons do in response to challenge is not power but bluff. They know we have much greater power. But they also realize that often we do not know how to use the power we have. So they use what tactics they can to keep us from getting them out. Seeing through their bluffing, and continuing to use the authority and power we have been given, is the name of the game.

When I suspect there might be a demon, I call for him to reveal himself by answering my questions. If the person has been having problems that I judge might be influenced by demons, I try to rouse the demon by calling him by the name of the problem. If fear is the problem, for example, I will call for a spirit of fear, usually after we have dealt, through inner healing, with the human roots of the problem on which the demon has been piggybacking. Or if the problem is worry, anger, self-hate, lust or pornography, I call that name. If the person has attempted suicide or had an abortion, I always find a spirit of death, suicide or abortion present. Often we have to call the demon's name several times before we get a response.

As a preliminary step, after I am pretty sure a demon is there but before challenging him directly, I often forbid any demons to speak in the first person when communicating with the person in whom they live. For years the person may have been hearing such statements as "I'm no good" or "I ought to kill myself" or "I don't believe demons can live in Christians" or "I can look at pornography [or drink alcohol or shoot drugs] without getting hooked on it." Since these statements start with *I,* the person has always assumed the thoughts were his or her own. But if these thoughts have been prompted by demons, as they often are, commanding them to refrain from using the first person results in new statements like "You're no good" or "You don't believe this stuff, do you?"

Recently I was teaching a class on inner healing and deliverance when a woman in the front row confessed that she had been hearing voices. Suspecting these were demons, I forbade them to use the first person and went on with my lecture. After a while the woman raised her hand to report that the voices were saying many of the same things to her, but were now using *you* rather than *I.* A man in the same class reported that he, too, began hearing *you* in such contexts, immediately after I gave my command to the demons in the woman.

In another class I spoke this command out to the whole class, just in case any of the members were carrying demons. One woman reported that as soon as I spoke out, she began to hear a whole series of *you* statements. This led her to suspect for the first time that she might be carrying demons, and it caused her to change her belief that demons cannot live in Christians. This event proved the first step in a glorious deliverance and radical change of life for her.

Though I will not here go into detail, it might be useful to note the steps we ordinarily follow in getting demons out.

1. The first step is always to pray, inviting the Holy Spirit to take over and to lead the session. I also ask for the right amount of authority and power to meet whatever challenge the enemy might bring. Next I usually bless the client with whatever the Lord brings to mind. He or she is usually at least in need of God's peace.

2. Claim authority over the place, time and people involved, and speak protection for all concerned from any revenge by the demons. Also, forbid any violence or any antics that might embarrass the client.

3. Do deep-level healing to get rid of the garbage and weaken the demons.

4. Challenge each demon by name (as suggested above). There will likely be several groups of demons, each with a head demon and helper demons in it. By quizzing the demons or through a word of knowledge, discover which are in charge and which are under them.

5. Command the head demons to line up with their helpers behind them. Bind all helper demons to the head demons.

6. Force the head demons to reveal if they have any further rights to be there. If they do, take away those rights through deep-level healing.

7. When they have no further rights, I like to ask Jesus or the angels to create a spiritual box to lock each group in. If any of the demons will not go into the boxes, this tells us they still have some right to stay. So we have to do more deep-level healing.

8. When they are all in their boxes, I send the boxes to the feet of Jesus and ask Him to separate the demons from the client as far as the East is from the West.

9. I then forbid any of the demons ever to come back or ever to send any others. Next I place Jesus' cross and His empty tomb between the demons and the person, to make sure they cannot get back.

10. We then bless the person with as many things as the Lord brings to our minds, especially things that are the opposite of the problems he or she was having.

God has blessed this approach enormously. Hundreds of His beloved servants are free now because He has led us to use His authority in this way. This approach, however, is not a magic formula. And there are other approaches that God uses, too.

Talking to Demons

You have noted that my colleagues and I engage in the controversial practice of talking to demons. The reason we do this is that we have found it the easiest and quickest way to find out information we would not know otherwise. As we minister, the demons are under the complete control of the Holy Spirit who, over and over again, forces them to reveal things that are against their own best interests. A typical question we ask demons is, "Does this person need to forgive anyone?" We find (because we can check up on it) that the demon's answer is almost always the truth. We then ask the person to forgive the one named. When the person deals with that important piece of garbage (the unforgiveness), the demon's strength is greatly reduced.

Do demons lie? Yes. But, interestingly enough, every scriptural account of demons speaking portrays them as telling the truth. And we find that under Holy Spirit pressure, they often reveal important information that we can use to defeat them. They are like hostile witnesses in court. You know they support the other side, so you weigh their answers and do not fully trust their testimony unless you can check up on it (which you frequently can). But by talking to demons just enough to get key information from them, we can keep track of them, gauge their strength by the strength of their voices and be much more certain at the end of the ministry session that we have gotten them out.

We also depend on words of knowledge coming directly from God, but using the demons to give us information enables many to be successful in deliverance who do not receive much information via words of knowledge. The important thing to remember is, it is the Holy Spirit getting information to us, even though it is through coercing the demons.

Who Is Targeted

If you were the enemy, whom would you target first? Pastors and other Christian leaders, of course. I have had frequent opportunity to cast demons out of Christian leaders who, either by inheritance or by foolish experimentation with the wrong activities, ended up carrying demons. One pastor, in order to gain respectability, had joined a Masonic lodge, not knowing this is one of the most evil organizations in the world. As I was working to find out what grip the demon had on the man, I asked the demon when he got in. "When he cursed God!" he replied. This surprised the pastor so much that he asked the demon when that was. The demon told him that all the Masonic commitments the pastor had made were to Lucifer, the god of Freemasonry.

Many who have no experience with demonized Christians refuse to believe demons can live in Christians. I wish this were true. But I have been involved personally in more than five hundred ministry sessions in which we delivered demons from people unmistakably committed to Christ. Demons living in Christians is, unfortunately, a fact, not a theory. It can be demonstrated like any other social scientific fact. What is theory is my assumption that demons cannot live in a Christian's spirit. They can live only in mind, emotions, body and will. Interestingly, these are the places where sin can also live in a Christian. I believe that when a person comes to Christ, the Holy Spirit takes up residence in his or her spirit (the central place in us) and banishes any demons that might be present from that place, though they may still have residence in the other parts of the person. When I ask demons if they live in the person's spirit, they always say no, and state that they had to get out of that part of the person when he or she came to Christ.

Since my occupation is teaching missionaries and international church leaders, I frequently get to cast demons out of these dear people. Many have inherited demons. Others have become demonized through cursing by the people they have worked among. On one mission station, I met at least four missionaries who had experimented with Satanism in their school days, and several who had been into communal experiments involving sexual promiscuity. Some were still struggling with pornography. What often happens to people with such backgrounds is that they get gloriously converted and give themselves for the Lord's work without getting cleaned up. The demons within them are smart enough to lie low until the people get involved in something really important to God's Kingdom, and then they sabotage them. I have met missionary after missionary who has had a crippling demonic experience at a crucial time in his or her ministry.

The fact that so many, including Christians, are demonized means there are many battles yet to be fought. The enemy is especially anxious to cripple believers to keep us from hurting him. But if we are to be engaged properly in spiritual warfare on behalf of our Master, we must equip and motivate ourselves and become active in using our authority in the cause of freedom.

God needs more of us using His authority in ministering deliverance. By doing so, we are imitating Jesus by freeing His creatures, especially those He has called to extend His Kingdom or feed His sheep. This is a loving thing to do, and God gives us the power and authority to do it.

Authority to Forgive

One of Jesus' surprising statements is recorded in John 20:21–23. After He told the disciples, "As the Father sent me, so I send you," He breathed on them, saying, "Receive the Holy Spirit," and added, "If you forgive people's sins, they are forgiven; if you do not forgive them, they are not forgiven." As Jesus forgave sins, so we are to forgive people's sins. This is an awesome responsibility and the sixth area of our authority in ministry.

Satan often cripples Christians through their guilt and failure to forgive themselves, even after they have ostensibly repented and given their sins to God. In ministry, therefore, God often leads us to pronounce as forgiven those who have already confessed their sins, or who do so during the ministry session. I usually ask

251

people if they have confessed all known sin before I pronounce them forgiven. The freedom such a pronouncement brings, then, may be dramatic.

Several years ago God led me to speak forgiveness to a woman who remarked, "I feel ten pounds lighter! Now I don't have to go on a diet!" She had been experiencing a heaviness in the chest that disappeared when I took the authority Jesus gives us and pronounced her forgiven. Often in such cases there are tears of joy, as a person who knows intellectually that God has forgiven him or her actually feels that forgiveness for the first time. Over the years I have seen several ministry sessions turn from so-so to spectacular after I, in response to a word of knowledge, pronounced the person forgiven.

But regardless of whether a person senses anything or not, transactions take place in the spiritual realm when we assert the authority Jesus has given us to pronounce forgiveness.

Authority to Raise from the Dead

The seventh area of authority is that over death. Jesus raised the widow's son from the dead (Luke 7:11–15), as well as Jairus' daughter (Luke 8:41–42, 49–56) and Lazarus (John 11:1–44). If we get to do whatever Jesus did, as He promised, raising people from the dead is included. Indeed, Jesus commanded His disciples to do so as He sent them out into ministry: "Heal the sick, bring the dead back to life, heal those who suffer from dreaded skin diseases, and drive out demons" (Matthew 10:8).

I have not had this privilege yet, but I know at least two people who have. The first is a Lutheran pastor who, while serving a church in Michigan, had the privilege of seeing two women come back to life while he was praying over them. One of them was in the hospital. The monitoring machines indicated that death had taken place, and the woman's skin had turned a brownish color. The nurses were calling the doctor to come and pronounce her dead. During the pastor's prayer, however, the woman's husband noticed her skin turning pink and healthy again. And as the pastor left the room, thinking his next job would be a funeral, the woman came back to life. I cannot forget the triumphal tone of voice of this pastor who, when concluding this account, exclaimed, "There were three people in our church last Easter who had risen from death—Jesus and these two ladies!"

The second person I know who has been used by God to raise people from the dead is a missionary working in Irian Jaya. She has been the human instrument in raising to life two children who had drowned. (At the time of the first one, she did not even believe healing is for today!) A boy had fallen into the river and been under water for about half an hour. When he was pulled out, he was quite dead, and the women began to wail over him. As this missionary reported the incident to me, she said something like, "I didn't know what to do, so I put a hand on the child and prayed that somehow God would help in the situation." And He did. The youngster came back to life!

About a year and a half later, this missionary had the opportunity to bring another drowning victim to life. Now both she and her husband are convinced God is still in the healing business. And the people they work among are convinced they are the most powerful shamans around, and the true God has become their God!

David Pytches records more than a dozen contemporary examples in his book *Spiritual Gifts in the Local Church* (Bethany, 1985), culled from various sources, of people who have been raised from the dead. One story, taken from Albert Hibbert's 1982 biography of Smith Wigglesworth (which reports "fourteen occasions when the dead were raised during Wigglesworth's ministry"), goes as follows:

> On one occasion he called at the home in which the family was mourning the loss of a five year old boy. Wigglesworth stood looking at the corpse in the coffin with tears running down his cheeks. Wigglesworth requested the father to leave him alone in the room. He locked the door behind the father, lifted the corpse from the coffin and stood it up in the corner. Wigglesworth rebuked death in the name of the Lord Jesus and commanded it to surrender its victim. An amazing miracle occurred when the child returned to life.
>
> On another occasion he was used to resuscitate a corpse. The man was raised however still suffering from the disease which killed him. Wigglesworth told the family that unless they repented and put matters right within their home, the man would die again. The family repented. Wigglesworth prayed for them and the Lord healed the man, who lived for thirty years more.
>
> pp. 232–233

God is still raising people from the dead. Don't be surprised if He uses you to do it sometime.

Authority over Higher-Level Spirits

With regard to higher-level spirits, the eighth area, I am not sure we really know how much authority we have. Some interpret a verse like Jude 9 as indicating that we should not get involved in confronting higher-level spirits directly. Jude 8 (see also 2 Peter 2:10–11) refers to people who "despise God's authority and insult

254

the glorious beings above," then goes on to say, "Not even the chief angel Michael did this. . . . Michael did not dare condemn the Devil with insulting words, but said, 'The Lord rebuke you!'" (verse 9).

Few Christian leaders dispute the fact that there are higher-level spirits at work constantly, attempting to thwart God's plans and programs. There is quite a bit of controversy, however, over what to do about these spirits, since neither Jesus nor Paul nor any other biblical leader (for example, Daniel in Daniel 10:13, or Moses and Joshua moving through and into pagan territory) seems to have been led to confront such higher-level spirits directly. Paul does state, however, that we are to battle "the wicked spiritual forces in the heavenly world, the rulers, authorities, and cosmic powers of this dark age" (Ephesians 6:12). Perhaps this verse means we are to oppose these higher-level beings directly.

Approaches to evangelism in Argentina and other places that involve direct attacks on higher-level spirits are producing impressive results. These results seem to be related to the breaking of the power of territorial spirits over the city or part of the city in which Christian meetings are held. One of the leaders encouraging this approach is Edgardo Silvoso. In his report on Argentina in C. Peter Wagner's *Engaging the Enemy* (Regal, 1991), Silvoso records the following:

> Until not too long ago, the average church in Argentina had less than 100 members. . . . All of that has changed lately. . . . Churches that used to have fifty members have grown to 1,000. Several churches have more than 5,000 people. . . . Vision of the Future ministers to 90,000 members. Hector Gimenez, a lay preacher, was able to plant a church of 20,000 members in downtown Buenos Aires in less than six months. Carlos Annacondia, Argentina's leading lay evangelist, has led over one

million people to a decision for Christ in less than four years. Yet, he is not the only one. There are at least a dozen evangelists and hundreds of younger preachers with the same degree of zeal who are efficiently preaching in every corner of the nation.

The church in Argentina has grown more in the last four years than in the previous one hundred.

p. 110

The apparent reason for this incredible growth is warfare prayer undergirded by a tremendous surge of unity among church leaders. This unity includes a commitment to break the powers of darkness over the nation through authority praying (that is, asserting authority over the spirit world in prayer). Annacondia and his team members spend countless hours in authority praying before his crusades start, in order to break the enemy's hold on a city. Then Annacondia "has patterned his crusade ministry around four 'times' of prayer" during each meeting. The first is with the new converts who have responded to his message. The second is for the demonized. The third is for the sick. The fourth is for people to be filled with the Holy Spirit. Silvoso reports, "I have estimated that of the two hours that Annacondia spends on the platform ministering, over one hour is actually spent in prayer." Under the platform he has a "prayer brigade" of about fifty people praying intensely during the whole meeting, which may last up to seven hours.

Silvoso continues:

> All kinds of prayers are offered in Argentina, but the most unique prayer is in the context of spiritual warfare. Christians seem to have two focuses in their prayers: God, to whom they address all honor and praise; and, Satan, whom they boldly and aggressively rebuke.

256

Believers subscribe to the view that prayer plays a vital, active role in God's plan of redemption. They claim that without the church's prayer God will not retake the territory invaded by Satan. They are quick to point out that every verse in the Bible dealing with prayer indicates that the action begins on earth. We must ask for Him to answer. We must knock for Him to open. We must bind and release for heaven to do the same. The action on earth not only precedes but to some extent determines the answer in heaven.

p. 113

When people pray like this, they expect God to take action. "They engage the enemy and they bind him. And then they move on and loot his camp."

Omar Cabrera, considered by some the dean of power evangelism in Argentina, consistently closets himself in a hotel room for five to seven days of aggressive prayer before opening up a new city. During that time, he prays for binding of the strong man, or prince, who controls the darkness of that particular "cosmos." Once he feels that this has been accomplished, he goes public, announcing to the people that now they are free to come to Christ. Like prisoners freed from a dungeon, thousands literally run to give their hearts to Christ.

Carlos Annacondia begins his crusades by showing the pastors how to take control over the area. The night before the beginning of a crusade, all workers participate in a prayer meeting so intense that it reminds one of Joshua and the people marching around Jericho. . . .

Floro Olivera, pastor of a Brethren church in San Justo, a suburb of Buenos Aires, and his elders decided to put a specific section of their town under spiritual authority. In a very short time they saw massive conversions coming out of that area. . . .

Eduardo Lorenzo and his fellow leaders at the Baptist church in Adrogue have been battling with a prince of darkness who controls the entire county where the church sits. They have already begun to see dramatic results not only in their own church but in the rest of the county as well.

pp. 113–114

When we read such impressive reports, resulting, as nearly as we can tell, from an authoritative approach to spiritual warfare against territorial spirits, it is hard to side with the skeptics.

It looks as though the enemy has specially infested certain places with both general and more specific kinds of power. (We often see certain sections of cities and countries, for example, characterized by specific sinful activities such as prostitution, gambling, abortion, homosexuality or deceit.) But if we Christians get together and assert our authority against Satan, things will change. As noted by the Argentineans, however, the activity that will result in such change has to start with us. We must knock, seek, bind and release before heaven acts—not because God is unwilling to take charge, but because the rules He has laid down require such ministry to be a joint venture.

Authority in ministry is an exciting aspect of our relationship with God. It is my prayer that the set of considerations raised in this chapter will challenge those of us who are not already experiencing the excitement of participating with Him in authoritative ministry to begin doing so. Nothing is so spiritually enriching yet personally humbling as being involved with God in doing things we know we cannot do ourselves!

Let's turn now to the use of God's authority in churches.

9

Authority
in Churches

I was conducting a seminar on healing and deliverance for a group of Taiwanese pastors when God led me to put together two verses I had never seen as related. Just thinking about the implications of this connection had such an impact on me that I decided to attempt to communicate them to the pastors through faith picturing.

The first of these verses occurs in the first book of the New Testament, at Matthew 16:18, in which Jesus states that He will build His Church on the foundation of Peter's confession, and it will not be overcome even by the power of death (called the "gates of hell" in many translations). Then, in the final book of the New Testament, at Revelation 3:20, we find Jesus communicating to the church of Laodicea that He now finds himself *out-*

side His own Church, knocking at the door, asking for permission to enter.

My question to these pastors was this: How did Jesus get to be outside His own Church? And if He is on the outside of *your* church, what are you going to do about it?

Because I wanted them to feel, not just think, their answers, I asked them to close their eyes and picture their church buildings with Jesus standing outside, knocking to get in. As they pictured that scene, I asked them to go to the door, open it and take Jesus by the hand, drawing Him inside. I asked them to lead Him up to the pulpit and give it to Him, returning the authority over the pulpit, and all that comes from it, to its rightful owner. Then they were to lead Him to the musical instruments, piano, organ, guitars, drums, whatever they used in their worship times, and give Him authority over the instruments and those who play them. Then to the place where the music director stands, and to give him or her to Jesus; and to the choir seats, picturing each choir member who sits there and giving every one to Him. And then down into the congregation, giving each seat and its occupant to Jesus.

Then I asked these pastors to go to their offices, or wherever they prayed or prepared for their opportunities to minister, and give everything here, too—all the people, books, computers, typewriters, telephones and office supplies—to Jesus. And their homes, giving each of their family members to Jesus. And themselves, so that Jesus could have complete authority over His Church, as well as His servant and family.

There were tears and even some wailing as we allowed the Holy Spirit to show us areas we had held back from our Master, and as we made the transactions that would put these areas in the right hands.

The Pastor as Spiritual Gatekeeper

The Scriptures are clear that people in authority, such as pastors and teachers, are responsible to God for what they do with that authority. The standard is very high. We are told that church leaders "must be without fault" (1 Timothy 3:2), that "teachers will be judged with greater strictness than others" (James 3:1), and that "they must give to God an account of their service" (Hebrews 13:17). Not only are pastors and teachers responsible for the way they handle the Word of God; they are accountable to God for the example they set for those under their supervision. The lives of church leaders are to be exemplary in every way, modeling the behavior of the Lord they claim to serve.

Pastors (called *elders* in 1 Timothy 5:17 and Titus 1:5) are responsible to assert authority within and through the church, with primary responsibility for prayer and ministering the Word (Acts 6:4). The senior pastor, as the top leader, holds ultimate authority and responsibility under God for all that goes on. His or her authority is not only from God but affirmed by an organization (whether a denomination or local congregation) through ordination. This position, therefore, contains important human dimensions.

The position of pastor also involves leaders in activity that carries great impact in the spiritual realm. The authority granted at the human level through ordination is taken seriously by the spirit world, whether or not the pastor has the proper gifting to fill that office. And pastors are the spiritual authorities under God over their churches, just as men are the spiritual authorities over their homes. Although some pastors (like some husbands and fathers) would rather not bear this enormous responsibility, there is no way out. It is theirs, assigned by God Himself.

This spiritual authority means the senior pastor is the gateway into and out of the church, just as the father is the gateway into and out of the family. What the pastor allows into the church, or allows to stay once there, has a right to be there. And sin allowed brings dire results to churches and their leaders, just as it did to Israel and her leaders throughout the Old Testament (recall Achan in Joshua 7 and the kings of Judah and Israel in 1 Kings 12 through 2 Kings 25). God has not changed His attitude toward sin or His requirements for those in authority.

The pastor must also lead the congregation in asserting its authority over whatever territory the Lord has given it responsibility for. (See the section "The Pastor's Commitment to the Church" for a discussion of this.)

I heard a sad story about a pastor who used his authority badly. He was accustomed, like most pastors, to being in complete control of Sunday services. One Sunday, however, a member of his church manifested a demon during the sermon. This disruption so upset the pastor that he went to his study after the service and made a pact with Satan: "If you'll promise never to do that again, I promise never to preach about you!" So for the sake of orderliness, this pastor compromised himself and his church.

The story, I hope, is unusual, but there are many pastors who either do not know what is really going on in their churches, or else they simply choose not to get involved in circumstances that require them to take authority. This seemed to be the case in the following true account (in which I have changed details to preserve anonymity).

A Hornets' Nest

A young man I will call Henry took a position as associate pastor in a small-town church. He was excited about the prospect of working with the young, dynamic senior pastor, who had a vision for spiritual renewal. Soon after Henry arrived, however, he realized that the senior pastor was very discouraged. Henry and his wife, who had some experience with spiritual warfare, prayed fervently about the senior pastor's discouragement, and sensed that the enemy was trying to destroy his ministry, probably because the pastor had attempted to bring renewal to the church. Seven months later he resigned and left, broken and beaten down.

Henry and his wife escalated their efforts in warfare prayer, asserting his authority as associate pastor against the enemy's activities, some of which seemed related to the fact that several leaders in the church were Freemasons. Soon a replacement senior pastor took over. Henry tried to share with him what he and his wife were discovering about the spiritual warfare going on in and around the church. But far from agreeing or even understanding, the new man explained all their concerns away in human terms. It became clear to Henry that the new senior pastor was not going to exercise his God-given authority over the congregation.

Henry had been asserting his own authority over the church in as many ways as he could. Among other things, he had begun going into the sanctuary weekly to pray over the space, the pulpits, the choir loft, the instruments, the pews, the classrooms and anything else he could think of. Church members began to remark that they sensed God at work during worship in a new way. Some were given new hope and expectancy for spiritual renewal.

Then Henry had a discussion with the senior pastor and made his position clear. All hell seemed to break loose! It was if a hornets' nest had been struck by a stick. Bizarre things began happening to Henry at the church. Attacks started coming from fellow staff people, from

263

church members, even from the senior pastor himself. It began to look as though the enemy had mounted a vicious counterattack, starting after the discussion with the senior pastor. And six months later that pastor persuaded the elders that the church could not afford two pastors, and Henry was asked to leave.

As soon as he did, the spiritual decay and apathy he had fought exerted new strength on the congregation. The last word I had on the church was that it is a shadow of its former self and has continued to slide rapidly downhill.

When Pastors Don't Take Authority

Sad to say, situations in which a pastor sides with the enemy, either consciously or unconsciously, are not uncommon. If the pastor does not exercise his or her authority on behalf of God's Kingdom, it will be exploited by Satan, as seems to have been the case here. A major part of the problem in this and many similar circumstances is that the senior pastor has little or no sensitivity to spiritual issues, but a naturalistic approach to ministry, more attuned to secular organizational and business practices than to the Holy Spirit and the spiritual warfare raging in and through the congregation.

A situation that, on the surface, looks a bit more manageable is referred to in Philippians 4:2–3. This is a brief plea from the apostle Paul that two women, Euodia and Syntyche, make peace with one another. He even urged the rest of the church to aid them in the process. Why would a disagreement between two women be of such consequence that the apostle Paul would take the time (while in prison yet!) to plead with them to make amends? As an apostle, church-planter and pastor to many, Paul knew a disagreement between two women who had "contended at [his] side in the cause of the gospel" (verse 3, NIV) could destroy the entire church. If leaders and founders could cause division within a church, there is little chance that those who knew of it would not also be affected. Furthermore, people new to the faith could lose heart and turn away.

Gossip, disagreement, jockeying for higher position, sin in people's lives, critical spirits and bitterness are just a few of the problems most of us have seen and experienced within a church. How Satan rejoices to see us fight one another rather than unite against him! It is the pastor's duty, as Paul's example shows, to ensure that such matters are dealt with swiftly, so that the enemy cannot gain a foothold in the entire church.

The Issue of Control

The control issue is a big one for pastors, elders, deacons, teachers, worship leaders and others used to being in charge. We often forget that the authority we have been given is a delegated authority. But ask yourself: When in our church services might the Holy Spirit have a chance to break in if He wanted to do something? We usually schedule things so tightly that we leave Him no opportunity. We are ordinarily guided more by the bulletin than by the Spirit.

One evening in Sydney, Australia, I learned how hard it is—but ultimately how good it is—to give up control. I was speaking at a Pentecostal church with about four hundred in attendance. I delivered my sermon, then told the people that we were going to invite the Holy Spirit to come and do whatever He wanted. Then I prayed, asking the Holy Spirit to come.

And we waited . . . and waited . . . and waited. I was determined that whatever happened was to be controlled by Him rather than me.

After what seemed an eternity, but was probably only five or ten minutes, a man toward the back raised his hand to say that he sensed someone in the congregation had a chest problem. I asked the group who that might be, and a man to my right in front raised a hand. I asked the man with the word of knowledge to come forward and pray with the man who had raised his hand. Then someone got another impression, and I was able to connect that person with another hurting person. And so on. The result was a marvelous ministry time, *out of my control.*

On another occasion I was leading a seminar of about 250 pastors and their wives on the South Pacific island of Truk. One evening, in order to demonstrate how to go about using the authority of Christ to minister healing, I decided to invite someone forward to be prayed for. God healed him dramatically in front of the group. Then I was at a loss as to what to do next. I did not want to call any more attention to myself, but felt there were many there whom God wanted to heal. So I asked the people to put their hands where it hurt and simply asked the Holy Spirit to come and do whatever He wanted. The result was far beyond anything I could have imagined. Probably more than one hundred people received healing that night. And again, *things were out of my control.*

In the average church, when would the Holy Spirit be able to do anything He wanted to do? How would He be able to work His way into the series of carefully scheduled events?

I asked a Presbyterian pastor this once, and he agreed that the schedule as written up in their weekly bulletin allowed no time for the Holy Spirit. "What should I do?" he asked.

I suggested that he appear in the pulpit some Sunday with nothing prepared, and simply tell the people he was going to turn things over to the Holy Spirit, and then wait until He did something.

"Oh, I couldn't do that," he replied.

Then I asked if he could relinquish his authority for ten or even five minutes.

He thought that over, and actually did give the Holy Spirit five minutes the next Sunday. The report I heard was that the time was well used by the Holy Spirit—but the pastor has not done it since.

We need to give Jesus not only the people and building and its contents, but also the time and schedule. He likes to be in control.

But so do we. So we seldom risk allowing the Holy Spirit to take charge. We need to learn to trust Him to take over, especially during ministry times. Unfortunately, we are afraid of silence, and He often allows a period of silence before He starts doing things. But it is worth the wait to see Him work when we take hands off.

Personnel

Under the pastors/elders are another group called deacons. The apostles delegated authority to these leaders, according to Acts 6:2–3, in areas of service to the needy, the handling of finances and like matters. Such leaders today may or may not be called deacons, depending on church polity. Their functions, however, require the delegation of authority by the pastors/elders.

Then there are other staff members to whom are delegated various responsibilities. Each is accountable to both the head pastor and God for the area over which he or she is given authority. The spirit world will respond to them according to the authority assigned them within the church polity and the responsibility vested in them by their leaders.

Given the low level of understanding of the spiritual implications of the positions people hold within church structures, it is good to hold training courses to increase awareness in this area. The enemy is vigilant to find and take advantage of those who do not know their authority.

Beyond the staff and church leaders, every church needs a core of intercessors. These are members of the congregation gifted in intercession whose job it is to pray regularly for the church, as God leads, and for specific requests coming from staff and members. Pastors should place a high priority on enlisting, training and making continual use of intercessors. To them can be delegated great authority for protection and stopping enemy activity within the congregation. They should also be involved to back in prayer any attacks on the enemy in areas like deliverance, healing and challenging territorial rights. In addition, each staff member should have personal intercessors as described in chapter 4. Many of the people who intercede for the church as a whole can double as personal intercessors.

The Sacraments in Spiritual Warfare

There is powerful authority, as we have seen, in obeying God. When He is obeyed, the enemy kingdom is put to flight. Carrying out the sacraments and other forms of dedication and initiation (for example, weddings, confirmations and dedications of buildings and hymnbooks) by those with God's authority to perform them can be powerful weapons in spiritual warfare. Although most church leaders value these rituals for their benefits at the human level, we often overlook the fact that the enemy takes hits when we conduct them.

We are commanded to baptize (Matthew 28:19). Baptism was a ritual used by the Jews to initiate Gentile converts into Judaism. Then John the Baptist used it to initiate fellow Jews (including Jesus) into the faith renewal movement he led. Baptism was also used commonly in the Greek mystery religions as an initiation ritual. Like the Lord's Supper, building dedications, weddings or any other ritual, baptismal rites can be empowered by those in authority who perform them, or they can be performed without empowerment.

All churches believe that some church ritual is appropriate for children soon after birth. Some churches perform dedications, some perform baptisms. Whatever the ritual, the influence on the child can be powerful when the pastor or priest uses his or her authority to dedicate the child to God and speak appropriate, God-revealed blessings over the child and family. The authority to speak powerfully comes from God and is delegated by the parents. We can be certain that such use of spiritual authority is taken seriously in the satanic kingdom. Though most pastors do bless as they dedicate babies, the ritual often seems to be merely a human coming-out party, rather than an intensely spiritual event.

Dedications and blessings ought to be conducted with greater seriousness than is often the case, and only after the pastor has been careful to receive from the Lord just which blessings to pass on to the child. Dedications and blessings should be prophetic, as was that of Jesus (Luke 2:22–38), perhaps involving words from others besides the pastor. Under the Holy Spirit's guidance, dedications might relate to life goals or occupation, and little ones might be blessed with such things as protection, early turning to Christ, faithfulness, long life and freedom from serious illness or accident.

Though we should not rely heavily on information gotten from demons, there is an interesting consistency to their statements concerning when they were forced to vacate a Christian's spirit (the central part of a human being where the Holy Spirit comes to live at conversion). I have asked many demons when they were forced out, expecting the usual answer: at the time the person came to Christ. On several occasions, however, demons have pointed to infant baptism or dedication as the time they had to leave.

At the time of a person's conversion, most churches believe some public ritual is again appropriate. Some baptize at this point. Others use a ceremony of confirmation or simply a testimony. Once again, a pastor should use his or her authority to challenge the enemy kingdom through prophetic utterances and blessings relating to the person's dedication. In addition, at both infant and adult dedications, the water used can be blessed and thus empowered to convey further blessing to the person.

Communion services can also be times when powerful blessings are conveyed to the participants. I have seen people fall under the power of the Holy Spirit when the elements have been consecrated with the power to heal or bring blessing at the deepest level of need. Several times, when I have not felt up to par (often for emotional reasons) while participating in a Communion service, I have blessed the elements myself with the ability to bring *me* peace. And it has happened.

The Jews practiced circumcision to obey God's command, on the one hand, and to enable authority figures to bless the child, on the other. Blessing was also practiced at weddings, and taken seriously. Genesis 48 and 49 record the way Jacob used his authority just before he died to make predictions in which he included blessings for his sons and grandsons—an event showing the prophetic dimension that such blessings can bear.

Liturgical churches often perform the Eucharist (or Communion) for purposes other than blessing those present. We who are low-church might well learn from them to use our authority to do the same, for special purposes such as breaking satanic strongholds, or hindering or helping certain causes. I believe using such a ritual applies the power of God to a situation in a special way.

A spectacular example of the use of Communion to change circumstances is recorded by Kenneth McAll in *Healing the Family Tree* (Sheldon, 1984). McAll and his wife were shipwrecked in 1972, just after experiencing a heavy storm while passing through the Bermuda Triangle. They found themselves "silently drifting" due to a burst boiler on the "banana boat" on which they were sailing.

McAll reports that as they drifted, both he and his wife heard a steady droning sound "which continued throughout the day and night." Knowing the area was famous for the number of ships and aircraft that have been destroyed there, often under mysterious circumstances, McAll began, after their rescue, to search for the reasons. He discovered that nearly two million slaves had been drowned in that area, cast overboard because the slavers felt they could not sell them. In response, McAll arranged for several "Jubilee Eucharists" to be performed by Anglican bishops and priests, both in England and in Bermuda, beginning in July 1977. These Eucharists were celebrated "for the specific release of all those who had met their untimely deaths in the Bermuda Triangle."

Though I believe McAll's assumption is wrong that they were releasing the souls of the dead, it seems clear that these empowered rituals have been effective in

271

breaking demonic power over the area, since to my knowledge there have been no unexplainable accidents in the area since that time.

The sacraments and other dedication and initiation rituals are empowered by God automatically at a certain level in response to our obedience. In addition (as we have seen), church leaders have the authority to bless physical objects, such as the Communion elements and the water of baptism, to convey spiritual power to the recipients. Leaders can, therefore, claim authority to further empower the elements for special purposes. These purposes may be to meet a specific need, such as for healing, to bring peace, or for some other blessing. Or they may be prophetic. Such an increase in empowerment can bring about major defeat of the enemy in the participants' lives.

Functions of a Church's Authority

In the life of any church, there are three major functions of authority. Let's look at each one.

1. To Prevent and Protect

This first function of a church's authority, preventing things from happening, is a protective function and has internal and external dimensions. Internally the authority needs to be exercised to prevent the enemy from carrying out his schemes among the members of the congregation. Prayer for protection is an important vehicle for this purpose. So is blessing. The members of the congregation should be blessed with protection regularly by their leaders.

Another important component of prevention and protection is teaching and prayer ministry (deep-level healing) to members and those applying for membership. Members of our congregations need to learn how to use their own authority to protect themselves. But before they learn this, they must get cleaned up spiritually. I am disturbed that we allow people to join our churches without checking to see if they are carrying crippling wounds or demons. We prepare them for membership by asking about any conversion experience or past church affiliation, and feeding them information about Christianity and the church. But many are hurting and many are carrying demons. Membership classes should include deep-level healing and, if necessary, deliverance. Imagine what a church would be like if people got cleaned up on the way in!

In addition, leaders and followers both should be putting on the armor of God (Ephesians 6:13–18) daily. A pastor friend of mine was feeling led to put on the spiritual armor regularly. As he prayed about it, he asked God how often he should put it on. The Lord answered, *As often as you put your clothes on.* So he does it daily.

One of my associates reports that he once asked a demon, "Where is the client's spiritual armor?" The demon replied, "It's on the floor at his feet. We never let him put it on. We hide it sometimes, or distract him to make sure he doesn't put it on. That's why he's so easy to control."

2. To Stop Enemy Attacks

The second function of church authority is stopping any attacks the enemy launches. Every congregation contains those vulnerable to satanic attack, especially since they do not usually get cleaned up on the way in. So every church should function as a spiritual hospital, seeking out those who need prayer ministry (including deliverance) and taking the initiative to bring healing to them. Such an approach can prevent further attack since it reduces vulnerability.

In addition, leaders and intercessors should be on the lookout for enemy attacks, and use their authority to put out whatever fires develop in the lives of their parishioners. As with prevention, so with stopping attacks. Instruction in how parishioners can assert their own authority is also a must.

3. To Mount Spiritual Attacks

In addition to ministering to individuals, churches need to mount corporate attacks on spiritual problems, both within the congregation and in the community. There may be times the enemy attacks a whole congregation, or substantial parts of it, with a problem. Often it seems that a wave of depression or unemployment or divorce has swept over a congregation. Such problems should be attacked by church leaders taking authority over the problem on behalf of those in the congregation suffering from it.

Usually, though, a church is so little threat to the enemy that he does little on any scale that might be noticed. He certainly does not want churches to wake up to his presence and activity, so he limits his work to individuals who have no idea that what is happening is not their own fault or the result of chance. Churches awakened to Satan's presence and activity, on the other hand, are attacked in big ways, at least until the leaders and membership get cleaned up spiritually to the point that they are not so vulnerable.

Each congregation should also tackle community problems. Once the leaders of a congregation have found out from the Lord the extent of the community they are responsible for (see below), they should take authority over any satanic stronghold within that territory. Churches can put out of business "adult" bookstores, prostitution rings, abortion clinics, homosexual activities, gambling operations, dope peddling, alcoholism, thievery and other sinful activities being carried on within their sphere of responsibility. And when all the churches in a city band together to assert their joint spiritual authority (as they have in Cincinnati over pornography), they can clean up whole cities.

The Pastor's Commitment to the Church

There is a direct relationship between the commitment of a pastor (or any leader) and the authority he or she wields in the spirit world. Pastors committed not to the church they serve, but to advancement or something else (such as money, prestige or an easy life), cannot expect the spirit world to take them seriously when they assert their authority over their own people and places, or over the community they purport to serve. This is an important lesson learned a few years ago by Pastor Bob Beckett of The Dwelling Place in Hemet, California. In the book *Breaking Strongholds in Your City* (edited by C. Peter Wagner, Regal, 1993), Beckett records his story. (The following information and quotations are taken from that book.)

For the first several years of his pastorate, Beckett says, "I had never seen myself anchored to this community." Rather, he had seen his position in Hemet as a stepping stone to a more prestigious position somewhere else. Then, he says, "the Lord [began] to stir within me a strong love for the land and its people," and he became concerned about seeing his church and city delivered from the enemy's power. The crucial point in

275

his ministry came when he heard the Lord asking him to define his commitment to his church. He records the next thing the Lord led him to realize:

> I could never begin to bring deliverance of any real and lasting significance to my own area if I was living here with my emotional and spiritual bags packed, always waiting for the day when the Lord would call me to a larger community with greater influence and significance.
>
> pp. 162–163

This lack of commitment affected Beckett's spiritual authority, both inside the church and within the community. He was able to plant a church that was like most other churches—basically a religious club. It was riddled with divisions and other "normal" problems. "If we were known for anything," he says, "we were known for church splits. We had experienced 5 splits in 18 years."

The community his church served was also known for several negative events. It was the site of an ancient Indian massacre, a tragic water company miscalculation that had drained the natural water from the valley (ruining it financially), occult and gang activity, violence and death.

In response to the Lord's prompting, however, Bob and his wife, Susan, announced to the congregation that they considered Hemet a lifetime call. They even purchased cemetery plots there. Once they made such a commitment, they began to see ministry results at the individual level. There were conversions, healings, deliverances and exciting church growth. Apparently their authority had been established within the congregation. But, they asked,

> Why were similar things not happening in our community? How could it be that our prayers for people

276

were answered but our prayers for Hemet and the surrounding area seemed ineffective? We looked to the north, the south, the east and the west from our church and saw little change. It seemed as if in some aspects our community was losing ground. Social conditions were deteriorating and we could sense encroaching darkness. We felt we were being faithful and diligent, but to little avail.

pp. 154–155

The Becketts decided that when they committed themselves to the church, they had also made what Bob calls a *territorial commitment* to Hemet. So they set out to discover what authority in and over a community might mean. He says,

If my city would ever know true deliverance from its ruling spirits of religious apathy, financial stinginess, occult idolatry and the like, it would have to start with Christian leaders making a commitment to the people and the land. Someone like me needed to begin by unpacking their bags and setting aside their dream of a more exciting ministry in the future. Pastors, lay leaders and whole churches must join, taking long-term territorial responsibility for the land they are living in!

p. 163

Years earlier Bob had begun to mark interesting phenomena with possible spiritual significance on a map of the area. Now he began to take seriously what the map seemed to show—that there were major satanic strongholds in and around their city. He and his staff began looking into the history of the city and surrounding areas, seeking to discover what he calls the "personality" of the city and looking for occult centers.

277

Recognizing the ties between the spiritual problems this research revealed and the "ground-level" people problems requiring repentance, Beckett led the church to sponsor a Strategic Warfare Conference in 1991. "At the conference," he writes, "we were able to put into practice this concept of repentance over our city, seeking God's forgiveness for social sins." Whites repented for their sins against Native Americans; Methodist and Pentecostal pastors apologized for their attitudes toward each other; a representative of the water company repented for its mistakes. In this ground-level move toward reconciliation, "years of division and hatred were broken in the spiritual realm [and] the principalities and powers received serious setbacks."

Next, Bob says, "while praying about the increasing gang violence in our community, we felt the need to establish a prayer canopy over our city." As Bob read Isaiah 33:20, he was impressed with the prediction that a tent that will never be moved would be erected over Jerusalem, with stakes driven into the ground to secure it. He "sensed the Lord was telling us to drive stakes into the ground in order to secure the spiritual canopy He wanted to spread over the city." So on a given Sunday, he announced to his congregation that those who wanted to join in should come to the church at 4:30 P.M. Bob announced:

> We would break into five groups. Four groups would accompany an elder with a stake to one of the four main entrances into our valley—all being highways. The fifth group would accompany my wife and me to the main intersection in the middle of town. At precisely 5:00 p.m., each elder would drive his stake into the ground as a memorial unto the Lord, and the resulting canopy of prayer would remain as our declaration of strategic intercessory warfare against the encroaching darkness.

At the same time, Susan and I, standing by the intersection in the center of town, would simultaneously lift up a praise offering unto the Lord as a center pole of the spiritual canopy.

pp. 166–167

From that day to this there has been a noticeable difference in the authority Beckett and the other pastors in town have been able to exercise, both in their churches and in their community. The lifting of a prayer canopy had what Beckett calls "a dramatic effect on the life of our own congregation." It also "has openly changed the spiritual face of our community." About 35 ministers in the community "now work together for evangelism," as well as sharing facilities and equipment, swapping pulpits and joining in joint tent revival meetings.

At least one other church, built on the site of an Indian massacre, has undergone a major transformation since the pastor and leaders took spiritual authority over their territory. They found that since the founding of that church in the early 1900s, violent death had occurred in every pastor's family except the last two. "We could not help but wonder," Beckett says, "if the violence and bloodshed in the past had defiled that piece of land and given a foothold for a spirit of violent death to operate." They also suspected that history had something to do with the fact that the neighborhood of the church "had become the geographical center for gang violence in the whole area." Beckett continues,

When the pastor learned about the Indian bloodshed and the history of violent deaths among pastors, he called a meeting of his elders and intercessors. They engaged in a time of sincere intercession and deep repentance for their land and their church.

279

What happened? Less than two months later, gang members began to come to the Lord. At least one walked into the church during the Sunday service and said, "I want to be saved!" Another gang leader, his mother, and then the entire family came to Christ. Gang violence in the area has dropped since then, although it has not yet disappeared entirely.

p. 160

How many pastors sacrifice much of their spiritual authority, as Beckett did, by not being fully committed to the churches they serve? It is common for pastors to hold the same attitude as many employees in other occupations: the desire to get ahead. In denomination after denomination, pastors serving smaller churches envy pastors with larger ones, and they work hard and pray for the day when they will "get promoted" to a larger church. Meanwhile, pastors with larger churches look down on those with smaller ones, since they consider the size of the church a badge of success and a mark of their approval by the Lord. Such attitudes delight Satan, who can poke holes in any church and in any pastor's authority, when that pastor is committed more to getting ahead than to serving the Lord.

Responsibility of the Church

It is important for a congregation and its leaders to discover, as Beckett did, what they have authority over. One obvious answer is the congregation itself. Such authority (as we noted earlier) involves preventing/protecting, stopping and, if necessary, attacking. The pastor and church leaders are responsible to assert their authority in the spirit world to prevent or stop whatever the enemy is doing in the lives of their members. And we can be sure the enemy is working any way he can to hinder and harass those who have committed themselves to Christ. A major concern of the leaders, then, should be to prevent and stop enemy activity among the flock. To be maximally effective in protecting the congregation and stopping attacks, leaders and those with intercessory gifts should be authority praying constantly for their members.

The responsibility for leaders and members of churches to clean up whatever the enemy is doing within their circles is implicit in the letters to the seven churches in Revelation 2 and 3. The letters were written to the angels, or perhaps the pastors, of these churches, pointing out strengths and weaknesses and encouraging them to persevere to the end to receive the rewards the Lord wanted to give them.

We learn from these letters the kinds of problems to watch out for. In Ephesus the problem the leaders needed to take authority over was the loss of their first love, apparently due to the presence of sin in their midst (Revelation 2:4–5). In Pergamum the problems were eating food offered to idols, immorality and following a cult (2:14–15). In Thyatira the leaders tolerated a woman who called herself a messenger of God but was misleading people by teaching immorality and the eating of food offered to idols (2:20–23). The Lord called the church in Sardis dead, in spite of their reputation for being alive (3:1). And in Laodicea the problem was lukewarmness in spiritual matters, with an accompanying materialistic way of life that deluded them into feeling they were rich, in spite of the fact that they were really "miserable and pitiful" spiritually (3:15–17).

Combining these messages warns us to look out for sin, compromising with idolatry, immorality, membership in cults, spiritual deadness, lukewarmness and loss of first love, misleading teaching within the church and materialism.

These first-century congregations were commended, on the other hand, for hard work, patience, discernment and perseverance in suffering (Ephesus, Revelation 2:2–3); for spiritual richness and steadfastness in the face of gossip and persecution (Smyrna, 2:9–10); for faithfulness in persecution (Pergamum, 2:13); for love, faithfulness, service, patience, growth in works and refusal to follow evil teaching (Thyatira, 2:19, 24); and for maintaining a little power, faithfulness to Jesus' teaching and endurance (Philadelphia, 3:8, 10). These are the traits leaders and intercessors in our churches today need to be concerned with, asserting their authority to protect against evil, to stop it and to bring about the characteristics for which the Lord commended the churches of Revelation.

Geographic Responsibility

A pastor called me several years ago and described some trouble his congregation was experiencing. In addition to more or less "normal" problems like divorce and bickering, a cult had arisen among the young people in his church, committed to the pagan god Dagon (1 Samuel 5). We decided to tackle this problem by conducting a seminar in which we taught on idolatry and ministered freedom to several people. Circumstances began to change in the church as the pastor and intercessors started to take seriously the satanic activity among their people, and to assert their authority over the enemy.

In addition to the internal authority church leaders are to exert, God has made churches the spiritual gatekeepers for the communities they serve. This means each church is responsible for the geographic or social territory God has assigned it. Church leaders are to assert their authority in the spirit world over this territory to cancel whatever authority the enemy claims within that space.

In order to fulfill our responsibility in this area, we must learn first what territory we have authority over. If we do not already know, we need to spend time in prayer to find out. God wants to reveal to us just what He holds us responsible for. For most churches, this involves a certain geographical area near the church building, plus some social space defined in terms of the personal relationships of its members. The authority to be wielded over these territories consists of the same prevention/protection, stopping and attacking activities we have been emphasizing. The primary means is intercession.

Another major factor, however, is understanding. Over and over, as we deal with demons, we find that a major source of their power is the ignorance of the person they live in. Likewise, as long as church leaders are unaware of their authority and responsibility over a specific geographic territory, the enemy can work without hindrance.

God's Commissioning

Once during a lull in a seminar, a pastor I will call Bill asked me how I thought his church should proceed in escalating its involvement in spiritual warfare. His was a small church, the only Protestant congregation for perhaps a square mile of their city. Both of us wondered if the fact that they had not been active in spiritual warfare might have something to do with their small size. As Bill's eyes were opened to the spiritual dimensions of the position of his church in the community, he began to look for ways they could move responsibly in the direction of becoming a greater threat to the enemy.

What came to me, as I asked the Lord for guidance in answering Bill's question, was that his small church was the gateway through which or around which any spiritual enemy must go to gain access to that community. So I asked him what was going on in his community. Bill indicated that the enemy had a pretty good foothold. My next question to him was this: "Do you think your church bears any responsibility for the present situation? Could it be that whatever the enemy is able to do in your church's backyard can be done only with your permission? Or because your church is ignoring it?"

I told Bill the story I recounted in chapter 5 of Steve Nicholson, the pastor in Evanston, Illinois, who felt led to claim certain territory for the Lord. According to C. Peter Wagner in *Engaging the Enemy*, Nicholson identified a certain street on the north, another on the south, and streets on the east and west as defining the territory he was claiming responsibility for and challenging enemy spirits over. As he prayed and fasted, a high-level demon identifying himself as a spirit of witchcraft appeared to him, saying he was in charge of that area and would not give him that much territory. Steve was able to break the spirit's grip, however, evidenced by the fact that immediately after this confrontation his church began to grow, largely through a steady flow of converts from witchcraft (most of whom, by the way, needed deliverance from demons).

My conclusion: that every congregation is commissioned by God to take and protect the territory in which it functions. My suggestion to Bill was that their church find out from the Lord what territory He holds them accountable for, attack sinful establishments within this territory through authority praying and run them out of business. We have the authority and responsibility to participate in the cleansing of our communities; and the experiments going on in Argentina, Hemet and elsewhere predict our success if we go about our attacks in the right way.

Authority over the History

Congregations can experience various kinds of dysfunction stemming from the fact that the enemy, at some time in the past, has been able to obtain rights in the Church. This situation parallels the "rats-and-garbage" condition in individuals whereby, because of agreements made with the enemy by their ancestors, demons have the right to live within them. It also parallels the situation when a person buys a new home in which past inhabitants gave the enemy rights.

To deal with such dysfunction, leaders in a church need to take authority over its past, just as the new owner of a home does, to cancel all past activities or agreements that gave the enemy rights. As with a home, those wielding God's authority in the present have the right to cancel any authority given to the enemy by past occupants. When problems like divisions, immorality, dissatisfaction and criticism flourish in a church, there may be a satanic grip there with roots in the past.

As we investigate the history of a congregation, we often find such problems as bickering, fighting, immorality on the part of pastors, dominance by certain families and other indications that Satan has been getting the best of the members and staff for generation after generation. When such problems occurred in the history of a congregation, the first step toward breaking the enemy's power is for the congregation, led by its leaders, to engage in identificational repentance. In this way they assume responsibility for the sins of the past members of the congregation and repent for them, as Nehemiah and Daniel did (Nehemiah 1; Daniel 9). The next step is for the leaders and intercessors to direct the congregation in authority praying to cancel the devil's rights over the congregation and its property. (John Dawson's book *Taking Our Cities for God*, although it deals specifically with cities, provides useful guidance for dealing with the historical influences on our churches.)

While Betsy Runkle-Edens was serving as associate pastor of a church in Ohio, she and her husband, Gary, became interested in discovering why their church and the one across the street (of the same denomination) had separated. They found that the one they served, Second Church, although it had experienced numerical growth during the 1950s and '60s, had never achieved spiritual vitality. The other one, First Church, had experienced some spiritual health but had remained small in numbers. Then they discovered that way back in 1836, a huge debate had surfaced at First Church over slavery and whether infants who die are damned. In anger, some of the members decided to leave and start their own church.

Although this bit of history appeared merely interesting and harmless at first, there was more to the story. Apparently from that day onward, members of the two churches continued in animosity toward one another. The churches stereotyped each other, competed for members and refused to cooperate down through the generations in reaching their community for Christ.

In praying about this, Gary and Betsy felt they heard the Holy Spirit saying that corporate healing was necessary before these churches could experience God's blessing. So they urged the senior pastors to consult with their respective elders about the possibility of mutual forgiveness and healing for the sins of their forefathers.

So far nothing has been done about the matter. Both churches continue to struggle, and I believe they will remain ineffective until they take such spiritual issues seriously and do something about them. The enemy has legitimate rights in these churches until they repent and use their authority to take those rights away from him.

Contrast the condition of these churches with several situations mediated by Ed Silvoso in which numbers of churches have agreed to pray together and repent to each other for past sins and competitiveness. They have also agreed to learn how to conduct spiritual warfare against the enemy—to fight the real enemy instead of each other. In Resistencia, Argentina, the results—in terms of conversions, church growth, mutual affection among church leaders and cooperation among the leaders to break the enemy's power through sinful establishments—have been phenomenal. The results have been similar with the churches in a California county and in several other places in Argentina and the United States where Silvoso has taught this approach.

When churches repent, cooperate and exercise their authority in concert, the Kingdom of God is enhanced in major ways, both within the churches and within the communities they serve.

A serious problem that affects many churches—which Betsy Runkle-Edens discovered while she was pastoring in Ohio—is that Freemasons have participated in planning and building churches and leading congregations. They especially like to lay the cornerstones and dedicate the buildings. Since this organization is committed to Satan (although without the knowledge of many, both inside and outside the organization), the enemy is able to gain considerable authority over a church through such dedications. In addition, many churches have several members, some in leadership positions, who belong to Masonic lodges.

It is no surprise, then, that many such churches are dying or have for years been spiritually ineffective. The power of the enemy gained through Masonic dedications can be canceled if leaders in the church use their authority to do so, but most of these pastors neither understand the problem nor know what to do about it. Until pastors and lay leaders gain understanding and act on it in their God-given authority, they can expect no renewal and little spiritual life.

Authority over the Property

We have mentioned the need for a pastor to take authority over a congregation, including its buildings, at the start of his or her ministry. But once satanic power over the history has been broken, it is important to keep asserting our authority, since demons are opportunistic, seeking and finding every opportunity to infect church buildings, their environs and furnishings. I do not know what all the rules are, but apparently it is necessary to claim authority over places regularly to assure that they are spiritually clean.

Several years ago several participants in a seminar and I were asked to check out a bell tower in the church building where we were meeting. Some felt there might be demonic influence in a room in that tower. And as we entered the room, even I, who do not usually feel such presences, felt something evil. Then we received two pieces of information that tended to confirm that the room needed spiritual cleansing. First, a runaway teenager had found a way to get into the church and had lived in that room for several weeks. Also, a musical and drama group that had experienced much dissension had used the room for practice and storing their instruments.

With these facts in mind, we asked the Holy Spirit what to do, and began authority praying according to His leading. We dealt with the history of the church and, with the authority of one of the pastors, claimed the room for Jesus Christ alone. Soon we all sensed the spiritual heaviness lift and the room take on a completely different feel.

During a seminar in a different place, one of the young women assisting in ministry had a disturbing experience when she left us. We were working to release someone from a demon, and this woman had to depart for another engagement. As she left the church, she experienced a powerful attack from the evil one, such that she could hardly move. Afterward she came running back into the church building, asking for someone to pray over her. Someone did, claiming protection for her as she left. We found out later that before we had arrived to start our seminar, the church's prayer team had prayed earnestly, taking authority over the inside of the church but paying no attention to the parking lot outside. When this woman left the church, then, she was apparently hit by some angry demons who could not get into the church building, but had rights to the parking lot by virtue of the fact that they had not been commanded to leave.

In another congregation, some unpleasant things began happening shortly after they received a carpet donated by a funeral home. The presence of the carpet was not considered, until in prayer someone sensed the Lord revealing that this was the cause. Thankfully the church had not yet installed the carpet. They disposed of it and the strange events stopped. They might have taken authority over the carpet and found they could thus cancel the enemy's power, but they chose to get rid of it because they felt God telling them to.

In another situation, a series of tragedies was probably averted when a pastor called me to ask whether I thought his church should rent a Masonic lodge on Sunday mornings for worship. I strongly advised against it, reasoning that although the Christians might be able to do spiritual housecleaning each Sunday, the fact that the Masons met there between Sundays, rededicating it regularly to Satan, meant they would reinfect it every week. And given the nature of that organization, such infection would be at a high level, making it risky for the church to meet there. They might find, for example, that they had failed to clean out a room completely of all evil presences—a room in which worship took place or a choir practiced or nursery children were tended to. This would put any vulnerable people in those groups at great risk.

I have mentioned teachers who experienced dramatic change in their students when they started to take authority over their classrooms in Jesus' name. The same applies to Sunday school teachers. If church buildings are prayed over properly, there should be no problem. But church buildings are primary targets for demons, since by infecting them, demons can cause disruption in God's camp. So we find that individuals, often young people, submit to temptation to sin on church property, thus giving the enemy rights to the places where they sinned. Earlier I mentioned the pastor's son who confessed to having had sexual relations in the balcony of his father's church. This incident, although unknown to the pastor, marked the start of a nosedive in his ministry. Sin committed by an individual in secret, as we learn from the story of Achan, can have disastrous effects on the nation or congregation of which he or she is part.

It is important, therefore, for us to cleanse the rooms spiritually whenever we use them, even if they are on church property, to protect against any possible interference. Church buildings should be cleansed regularly in case people have carried in demons on their persons, or if demons have gained the right to enter by some other means. It is possible the enemy sends his agents with street people who come for help during the week. And, of course, in most churches a fair number of those who attend are carrying demons.

When demons get into churches, there are certain places they seem to congregate more than other places. A friend with the gift of discernment, who has been involved in cleansing several churches, finds that the three greatest concentrations of demons are in the nursery, in the part of the church office where the records and offerings are processed and in the musical instruments. Demons are also frequently present in the library and around the pulpit. At one church powerful demons of depression were found working at every entrance to the building. In attempting to rid at least one church of these demons, my friend found they would not budge when he commanded them to leave. They would leave only when the pastor asserted his authority over them.

In addition to the ability of demons to contaminate church buildings, they can infest the furnishings of a church. In churches for which families have purchased pews or windows, enemy agents can be given rights to those items by virtue of their rights in the families—unless, of course, the authority of Jesus has been used to cleanse them. I have already suggested the possibility of a carpet being infested. And we have noted that musical instruments are a likely place for demons to hang out. So are the seats of disgruntled choir members—or, for that matter, discontented members of the congregation. At one of my seminars, the leader of a Christian musical group reported a dramatic change in the results of their concerts when they started blessing their instruments. The blessings probably broke any enemy power that was there, and added God's power.

Being Alert

Two things should be clear by now concerning church leadership and the other aspects of authority we have dealt with: First, we are at war; and second, we have great authority to win regularly in confrontations with the enemy. Since Satan's main weapon is our ignorance, I hope and pray that the kind of information we have been discussing will awaken us to wield the weapons God has given us. There is much we do not know about spiritual warfare. But I hope this presentation will alert us to some of the principles that seem to be at work, as well as to what we can do by way of experimentation to find success.

We who are in church leadership should not be frantic or fearful about the challenges of the enemy. We should, rather, take care to exercise our authority regularly over both our people and our property and furnishings. We must recognize that enemy spirits have a job to do—to mess us up—and that they are at it fulltime. We need to walk in authority day in and day out, therefore, always mindful of the enemy's schemes (2 Corinthians 2:11). Our awareness of the warfare we are in should make it as natural as breathing to assert our authority by claiming God's presence and power, in and over us and our surroundings.

Now let's wrap up our discussion by turning to a few more general matters, including the relationship of authority thinking to the kind of Christianity Jesus intends to be normal.

10

Our Authority
Is Great

Once there was a Man who came into the world sent by God the Father to bring freedom from captivity (Luke 4:18) and to be lifted up so He could draw all the peoples of the world to Himself (John 12:32). This was an incredible assignment. There were so many people to help. The enemy was so active and effective. Those in power were so uncaring, and in the habit of misusing their power to benefit themselves alone. And Jesus felt such compassion for those who were hurting (Matthew 9:36; 14:14).

Where was truth? Where was honesty? Where were those who cared for the oppressed? Who cared at all to do God's will?

The situation was enough to keep the anxiety level of the strongest caring person very high; enough to lead to impatience, frustration, anger and even violence if people did not see things His way and get on board His program.

But Jesus knew who He was, where He had come from and where He was going. Knowing these things, He was secure in Himself and able to exercise the authority granted Him by the Father in spite of criticism and opposition. With this knowledge to undergird Him, Jesus went about His Father's business with an admirable singleness of purpose.

He was disappointed at times, especially with the disciples, and angry, especially at the religious leaders who oppressed rather than helped the hurting. He got tired, especially on days when the crowds would not let Him alone, and lonely for the presence of the Father. And He hurt with compassion for the sheep wandering without a shepherd (Matthew 9:36).

But with a world to win, and only three years to do His job, He never got frantic! He did what the Father showed Him to do. He healed many but walked right past many others. He cast out demons from many, but there must have been many more He never helped. He spoke gladly to the crowds at times, but at other times ran away from them.

And He is our model. What better message could this book convey than to challenge us to be what Jesus was and do what He did? Oh, that we would have the security He had, knowing who we are and why we are here! And the commitment to do the will of the Father, whatever opposition and misunderstanding we have to put up with. And the ability to feel His compassion for those around us in enemy captivity.

We Are at War

We have seen clearly that we are at war against "the wicked spiritual forces in the heavenly world" (Ephesians 6:12). It is also clear by now that the context in which we are to operate authoritatively is one of warfare between the kingdoms. Jesus has put uniforms on us, given us weapons and commissioned us to fight. We know who gets to win. But for reasons we do not understand, although Jesus has won the victory, the war is not yet over. Many battles still need to be fought. Many prisoners who have been taken need to be set free (Luke 4:18–19).

But we have at least two enemies, not one. Satan and his demonic helpers, of course, constitute an ever-present challenge. The other enemy is his chief weapon: ignorance. Although Paul said, "We are not unaware of [Satan's] schemes" (2 Corinthians 2:11, NIV), most American Christians today, even those who know their Bibles best, are almost totally unaware of his schemes, and of the authority we have been given to thwart them.

Such widespread ignorance makes us sad, but we can be happy about the fact that we see at least the beginnings of a movement toward greater spiritual awareness. Some are even speaking of a worldwide movement of the Holy Spirit. Incredible things are occurring around the globe, even as I write, and some of them are happening in the United States. Signs and wonders, healings and deliverances—often accompanied by people turning to Christ in numbers unprecedented in human history—are being reported from China and the Muslim world.

And in the U.S., certain churches are discovering the importance of the Holy Spirit, intercessory prayer, contemporary worship, healing, spiritual warfare and even fasting. As I write, I have just come back from an incredible weekend seminar in an Episcopal church that is becoming biblically normal. And I get to conduct a dozen or more such seminars per year in Presbyterian, Methodist, Baptist, independent, even Nazarene church contexts. It is unlikely that such non- or even anti-charismatic groups would have been open to people working overtly in the power of the Holy Spirit a generation ago. But God seems to be "breaking loose" these days in many interesting and unpredictable places. A hunger for spiritual vitality on the part of many Christian leaders and ordinary Christian followers seems to be coinciding with the willingness of God to work in power anywhere He is invited.

One indication of this outpouring of the Spirit in our day is the rise of a movement of Christian men toward *reclaiming their rightful authority,* at least at the human level. Leading the way is the Promise Keepers. In a land where women have outnumbered men in churches for decades and, by default, have had to take the leadership God expects men to take, this is a breath of fresh air. Christian men and women alike are realizing that if God is to come and heal our land, we must exercise our God-given authority over homes, families, churches, communities and beyond. The Promise Keepers movement is a start in the right direction. It remains to be seen how far it will go in leading men beyond the more human dimensions of authority-taking.

We should pray that this and other movements will carry their members all the way past the spiritual ignorance that has characterized American Christianity.

Normal Christianity

As I began to move in the authority Jesus gives us, I began to recognize that the Christianity I had been living was sub-biblical and, therefore, subnormal. We are not intended to live as Christians the way most of us have been functioning—with little or no recognition of what is going on in the invisible spiritual world. As this dimension was opened up to me, I began to become more what a normal, biblical Christian ought to be.

I have tried in these pages to suggest various aspects of what I think normal Christianity should look like. By way of summary, then, along with some amplification, let me suggest three major components of normalcy.

1. Staying Close to Jesus

I have emphasized throughout this volume that if we are to be normal Christians, *we must stay close to Jesus in the same way He stayed close to the Father.* Our aim in our relationship with God should be nothing short of total intimacy—the kind Jesus practiced. He received His power from being filled with the Holy Spirit. His authority, however, sprang from His intimacy with the Father. He spent hours and hours in prayer, keeping in close contact with the Father. In this way He kept His will lined up with the Father's, seeing to it that He never did anything except on the Father's authority (John 5:19; 7:16–18).

Jesus is the Vine, we are branches. As with grapevines, both vine and branches are important to the bearing of fruit. Neither can function by itself. Branches in particular cannot function or even live by themselves. As Jesus said:

> "Remain united to me, and I will remain united to you. A branch cannot bear fruit by itself; it can do so only if it remains in the vine. In the same way you can-

not bear fruit unless you remain in me . . . for you can do nothing without me."

John 15:4–5

This means spending time with Jesus in prayer. It also means listening constantly for His voice, whether through the Scriptures, through people, through reading or directly. We need to keep on good terms with Him, growing in our commitment and staying close to Him. Just as it was necessary for my son to keep on good terms with me if he was to continue to have permission to use my credit card, so it is with us and Jesus. We should be in constant conversation with our Lord, friend to friend (John 15:15), as those chosen to be with Him. For He seeks to relate to us as He did to the apostles, to whom He said,

"I have chosen you *to be with me.* . . . I will also send you out to preach, and you will have authority to drive out demons."

Mark 3:14–15 (italics added)

Note the order of the reasons Jesus gave for choosing the Twelve: first, *to be with Him,* and only then to preach and drive out demons. Relationship first, ministry second. As in the beginning we were made for a close relationship with God, so Jesus chose twelve to be closely related to Him, His friends. They would walk and talk with Him, not as servants but as those who shared the Kingdom with Him. *That Kingdom would be theirs as well as His.* Jesus would share with them all the knowledge the Father shared with Him (John 15:15). And they could ask Him for anything so long as they stuck close to Him (John 15:7), since their relationship was more His choice than theirs (John 15:16).

298

God's power is there for us through the filling of the Holy Spirit. But keeping our wills lined up with God's can be another matter. This comes for us, as with Jesus, from spending time with God in private and listening to Him as we seek to represent Him in ministry and in all other facets of our lives. Jesus' success rate in ministry was one hundred percent since He always lined His will up with that of the Father. Our record is considerably less than His. The difference, I believe, lies in our ability to hear and follow the Father's voice. For me the biggest challenge in healing ministry is not in the area of power, but in the area of the intimacy of my relationship with the Father—a relationship that is essential if we are to coordinate our wills successfully with His.

The major external fruit of our intimate relationship with the Father is love. As we mature in intimacy, we mature in love—love for God and love for all whom God loves. We are, of course, to love and minister to those who are hurting. This has been a constant theme here as we have dealt with our authority under Christ. What we have not emphasized so far is that this intimacy requirement mandates us also to practice an intense love toward God's people, our brothers and sisters. Reminding us of this requirement, and its relationship to the ability of God to flow His power through us, Jack Deere says in *Surprised by the Power of the Spirit:*

> Spiritually mature Christians love God and his people passionately, and they hate anything that takes them away from God. Only in the context of such love will Bible knowledge and the gifts of the Spirit ever achieve their divine purposes. The power of the Spirit can flow unhindered through passionate love for God and his children.

p. 206

There is one aspect of the relationship of intimacy to authority that I find quite puzzling. People who seem to have gone off-track in their spiritual lives retain what looks like the same amount of power and authority they had when they were faithful and better motivated. Could it be that Romans 11:29—translated in the NIV as "God's gifts and his call are irrevocable"—applies here? If so, those who once were given spectacular gifts get to keep them even though they are no longer faithful to the Master. Perhaps, though, these are the ones Jesus says will not make it:

> "Not everyone who calls me 'Lord, Lord' will enter the Kingdom of heaven, but only those who do what my Father in heaven wants them to do. When Judgment Day comes, many will say to me, 'Lord, Lord! In your name we spoke God's message, by your name we drove out many demons and performed many miracles!' Then I will say to them, 'I never knew you. Get away from me, you wicked people!'"
>
> Matthew 7:21–23

With this as a warning, it behooves us to do our best to keep close to Jesus so we can participate in His life and work as God intended us to do—on His terms rather than ours.

2. Knowing Who We Are

Second, we need to underline what we have said throughout this book: *We must know who we are and the authority that entails.* We are children of the King! Royal blood flows in our veins. We have the authority to come boldly and confidently into His presence (Hebrews 4:16) and call God "Abba," Dad. We do not have to fear Him as Isaiah did (Isaiah 6:5). Further, we know we are loved by God because of who we are, not because of anything we may accomplish. As John says, "See how much the Father has loved us! His love is so great that we are called God's children—and so, in fact, we are" (1 John 3:1).

One mind-blowing aspect of our status is the trust God puts in us by granting us this position, and the authority inherent in it. When Jesus gave His disciples authority and power, and then sent them out to minister, He trusted them. (Would you have trusted the disciples with anything, especially with authority and power?) When Jesus reinstated Peter, He trusted him and gave him authority to look after His sheep (John 21:15–19). When He left the earth, He entrusted us with the Holy Spirit and the authority that goes along with His presence in us, predicting that with Him we "will do what [Jesus did]—yes, [we] will do even greater things" than He did (John 14:12).

Jesus trusted the disciples and us so much that He authorizes us to be called *His friends,* not slaves, because He has entrusted us with "everything I heard from my Father" (John 15:15). It is, therefore, our Kingdom as well as His (Luke 12:32; 22:29–30).

3. Knowing We Are at War

A third element crucial to Christian normalcy is that *we must recognize we are at war and behave accordingly.* We are to put on the armor of God (Ephesians 6:13–18) and join the ranks of God's shock troops, fighting on His behalf behind enemy lines. For according to 1 John 5:19, "The whole world is under the rule of the Evil One." As soldiers we are to be obedient to our leader and disciplined in our personal lives. We should not be running or hiding, trying to avoid the war. We must enter it actively, seeking victories for our Master in His war with our enemy.

In warfare we risk the possibility of defeat. Even in our war, not all battles are won, although ultimate victory is sure. But even when we are bested in battle, we are fighting. I have confessed that, during nearly forty years of my Christian life, God wanted me to fight the enemy but I was unprepared and hiding. For years I barely knew there was a war being waged. I was probably more of a hindrance than a help to the war effort.

Biblically normal Christianity requires that we wake up to the reality of the war and learn to use the weapons God has given us to fight the real enemy. Our churches have largely been living and working at the natural or human level. Some have been doing a good job at that level. But normal, biblical Christianity demands that we live and work at the supernatural level. Only at this level can we effectively fight our enemy who lives and works at that level. For

> The weapons we use in our fight are not the world's weapons but God's powerful weapons, which we use to destroy strongholds. We destroy false arguments; we pull down every proud obstacle that is raised against the knowledge of God; we take every thought captive and make it obey Christ.
>
> 2 Corinthians 10:4–5

These verses speak of a different level of warfare than we are used to fighting on, and a different caliber of weapons than we are used to wielding. But we have the authority to fight at that level and use that kind of weapon. Now let's learn how—and become normal.

Authority in Allegiance, Truth and Power

There are at least three crucial dimensions to Christian life and witness: allegiance, truth and power.

1. Allegiance to Christ

Allegiance to Christ, in contrast with any other allegiance, is the starting point for the relationship with Jesus that saves us and facilitates the authority we have been discussing. This allegiance also assures us of the quality of life Jesus promised when He said, "I have come in order that you might have life—life in all its fullness" (John 10:10). We have the authority to be part of God's family (John 1:12) and to live this abundant life even while living in enemy territory. And when Jesus returns, we have the right to live forever with Him.

Jesus put this allegiance first, and considered the intimacy with Him that flows from it in His choosing of His closest followers. Mark 3:14–15 records that Jesus "chose twelve, whom He named apostles. 'I have chosen you *to be with me,'* he told them. 'I will also send you out to preach, and you will have authority to drive out demons'" (italics added). Once again, note the order: These men were chosen first to be close to Him, and only then to preach and work in authority in relation to demons. So authority starts with allegiance/commitment that leads to closeness in a relationship with Jesus.

Allegiance to Christ ———— Leads to ———→ Relationship with Christ

The relationship flowing from our allegiance to Christ is foundational to the authority in which we walk as we seek to live the fruits of the Spirit (Galatians 5:22–23). This relationship provides us with the authority to love the unlovable, to be joyful in the midst of gloom, to be peaceful when things are falling apart, to be patient when things look hopeless, and all in all to live righteous lives in an evil world. In short, our allegiance to Christ provides us with the authority to live as He did.

In addition, our authority to win victories over the enemy is calibrated to the strength of our commitment to our Master. The enemy spirit world knows just how committed we are, and is able to work in and around us wherever there is a weakness. Our level of commitment speaks eloquently to the evil spirit world, granting us great authority if our commitment is great and less authority if our commitment is weak.

Our allegiance to Christ also gives us the authority to challenge other allegiances, both in ourselves and in others. There are many possible allegiances. Some are weak (for example, to a brand of soap or toothpaste), but a few are strong. If we are pressured to change something to which we are weakly committed (like our soap), we change. On the other hand, we would rather die than break some of our strong allegiances (for example, to Jesus Christ, family, job). We need to challenge all lesser allegiances to make sure our commitment to Jesus is at the top.

One of the enemy's priorities is getting us to use our faculties to commit ourselves more to other allegiances than to Jesus Christ. (The temptation in American society might be to make our job our primary allegiance.) This weakens our authority. In the society in which Jesus worked, the primary allegiance of most people was family. So in His teaching He appealed for people to make

Him their primary allegiance (Matthew 8:21–22; Luke 14:26), even to the point of suffering and dying for Him.

2. God's Truth

The second crucial dimension of our Christian life and witness is *truth*. God's truth provides the knowledge and understanding we need to operate in the authority we have been given. Jesus taught truth with authority (Matthew 7:29) and truth about authority. With Him we have the authority to handle God's truth, to experience it, to speak it, to teach it.

One fact we dare not miss in a discussion of truth, however, is that the Greek words for *truth* and *knowledge* imply that these have been learned by experience. The Scriptures are not talking about intellectual or theoretical truth and knowledge. They are advocating an understanding of truth that has been gained by experience. It is the truth experienced, not simply thought, that will set us free (John 8:32). And as the preceding verse says, the basis of this experience is obedience. We can count on the Holy Spirit to lead us in this quest for understanding (John 16:13).

Truth ——————— Leads to ——————→ Understanding
(Experienced)

Like Jesus, we are to confront ignorance and error with God's truth. We cannot effectively confront an allegiance with truth. One allegiance can be confronted only with another allegiance. Nor can we confront power with truth. Power can be challenged effectively only with power. Whenever there is ignorance concerning any issue, however, including ignorance about either allegiances or power, we are to learn and speak truth, as Jesus did. (Learning the truth about false allegiances or counterfeit power can be a meaningful start toward confronting them in kind.)

In Jesus' ministry, teaching truth was what He spent the most time doing, combating the ignorance and error around Him. Likewise in this book I have attempted to teach truth to supplant the ignorance and error in most of our churches concerning the subject of authority.

Truth ———————— Combats ———————▶ Ignorance, Error

The fact that our authority is grounded in truth is not to be taken lightly. It is the authority granted by the True One who frees people, in contrast with the domination and captivity our enemy brings about through deceit and lies. Much of what the world believes and practices is based on lies such as that the most important goals of life are material and temporal; or that God and spiritual things are not important, since only what we can see and touch is real; or that we, not God, are the masters of our fate; and so on. The right to be connected to the Source of truth, and to speak and live that truth in a world like this, is an inestimable privilege.

That privilege carries with it a great responsibility, however—the responsibility that goes with all authority: to use what we are given rightly. As 2 Timothy 2:15 instructs us, we are to win God's approval of our use of His authority by being those "who correctly [teach] the message of God's truth."

3. Authority to Use God's Power

The third of our crucial dimensions, the authority to use *God's power* for God's purposes, is our major concern in this book. A primary function of spiritual authority is to enable us to work in God's power in a variety of ways here on earth. These ways are prominent throughout the chapters of this book. The aim of spiritual power used in the authority of Jesus Christ is freedom. Our enemy holds countless of God's people, not to mention those outside the Kingdom, in captivity, but we have the authority to free them.

All Three Elements in Balance

Although each of these dimensions—allegiance feeding relationship, truth leading to understanding, and power bringing freedom—is distinct, Jesus interrelated them constantly as He ministered to those around Him. When He taught, He taught truth about both allegiance and power. When He healed, He used the true power of the true God to whom He was totally committed (allegiance) and with whom He had a close relationship. When He appealed for allegiance (for example, Matthew 11:28), it was on the basis of God's truth and in God's power. The interrelationship among these elements formed the basis for Jesus' authority, and it forms the basis for ours. If our authority to work in the power of Christ is authentic, it must be conditioned by wholehearted commitment to Him and a total concern for His truth. Thus, allegiance and truth serve as the backdrop to the proper use of spiritual authority and power.

But we need to guard against the tendency to become unbalanced or deficient, either by overemphasizing or by ignoring any of these three focal elements of our Christian experience. Evangelicals have often concentrated on allegiance and truth and neglected power, keeping two strong arrows in our quiver and ignoring the third. We have gone a long way with the two arrows, but without the freedom that comes only by confronting the enemy's power with God's, our approach has suffered.

In reaction, Pentecostals and charismatics have so often focused on power that the importance of truth and allegiance has gotten lost in the shuffle. Not that these groups have ignored allegiance and truth. They have not. But power, especially when surrounded by a lot of emotion, can distract from other important emphases. And it has often been allowed to distract.

Either approach is off-balance and unbiblical. A fully biblical expression of Christianity emphasizes all three crucial dimensions in balance. We should make sure to use all that God has given us in each of these important areas, as Jesus did.

We Must Continue to Experiment

I have pointed out that there is a lot about the spirit world we do not understand. It used to be that, although many had ideas and practices in this arena that worked, they kept them secret or shared them only within a limited circle of acquaintances. But today more and more people are venturing into this realm, and learning and writing about it. And whenever people begin sharing ideas, theories and experiments more openly, the process of learning escalates. Someone advances an idea and someone else critiques it, offering what he or she considers a better approach. Then someone else comes along with a radically different suggestion, and different traditions develop, each practicing its own approach and conducting experiments based on its own theories. In this way new ideas and techniques get developed, less effective ones get dropped and science moves forward.

If there is the same regularity in the interactions between the spirit and human worlds that there is in the physical world (and I believe there is), we can speak of developing a science of the spirit realm by means of the same process described above. Thus, I make no excuses for experimentation. As with the physical and human worlds, where God has left much for us to discover on our own (that is, without the benefit of special revelation), so in the spirit world. We must start with whatever the Bible shows us, but there is much more to discover through practice, theorizing and experimentation.

We know from the Gospels, for example, that Jesus gives His followers authority and power. We read in the Scripture some of what Jesus and the apostles did with that authority and power. But the descriptions of those events are simply outlines of what happened. We are told few details of what they did as they healed or delivered people from demons. Nor are we given such information as how long it took, or whether they or others did any follow-up to bring the freed people to complete wholeness.

What we learn from experience, then, are insights like these:

Often authority-prayer events take quite a bit of time.

Often healings are not immediate.

Often the use of visualization helps bring about healing that seems to come in no other way.

Often getting information from demons helps to assist in deliverance.

Often the person who has been freed needs to work hard and have considerable support to consolidate the gains made during the prayer ministry time.

Scripture does not answer all our questions as we assert the authority Jesus has trusted us with. So we experiment, praying all the while that we are not going beyond what pleases God, and we develop practices that are not explicit in Scripture but that work consistently to set captives free. Often we are criticized by those who feel we go too far. Usually these people have little or no experience, and would never launch out themselves to use the authority and power Jesus gives us.

A typical critique was leveled at me and several others recently by some well-meaning, thoughtful people who accused us of being unbiblical in our use of God's authority. It is all right to critique ministries like ours for, as I said, that is how we learn, and how a science of the spirit realm will be developed. But these people had zero experience in most of the areas in which they found our approaches off-base. And, as nearly as I can tell, they do not plan to tackle these areas in practice, only in theory.

In a meeting with one of these critics, I suggested that it was difficult to take his criticisms seriously, given the fact that he has never faced most of the problems we deal with regularly in this ministry. As we do, we soon run out of biblical information concerning what Jesus or the apostles did in such situations. So we are forced to use our own creativity under the guidance of the Holy Spirit, and we do.

"When you have worked with 25 demonized people," I said to this critic, "and discover that you, too, must go beyond approaches specifically indicated in the Bible, let's talk again."

If he ever does what I suggest, our conversation and relationship will be considerably different.

I continue to take critiques like his seriously, but I will not stop working in Jesus' authority merely because people do not like what I am doing. If I must choose between helping a person to freedom by using approaches not found in Scripture (though not anti-scriptural) or else allowing that person to remain in bondage, I choose to help.

The fact that God blesses our efforts so regularly, using them to bring freedom to people in amazing ways, encourages us to continue in both ministering and experimenting to find better ways to help people, in spite of the criticism. I understand that D. L. Moody said once in response to a person criticizing his evangelistic methods, "I like the way I do it better than the way you don't do it."

How to Put These Ideas into Practice

When I teach on the subject of spiritual authority, those who buy what I have to say often ask, "How do I get started?" They have usually been unaware that they are living in enemy territory and are being harassed by Satan. When these facts are pointed out, however, they can often identify circumstances in their lives that they suspect are the result of enemy activity. So what do they do now?

1. Be Aware

The first issue is awareness. Like almost everything else we do, awareness is a matter of habit. We have learned as part of our Western worldview to assume that nothing we cannot see can hurt us. So we are habitually unaware of the invisible world. This habit must be changed if the material in this book is to be of any use to us. We have noted the assumption of the apostle Paul, articulated in 2 Corinthians 2:11, that we are aware of the enemy's schemes. But, in fact, we are not until we force ourselves to become aware of that dimension of our human condition.

In considering the matter of awareness, some refer to those who have gone too far. They say, "I don't want to be one of those who believe there's a demon under every rock and behind every bush." Nor do I. But I think it is important to find out which rocks and bushes demons *are* hiding behind. It is not wise to turn aside from the whole matter just because some carry it too far. Satan loves us to go to one extreme or the other.

So let me suggest that we risk overdoing things for a while, in order to school ourselves to the fact that there are malevolent beings out there working full-time to try to mess up our lives. I have found it helpful to go through a little ritual each morning that, on the one hand, brings protection, and on the other hand, keeps me alert to the presence of the demonic world and its devices. I suggest saying something like this:

> In the name of Jesus, I claim protection from any enemy spirits that seek to hurt or harass me or my family. I forbid them to affect me or any of my family spiritually, emotionally, physically or in any other way.

2. Claim What Is Yours

As our awareness grows, we need to learn to claim what is rightfully ours. By this I mean that we should claim such things as protection from harm and freedom from harassment. Throughout the day I try to increase my consciousness of the fact that I live in a hostile world, by calmly claiming God's protection as I take my daily walk, when I get into my car and at any other times there might be danger or risk.

Claiming our rights does not mean we have to remain conscious continually of the threat of the spirit world.

I claim protection as I get into my car, for instance (or soon after), and go about my business without further concern unless I perceive danger, like a dangerous intersection or being crowded by another car. Then I claim protection again—usually saying something like, "In Jesus' name I claim safety and protection"—knowing that both God and the enemy spirit world are listening, and that angels are carrying out God's orders.

When it seems that I am being harassed or interfered with in some way, I use the expression I recommended earlier: "If this is the enemy, stop it!" This helps not only with arguments coming on, but with disruptions of public meetings, even headaches or occasional physical problems, if they are caused by demons. (Some are, many are not.) People tell me that sometimes when they experience emotional downs, they are able to get over them by breaking the enemy's power in this way. Even lustful thoughts or thoughts of anger and bitterness can be banished by commanding the enemy to stop feeding them into one's mind.

3. *Assert Your Authority to Change Things*

Building on our awareness and the claiming of our rights, we can move to asserting our authority to change things. I have spoken of the authority God has given us to bless, bring healing, deliver from demons and forgive. I have also mentioned the canceling of enemy rights to places, property, artifacts, music and other things that have been dedicated to him. We have also discussed the authority to cancel rights obtained through curses, vows, sin and in other ways. All these are changes brought about as we assert our authority.

Jesus used His authority at least once to change the weather. Maybe we can, too. I have experimented with

313

this use of our authority. On two occasions the weather changed soon (one immediately, one later) after I commanded it to. I do not know if my command did it or not. On numerous other occasions, I have commanded weather to change and it has not!

Jesus also used His authority to multiply food. I have heard of at least three instances in recent years of the multiplication of food. One occurred in Colombia when some missionaries had prepared food in individual portions for a gathering of low-income people. If I remember correctly, about twice as many as they had planned for showed up, but each received an individual portion.

One of the major purposes of this book has been to alert us to the many areas of life in which I believe Jesus wants us to assert our authority. Let me remind us that we are continually to use the credit card Jesus has given us in our day-to-day activities. Although we must be careful to use that authority responsibly—not arrogantly, pridefully, emotionally or obtrusively—we are to use it at all times.

We are also to assert this authority in our families. Whatever our status in the family, we have others to be concerned about. The enemy is fond of attacking the weakest and least protected. We are responsible to use our authority to protect whoever is under our authority, and probably others as well, at least on occasion. We have considered suggestions as to how heads of households can protect those under their authority. And we have pointed out that there seem to be counter-rules by which those with lesser authority can protect themselves and even have influence on those with greater authority. For the many women who find themselves in disadvantageous positions with respect to authority, the use of 1 Corinthians 7:14 as the basis for asserting authority can be very effective.

We have spoken of the use of authority in ministry. I have not gone into the detail I might have in this area because I have written several other books on the subject. (*Christianity with Power* offers a general treatment of the use of authority in ministry. *Deep Wounds, Deep Healing* explores ways to use our authority in a ministry of deep-level healing that gets at problems of an emotional or spiritual nature. *Defeating Dark Angels* speaks of our use of Jesus' authority in dealing with demonization. And a broader use of authority in dealing, for example, with territorial matters is treated in the compilation *Behind Enemy Lines*.)

I hope chapter 9 has been helpful in applying an understanding of spiritual authority to the Church. I tried to raise certain issues that most pastors seem not to recognize concerning their authority and its use. And finally I have commented on our need to claim the authority of our Lord and Master in the places where we work. Circumstances change in the classroom, in the office, even in places where we enjoy coffee breaks, when someone takes the authority Jesus gives us to kick out whatever enemy spirits may be infecting the place.

Do We Know the Enemy's Schemes?

I am concerned that we know what our enemy is up to. Awareness is crucial. No army goes into battle without studying their enemy thoroughly. And from what Paul said in 2 Corinthians 2:11, it looks as though God expects us to be onto our enemy and his devices. Since he works full-time to thwart what God is doing in, with and through us, no weak-kneed, mild-mannered approach to defeating him will work. Though we are to be gentle toward people, in relation to the enemy of our souls we are to conduct all-out warfare.

Let's learn his schemes and how to use the authority God gives us to speak God's power when and wherever we can, to squelch what the enemy is doing or wants to do. In our hands is the credit card of *In Jesus' name,* backed by the authority of Jesus' resurrection defeat of Satan and all his followers. Let's use it.

I pray that this book will be effective in challenging you to be and do all that God wants you to be and do, in and with His authority. I bless you to that end.

APPENDIX

Authority in the Bible

Edited from a paper by D. Michael Crow

The concept of authority predates history. The royal dignity and creative power of God originated from His "throne," which was established "from all eternity" (Psalm 93:1–2, NIV). Authority is of the very nature of God.

When the Eternal One created humankind in His image, immediately they were told, both male and female, "to have dominion." The inclination to exercise authority is part of the undefiled *imago Dei*. Sadly this was corrupted by the Fall, resulting in the misuse of authority to dominate, enslave and commit unspeakable cruelty from that day till this.

In redeeming humankind, Jesus emptied Himself of divine authority. He allowed Himself to suffer some of the worst atrocities of sin-distorted human authority, in order to liberate humanity from the tyranny of its authority-distorting master. Following His resurrection, Jesus reclaimed His universal and absolute authority (Matthew 28:18). He then turned and mandated to those who submit to His authority that we express that authority in a way consonant with His own character and purpose (Matthew 28:19–20).

This we are to do until the day when every person acknowledges the supremacy of that authority in Jesus Christ (Philippians 2:5–11). Having abolished every false and opposing authority, He will then surrender the Kingdom *in toto* to His Father (1 Corinthians 15:24), thus bringing the universe into complete alignment with His authority, transcendent over all.

Authority is thus inherently human, because it is inherently divine. It is corrupted in fallen creatures, yet redeemable through the new creation. Authority is not simply a social convention; it originates with God. Independent of Him, it can produce hell on earth. In submission to Him, it expresses the beauties of the divine nature.

Authority is expressed in a thousand ways, a thousand times a day, in normal social interaction, yet for it to be truly expressive of God's nature, it must be synchronized and harmonized with His will. Though this authority is expressed in a fallen way now, God is still able to weave its discordant notes into His celestial symphony.

Ultimately God will bring final resolution to this present terrestrial cacophony. In the meantime we live in eschatological suspension, between one movement and the last, and it is our duty to harmonize our instruments with His. As we do so, we express His authority, true spiritual authority, ascending in a harmonious crescendo with the rest of His obedient creation, a jubilant anthem of praise to the Eternal One enthroned on high.

Authority in the Old Testament

The primary Hebrew word in the Old Testament for "authority," according to *Strong's Concordance,* is *toqeph* ("might" or, figuratively, "positiveness"), which is translated "authority" or "power." It is based on the primary root word *taqaph* (to "overpower"), which is translated "prevail [against]." The related Chaldean word *teqoph* ("power") corresponds to *toqeph* and is often translated "might" or "strength." It is usually used in the Old Testament with reference to governmental authority.

Authority in the New Testament

The most prominent Greek word for *authority* in the New Testament is *exousia.* The following is based on W. Foerster's discussion in *Theological Dictionary of the New Testament* (Eerdmans, 1985) of the function of the concept in ordinary Greek usage, in Jewish and New Testament usage and as a New Testament concept.

In Ordinary Greek Usage

The basic meaning of *exousia* was the "ability" to perform an action. Following from this are meanings such as the "right," "authority" or "permission" conferred by a higher court. These rights are granted either by government or through social relationships (for example, that of parents, masters or slave-owners).

Since such authority would be meaningless without real power, the term sometimes means essentially the same as *dunamis,* though *dunamis* points to a more external power, while *exousia* has a more inward reference. The term may even be used with reference to self-asserted freedom from law, though it most often assumes a legally ordered context. Derived from *exou-sia* are meanings such as "authoritative position," "of-fice-bearers" (plural), "laudatory address," "crowd" and "pomp."

In Jewish and New Testament Usage

Greek-speaking Jewish people used *exousia* in simi-lar ways, to denote "permission," "authority" or "right." In the Jewish philosopher Philo's writings, we find *ex-ousia* used to refer to the absolute power of the king or of God.

In the Greek translation known as the Septuagint (ab-breviated LXX), the version used by New Testament writers, *exousia* is used to mean both legal "right," "au-thority," etc., and that given by God (for example, in the Law). In Daniel and Maccabees, it refers to the *power* of God or the king.

The New Testament authors largely follow LXX usage. *Exousia* is the power of God, that given to Jesus, or that given by Jesus to His disciples. It is also the power of government (for example, the Sanhedrin in Acts 9:14, or Herod in Luke 23:7), the power of self-determination (Acts 5:4), the power of kings (Revelation 17:12) and "the [spiritual or governmental] authorities [plural] that exist" (Romans 13:1; see Luke 12:11). A sphere over which authority is exercised is often in focus, such as the state (Luke 23:7), the domain of spirits (Ephesians 2:2) or the spiritual powers (1 Corinthians 15:24; Ephe-sians 1:21; Colossians 1:16; 1 Peter 3:22).

As we would expect of those thinking Hebrew but speaking Greek, the meanings of the Hebrew words that *exousia* translates get carried over into the Greek term. Among these are "power of disposal," "possession," "commission," "right," "freedom" and "government" (singular), in addition to the kingly power of God.

The New Testament Concept of Exousia

In the New Testament there seem to be three basic assumptions or implications underlying the use of *exousia*. First, those with *exousia* have the right, freedom and power to decide. Second, such a right occurs within the context of relationships ordered by and ruled over by God. And third, such authority, since it is given by God, implies freedom for the community to act under that authority.

The primary denotation of *exousia* relates to activities that are the prerogative of God alone since He is the source of all power and legality (Luke 12:5; Acts 1:7; Romans 9:21; Jude 25). God has authority over nature (Revelation 14:18). The empowerment of natural forces, then, comes from God (Revelation 6:8; 9:3, 10, 19; 16:9; 18:1). God's sphere of authority also circumscribes that of Satan (Acts 26:18; Colossians 1:13). The most surprising thing about Satan and evil is not his power but the fact that God holds the trump cards to overrule him (compare Luke 4:6 and 22:53 with Revelation 13:5, 7).

Exousia in Jesus' ministry points to His God-given rights and power, accompanied by His freedom to carry out His mandate (Matthew 28:18; Revelation 12:10). His was a cosmic power enfleshed in human form (Matthew 11:27; John 1:12; 17:2; and at the Judgment, John 5:27). Jesus exercised His *exousia* within the limits of His commission to forgive sins (Mark 2:10), to expel demons (Mark 3:15) and to teach (Matthew 7:29; 9:8; Mark 11:28; Luke 4:36). The context in which this power is asserted is the Kingdom brought near by Christ the King.

The Church depends on Christ for her authority and empowerment. Our rights as individuals come from Him (John 1:12; Revelation 22:14). The authority of the apostles comes from the Lord (2 Corinthians 10:8); they must, therefore, use it responsibly (Mark 13:34; 1 Corinthians 9:4ff), for it comes with freedom (1 Corinthians 6:12; 8:9; 10:23) and can be used unlovingly (Romans 14:14–15). Among heretical groups such as the Gnostics, we find this freedom misused, even to the extent (obvious in apocryphal Acts) of *exousia* being regarded as a magical power used for one's own ends.

A usage found in the New Testament, though in neither Hellenism nor Gnosticism, is for *exousia* to refer to supernatural powers. This usage has Jewish roots. *Exousiai* (plural) is used to refer to cosmic powers, distinct from *daimones* (demons) but not clearly different from *archai* (kingdoms). Paul speaks of "authorities" that strongly influence human life. These stand between God and us, are fallen but recognize the sovereignty of Christ over creation (Colossians 1:15–16). Their existence creates tension but, since they are unequal to God, they can never separate us from Christ.

There is much discussion and division over the meaning of the connection Paul makes between a woman covering her head (or veiling her face) and the angels (1 Corinthians 11:10). The angels seem to be assigned to guard or protect the natural order, part of which requires that a woman be under her husband's authority, as shown by the covering.

Authority Terminology in Scripture

A close examination of all the Bible says about authority could fill volumes. I am limiting this study, therefore, to what I call "authority terminology"—that is, words such as *authority, authorities, authorized* and *authoriza-tion.* I am not studying each occurrence of authority terminology in the Bible, nor am I looking at authority terminology in the original languages (Hebrew, Aramaic and Greek), only in the English of the New International Version. I simply want to overview the progressive conceptualization of authority as biblical revelation progressed.

Authority Terminology in the Old Testament

The biblical data indicates that authority terminology took on greater and greater *conceptual* significance throughout biblical history. During the entire Old Testament history, from the time of Abraham until the destruction of Jerusalem (approximately 1,100 years), authority terminology is used only five times: three times in the Torah, and once each in the prophets Isaiah and Jeremiah.

During the exilic and post-exilic periods, dating from the destruction of Jerusalem in 587 B.C.E., the dedication of the rebuilt Temple in 515 B.C.E. and until the fourth return of the Jews to Jerusalem under Ezra sometime between 458 and 398 B.C.E.—a period of approximately 150 years—the frequency increases to ten times, with authority terminology used five times in each period.

Authority Terminology in the New Testament

When we come to the era of the New Testament, which lasted only fifty to sixty years, there is a dramatic increase in the use of authority terminology. The four historical New Testament writers use authority terminology 46 times (eleven times in Matthew, ten times in Mark, thirteen times in Luke, six times in Acts, and six times in John), usually in relation to Jesus.

The general epistles and Revelation account for twenty occurrences of authority terminology (once in Hebrews, four times in Peter, three times in Jude and twelve times in Revelation).

Authority Terminology in Paul

The most frequent use of authority terminology in a single biblical author is found in Paul, whose extant literary career lasted only fifteen years. Authority terminology occurs in Paul's writings at least 38 times (only 24 times in the NIV)—more than the entire Old Testament combined.

Clearly what began as a vague concept in Old Testament times took on greater and greater conceptual significance in New Testament times, culminating with Paul. He was, according to Hans von Campenhausen in *Ecclesiastical Authority and Spiritual Power in the Church of the First Three Centuries* (Stanford University Press, 1969), "the true founder and discoverer of the Christian concept of authority." This makes Paul one of our most important sources for a biblical understanding of spiritual authority.

The 38 times Paul uses authority terminology in his writings include 31 uses of the word *exousia* and seven times when another word is used. (When a word other than *exousia* is used, the verse is asterisked both below and when the verses are written out later in this appendix.) The authority terminology carries twelve different meanings:

1. Christ's triumph over cosmic authorities (1 Corinthians 15:24; Ephesians 1:21; Colossians 2:10, 15).

324

2. The Church's battle with cosmic authorities (Ephesians 2:2; 3:10; 6:12; Colossians 1:13, 16).
3. Authority and the Law (Romans 7:1).
4. Governmental authority (Romans 13:1 [three times], 2, 3, *5, *6; *1 Timothy 2:2; Titus 3:1).
5. Authority as the legitimate "right" of God's servants (1 Corinthians 9:4, 5, 6, 12 [twice], 18; 2 Thessalonians 3:9).
6. Authority in teaching (*1 Thessalonians 4:2; *Titus 2:15).
7. Ministry authority (2 Corinthians 10:8; 13:10).
8. Authority as personal self-control (1 Corinthians 7:37).
9. Authority and personal liberty (1 Corinthians 6:12; 8:9).
10. Women and authority (1 Corinthians 11:10; *1 Timothy 2:12).
11. Authority of God over people (Romans 9:21).
12. Authority over each other's bodies in marriage (1 Corinthians 7:4).

Verses Employing Authority Terminology

Following is a reading of every verse in the Bible utilizing "authority terminology" in the NIV translation.

In the Pentateuch

Genesis 41:35: "They should collect all the food of these good years that are coming and store up the grain under the *authority* of Pharaoh, to be kept in the cities for food."

Numbers 27:20: "Give him some of your *authority* so the whole Israelite community will obey him."

Deuteronomy 1:15: "So I took the leading men of your tribes, wise and respected men, and appointed them to have *authority* over you—as commanders of thousands, of hundreds, of fifties and of tens and as tribal officials."

In the Historical Books

Ezra 3:7: Then they gave money to the masons and carpenters, and gave food and drink and oil to the people of Sidon and Tyre, so that they would bring cedar logs by sea from Lebanon to Joppa, as *authorized* by Cyrus king of Persia.

Ezra 5:3: At that time Tattenai, governor of Trans-Euphrates, and Shethar-Bozenai and their associates went to them and asked, "Who *authorized* you to rebuild this temple and restore this structure?"

Ezra 5:9: We questioned the elders and asked them, "Who *authorized* you to rebuild this temple and restore this structure?"

Ezra 7:24: You are also to know that you have no *authority* to impose taxes, tribute or duty on any of the priests, Levites, singers, gatekeepers, temple servants or other workers at this house of God.

Nehemiah 3:7: Next to them, repairs were made by men from Gibeon and Mizpah—Melatiah of Gibeon and Jadon of Meronoth—places under the *authority* of the governor of Trans-Euphrates.

Esther 9:29: So Queen Esther, daughter of Abihail, along with Mordecai the Jew, wrote with full *authority* to confirm this second letter concerning Purim.

In the Prophets

Isaiah 22:21: "I will clothe him with your robe and fasten your sash around him and hand your *authority* over to him. He will be a father to those who live in Jerusalem and to the house of Judah."

Jeremiah 5:31: "The prophets prophesy lies, the priests rule by their own *authority,* and my people love it this way. But what will you do in the end?"

Daniel 4:31: The words were still on his lips when a voice came from heaven, "This is what is decreed for you, King Nebuchadnezzar: Your royal *authority* has been taken from you."

Daniel 7:6 "After that, I looked, and there before me was another beast, one that looked like a leopard. And on its back it had four wings like those of a bird. This beast had four heads, and it was given *authority* to rule."

Daniel 7:12: "(The other beasts had been stripped of their *authority,* but were allowed to live for a period of time.)"

Daniel 7:14: "He was given *authority,* glory and sovereign power; all peoples, nations and men of every language worshiped him. His dominion is an everlasting dominion that will not pass away, and his kingdom is one that will never be destroyed."

In the Gospels

Matthew 7:29: Because he taught as one who had *authority,* and not as their teachers of the law.

Matthew 8:9: "For I myself am a man under *authority,* with soldiers under me. I tell this one, 'Go,' and he goes; and that one, 'Come,' and he comes. I say to my servant, 'Do this,' and he does it."

Matthew 9:6: "But so that you may know that the Son of Man has *authority* on earth to forgive sins. . . ." Then he said to the paralytic, "Get up, take your mat and go home."

Matthew 9:8: When the crowd saw this, they were filled with awe; and they praised God, who had given such *authority* to men.

Matthew 10:1: He called his twelve disciples to him and gave them *authority* to drive out evil spirits and to heal every disease and sickness.

Matthew 20:25: Jesus called them together and said, "You know that the rulers of the Gentiles lord it over them, and their high officials exercise *authority* over them."

Matthew 21:23: Jesus entered the temple courts, and, while he was teaching, the chief priests and the elders of the people came to him. "By what *authority* are you doing these things?" they asked. "And who gave you this *authority?*"

Matthew 21:24: Jesus replied, "I will also ask you one question. If you answer me, I will tell you by what *authority* I am doing these things."

Matthew 21:27: So they answered Jesus, "We don't know." Then he said, "Neither will I tell you by what *authority* I am doing these things."

Matthew 28:18: Then Jesus came to them and said, "All *authority* in heaven and on earth has been given to me."

Mark 1:22: The people were amazed at his teaching, because he taught them as one who had *authority,* not as the teachers of the law.

Mark 1:27: The people were all so amazed that they asked each other, "What is this? A new teaching—and with *authority!* He even gives orders to evil spirits and they obey him."

Mark 2:10: "But that you may know that the Son of Man has *authority* on earth to forgive sins. . . ." He said to the paralytic. . . .

Mark 3:15: And to have *authority* to drive out demons.

Mark 6:7: Calling the Twelve to him, he sent them out two by two and gave them *authority* over evil spirits.

Mark 10:42: Jesus called them together and said, "You know that those who are regarded as rulers of the Gentiles lord it over them, and their high officials exercise *authority* over them."

Mark 11:28: "By what *authority* are you doing these things?" they asked. "And who gave you *authority* to do this?"

Mark 11:29: Jesus replied, "I will ask you one question. Answer me, and I will tell you by what *authority* I am doing these things."

Mark 11:33: So they answered Jesus, "We don't know." Jesus said, "Neither will I tell you by what *authority* I am doing these things."

Luke 4:6: And he said to him, "I will give you all their *authority* and splendor, for it has been given to me, and I can give it to anyone I want to."

Luke 4:32: They were amazed at his teaching, because his message had *authority*.

Luke 4:36: All the people were amazed and said to each other, "What is this teaching? With *authority* and power he gives orders to evil spirits and they come out!"

Luke 5:24: "But that you may know that the Son of Man has *authority* on earth to forgive sins. . . ." He said to the paralyzed man, "I tell you, get up, take your mat and go home."

Luke 7:8: "For I myself am a man under *authority*, with soldiers under me. I tell this one, 'Go,' and he goes; and that one, 'Come,' and he comes. I say to my servant, 'Do this,' and he does it."

Luke 9:1: When Jesus had called the Twelve together, he gave them power and *authority* to drive out all demons and to cure diseases.

Luke 10:19: "I have given you *authority* to trample on snakes and scorpions and to overcome all the power of the enemy; nothing will harm you."

Luke 12:11: "When you are brought before synagogues, rulers and *authorities,* do not worry about how you will defend yourselves or what you will say."

Luke 20:2: "Tell us by what *authority* you are doing these things," they said. "Who gave you this *authority?*"

Luke 20:8: Jesus said, "Neither will I tell you by what *authority* I am doing these things."

Luke 20:20: Keeping a close watch on him, they sent spies, who pretended to be honest. They hoped to catch Jesus in something he said so that they might hand him over to the power and *authority* of the governor.

Luke 22:25: Jesus said to them, "The kings of the Gentiles lord it over them; and those who exercise *authority* over them call themselves Benefactors."

John 2:18: Then the Jews demanded of him, "What miraculous sign can you show us to prove your *authority* to do all this?"

John 5:27: "And he has given him *authority* to judge because he is the Son of Man."

John 7:26: "Here he is, speaking publicly, and they are not saying a word to him. Have the *authorities* really concluded that he is the Christ?"

John 10:18: "No one takes it from me, but I lay it down of my own accord. I have *authority* to lay it down and *authority* to take it up again. This command I received from my Father."

John 17:2: "For you granted him *authority* over all people that he might give eternal life to all those you have given him."

In Acts

Acts 1:7: He said to them: "It is not for you to know the times or dates the Father has set by his own *authority.*"

Acts 9:14: "And he has come here with *authority* from the chief priests to arrest all who call on your name."

Acts 15:24: "We have heard that some went out from us without our *authorization* and disturbed you, troubling your minds by what they said."

Acts 16:19: When the owners of the slave girl realized that their hope of making money was gone, they seized Paul and Silas and dragged them into the marketplace to face the *authorities.*

Acts 26:10: "And that is just what I did in Jerusalem. On the *authority* of the chief priests I put many of the saints in prison, and when they were put to death, I cast my vote against them."

Acts 26:12: "On one of these journeys I was going to Damascus with the *authority* and commission of the chief priests."

In the Pauline Epistles

*Romans 7:1: Do you not know, brothers—for I am speaking to men who know the law—that the law has *authority* over a man only as long as he lives?

Romans 9:21: Does not the potter have the *right* to make out of the same lump of clay some pottery for noble purposes and some for common use?

Romans 13:1: Everyone must submit himself to the governing *authorities,* for there is no *authority* except that which God has established. The *authorities* that exist have been established by God.

Romans 13:2: Consequently, he who rebels against the *authority* is rebelling against what God has instituted, and those who do so will bring judgment on themselves.

Romans 13:3: For rulers hold no terror for those who do right, but for those who do wrong. Do you want to be free from fear of the one in *authority?* Then do what is right and he will commend you.

*Romans 13:5: Therefore, it is necessary to submit to the *authorities,* not only because of possible punishment but also because of conscience.

*Romans 13:6: This is also why you pay taxes, for the *authorities* are God's servants, who give their full time to governing.

1 Corinthians 6:12: "Everything is permissible for me"—but not everything is beneficial. "Everything is permissible for me"—but *I will not be mastered* by anything.

1 Corinthians 7:4: The wife's body does not *belong* to her alone but also to her husband. In the same way, the husband's body does not *belong* to him alone but also to his wife.

1 Corinthians 7:37: But the man who has settled the matter in his own mind, who is under no compulsion but has *control* over his own will, and who has made up his mind not to marry the virgin—this man also does the right thing.

1 Corinthians 8:9: Be careful, however, that the exercise of your *freedom* does not become a stumbling block to the weak.

1 Corinthians 9:4: Don't we have the *right* to food and drink?

1 Corinthians 9:5: Don't we have the *right* to take a believing wife along with us, as do the other apostles and the Lord's brothers and Cephas?

1 Corinthians 9:6: Or is it only I and Barnabas who must work for a living? (Lit: who have not the *authority* not to work).

1 Corinthians 9:12: If others have this *right* of support from you, shouldn't we have *it [the right]* all the more?

1 Corinthians 9:18: What then is my reward? Just this: that in preaching the gospel I may offer it free of charge, and so not make use of my *rights* in preaching it.

1 Corinthians 11:10: For this reason, and because of the angels, the woman ought to have a sign of *authority* on her head.

1 Corinthians 15:24: Then the end will come, when he hands over the kingdom to God the Father after he has destroyed all dominion, *authority* and power.

2 Corinthians 10:8: For even if I boast somewhat freely about the *authority* the Lord gave us for building you up rather than pulling you down, I will not be ashamed of it.

2 Corinthians 13:10: This is why I write these things when I am absent, that when I come I may not have to be harsh in my use of *authority*—the *authority* the Lord gave me for building you up, not for tearing you down.

Ephesians 1:21: Far above all rule and *authority,* power and dominion, and every title that can be given, not only in the present age but also in the one to come.

Ephesians 2:2: In which you used to live when you followed the ways of this world and of the ruler of the *kingdom* of the air, the spirit who is now at work in those who are disobedient.

Ephesians 3:10: His intent was that now, through the church, the manifold wisdom of God should be made known to the rulers and *authorities* in the heavenly realms.

Ephesians 6:12: For our struggle is not against flesh and blood, but against the rulers, against the *authorities,* against the powers of this dark world and against the spiritual forces of evil in the heavenly realms.

Colossians 1:13: For he has rescued us from the *dominion* of darkness and brought us into the kingdom of the Son he loves.

Colossians 1:16: For by him all things were created: things in heaven and on earth, visible and invisible, whether thrones or powers or rulers or *authorities;* all things were created by him and for him.

Colossians 2:10: And you have been given fullness in Christ, who is the head over every power and *authority.*

Colossians 2:15: And having disarmed the powers and *authorities,* he made a public spectacle of them, triumphing over them by the cross.

*1 Thessalonians 4:2: For you know what instructions we gave you by the *authority* of the Lord Jesus.

2 Thessalonians 3:9: We did this, not because we do not have the *right* to such help, but in order to make ourselves a model for you to follow.

*1 Timothy 2:2: For kings and all those in *authority,* that we may live peaceful and quiet lives in all godliness and holiness.

*1 Timothy 2:12: I do not permit a woman to teach or to have *authority* over a man; she must be silent.

*Titus 2:15: These, then, are the things you should teach. Encourage and rebuke with all *authority.* Do not let anyone despise you.

Titus 3:1: Remind the people to be subject to rulers and *authorities,* to be obedient, to be ready to do whatever is good.

In the General Epistles

Hebrews 13:17: Obey your leaders and submit to their *authority.* They keep watch over you as men who must give an account. Obey them so that their work will be a joy, not a burden, for that would be of no advantage to you.

1 Peter 2:13: Submit yourselves for the Lord's sake to every *authority* instituted among men: whether to the king, as the supreme *authority.* . . .

1 Peter 3:22: Who has gone into heaven and is at God's right hand—with angels, *authorities* and powers in submission to him.

2 Peter 2:10: This is especially true of those who follow the corrupt desire of the sinful nature and despise *authority.* Bold and arrogant, these men are not afraid to slander celestial beings.

Jude 1:6: And the angels who did not keep their positions of *authority* but abandoned their own home—these he has kept in darkness, bound with everlasting chains for judgment on the great Day.

Jude 1:8: In the very same way, these dreamers pollute their own bodies, reject *authority* and slander celestial beings.

Jude 1:25: To the only God our Savior be glory, majesty, power and *authority,* through Jesus Christ our Lord, before all ages, now and forevermore! Amen.

In Revelation

Revelation 2:26: "To him who overcomes and does my will to the end, I will give *authority* over the nations."

Revelation 2:27: "'He will rule them with an iron scepter; he will dash them to pieces like pottery'—just as I have received *authority* from my Father."

Revelation 12:10: Then I heard a loud voice in heaven say: "Now have come the salvation and the power and the kingdom of our God, and the *authority* of his Christ. For the accuser of our brothers, who accuses them before our God day and night, has been hurled down."

Revelation 13:2: The beast I saw resembled a leopard, but had feet like those of a bear and a mouth like that of a lion. The dragon gave the beast his power and his throne and great *authority.*

Revelation 13:4: Men worshiped the dragon because he had given *authority* to the beast, and they also worshiped the beast and asked, "Who is like the beast? Who can make war against him?"

Revelation 13:5: The beast was given a mouth to utter proud words and blasphemies and to exercise his *authority* for forty-two months.

Revelation 13:7: He was given power to make war against the saints and to conquer them. And he was given *authority* over every tribe, people, language and nation.

Revelation 13:12: He exercised all the *authority* of the first beast on his behalf, and made the earth and its inhabitants worship the first beast, whose fatal wound had been healed.

Revelation 17:12: "The ten horns you saw are ten kings who have not yet received a kingdom, but who for one hour will receive *authority* as kings along with the beast."

Revelation 17:13: "They have one purpose and will give their power and *authority* to the beast."

Revelation 18:1: After this I saw another angel coming down from heaven. He had great *authority,* and the earth was illuminated by his splendor.

Revelation 20:4: I saw thrones on which were seated those who had been given *authority* to judge. And I saw the souls of those who had been beheaded because of their testimony for Jesus and because of the word of God. They had not worshiped the beast or his image and had not received his mark on their foreheads or their hands. They came to life and reigned with Christ a thousand years.

Bibliography

Beckett, Bob, with Rebecca Wagner Sytsema. *Commitment to Conquer.* Grand Rapids: Chosen, 1997.

Bubeck, Mark L. *The Adversary.* Chicago: Moody, 1975.

Cho, Paul Y. *Prayer: Key to Revival.* Dallas: Word, 1984.

Clinton, J. Robert. *The Making of a Leader.* Colorado Springs: NavPress, 1988.

———. *Leadership Emergence Theory.* Altadena, Calif.: Barnabas Resources, 1989.

Crow, D. Michael. "Spiritual Authority: Theoretical, Biblical, Historical." A doctoral tutorial paper presented at Fuller Seminary, 1996.

Dawson, John. *Taking Our Cities for God.* Lake Mary, Fla.: Creation House, 1989.

Deere, Jack. *Surprised by the Power of the Spirit.* Grand Rapids: Zondervan, 1993.

Foerster, W. *Theological Dictionary of the New Testament: Abridged in One Volume.* Gerhard Kittel and Gerhard Friedrich, eds., G. W. Bromiley, trans. Grand Rapids: Eerdmans, 1985.

Foster, Richard J. *Celebration of Discipline.* New York: Harper & Row, 1978.

Hibbert, Albert. *The Secret of His Power.* Tulsa: Harrison House, 1982.

Kraft, Charles H. "Christian Animism or God-Given Authority," in *Spiritual Power and Missions.* E. Rommen, ed. Pasadena, Calif.: William Carey Library, 1995.

———. *Christianity with Power.* Ann Arbor, Mich.: Servant, 1989.

———. *Behind Enemy Lines.* Ann Arbor, Mich.: Servant, 1994.

———. *Deep Wounds, Deep Healing.* Ann Arbor, Mich.: Servant, 1993.

———. *Defeating Dark Angels.* Ann Arbor, Mich.: Servant, 1992.

MacNutt, Francis and Judith. *Praying for Your Unborn Child.* New York: Doubleday, 1988.

McAll, Kenneth. *Healing the Family Tree*. London: Sheldon Press, 1982 (rev. ed., 1984).

Murphy, Ed. "From My Experience: My Daughter Demonized?" in *Equipping the Saints*, Vol. 4, No. 1, Winter 1990.

Nee, Watchman. *Spiritual Authority*. New York: Christian Fellowship Publishers, 1972 [1948].

Pytches, David. *Spiritual Gifts in the Local Church*. Minneapolis: Bethany, 1985.

Sandford, John and Paula. *Healing the Wounded Spirit*. Tulsa: Victory House, 1985.

Sherman, Dean. *Spiritual Warfare for Every Christian*. Seattle: Frontline Communications (YWAM), 1990.

Silvoso, Edgardo. "Prayer Power in Argentina" in *Engaging the Enemy*. C. Peter Wagner, ed. Ventura, Calif.: Regal, 1991.

Strong, James. *Strong's Exhaustive Concordance: Compact Edition*. Grand Rapids: Baker, 1981.

Verny, Thomas, and John Kelly. *The Secret Life of the Unborn Child*. New York: Dell, 1981.

Von Campenhausen, Hans. *Ecclesiastical Authority and Spiritual Power in the Church of the First Three Centuries*. J. A. Baker, trans. Stanford, Calif.: Stanford University Press, 1969.

Waetjen, Herman C. "Binding and Loosing" in *Evangelical Dictionary of Theology*. Walter A. Elwell, ed. Grand Rapids: Baker, 1984.

Wagner, C. Peter. *Engaging the Enemy*. Ventura, Calif.: Regal, 1991.

———. *Prayer Shield*. Ventura, Calif.: Regal, 1992.

———. "Territorial Spirits" in *Wrestling with Dark Angels*. C. Peter Wagner and Douglas Pennoyer, eds. Ventura, Calif.: Regal, 1990.

Merriam Webster's Collegiate Dictionary. Springfield, Mass.: G & C Merriam, Tenth Edition, 1993.

Wimber, John. *Power Healing*. San Francisco: Harper & Row, 1987.

Wink, Walter. *Unmasking the Powers*. Philadelphia: Fortress, 1986.

Wright, Nigel. *The Satan Syndrome*. Grand Rapids: Zondervan, 1990.

Subject Index

Abba, 43
abuse, 234
accountability, 73–78, 116–17
Adam and Eve, 20
adoption, 41–42, 43–44,
alertness, 292
allegiances, 304–5
allegiance to Christ, 303–5
ancestral vows, 162, 236
angels: authority of, 17–18; hi-
    erarchy of, 132–34; protec-
    tion by, 28
animism, 101–2
Annacondia, Carlos, 255–56
archangels, 132–33
asking prayer, 50
asserting authority, 52–53,
    176–81, 313–15
attack, satanic, 26–28, 273–74
attacking the enemy, 57–58,
    274–75
authority: characteristics of,
    107–8; counteracting,
    149–51; defined, 67; misuse
    of, 69–73, 79–80, 95–103;

over the past, 163–170; of
the position, 87–88; possession of, 45; prerequisites to,
110–17; in the present,
171–73; types of, 125–26;
vocal assertion of, 52–53
authority patterns, 136–37,
138–39
authority praying, 49–52, 86–87
awareness, 292, 295, 311–12,
315–16

babysitters, 216–17
balance, 307–8
baptism, 269, 270
Beckett, Bob, 275–80
Bermuda Triangle, 271–72
Bible, 10–12, 98–99, 178–80
binding and loosing, 61–63
binding Satan, 62
blessing: of children, 269; effec-
tiveness of, 59–60; empowerment of, 141–42; of items
used by others, 60–61; Jesus'
practice of, 224–25, 228–29;

Scripture Index

Dr. Charles H. Kraft is professor of anthropology and intercultural communication at Fuller Theological Seminary and the author of 21 books, including *Christianity with Power; Behind Enemy Lines; Deep Wounds, Deep Healing;* and *Defeating Dark Angels.* A graduate of Wheaton College, Ashland Theological Seminary and Hartford Seminary Foundation, he was a missionary in Nigeria under Church of the Brethren Mission. He and his wife, Marguerite, have four grown children.